"Childhood in general and schooling in particular are often seen as things that are done to children. Based on meticulous research, Cunningham and Lavalette correct this imbalance, detailing five waves of school student strikes. This is a must-read for anyone interested in the history of education and childhood."

—*Alan Gibbons, multi-award winning author*

"A truly revelatory account of school kids' rebellion and political dissidence. *Schools Out!* is both rigorous and captivating; inspiring reading in these dark days."

—*John Newsinger, Professor of History, Bath Spa University*

"This is a path-breaking book. Famous episodes like Burston have been celebrated before but no one has tried to cover the stories of school kids' resistance from 1889 to Stop the War. Extensively researched and told with passion it is a real page turner. An unusual claim to make for a piece of social history!"

—*John Charlton, socialist historian and activist, author of* It Just Went Like Tinder *and father of six dissenting children!*

"The history of school student protest is hidden and yet it has played a part in all the big upsurges in struggle over the last 100 years. This book shows how school students have played a living, breathing role in working class history. It will be a fascinating read for teachers and all those who work with school students and young people—it emphasises the role young people can play in shaping their own worlds."

—*Jess Edwards, Joint Divisional Secretary, Lambeth NUT*

"Public rhetoric on childhood has recently been overwhelmingly negative. Children are invariably said to be menaced by traffickers, internet pornographers, incompetent parents, bad teachers and clothing manufacturers eager to sexualise them. They are also widely held to be uninterested in politics. This admirable book confronts these dreary misrepresentations. Michael Lavalette and Steve Cunningham, known for their important work on child labour, show here how children have long been, and continue to be, active on their own account, politically aware and prepared to defy their teachers in the face of perceived injustice. The book is readable and impressive in its historical and cross cultural compass and it's a worthy contribution to a literature through which children are becoming no longer hidden from history or excluded from political consideration. I strongly recommend it."

—*Stephen Wagg, Professor at Leeds Beckett University and co-editor* Thatcher's Grandchildren? Politics and Childhood in the 21st Century

"Although children's 'agency', 'participation' and 'rights' have become well-established conceptual touchstones in the discourses of the social sciences, they are rarely applied in ways that genuinely unsettle conventional understandings of child-adult relations and/or the power of social institutions. Not so with this book. By analysing both historical and contemporary manifestations of children's agential capacities to organise 'student strikes', Cunningham and Lavalette challenge received orthodoxies and provoke new ways of thinking. *Schools Out!* is a must-read for any scholar or student of childhood and youth studies."

—*Professor Barry Goldson, Department of Sociology, Social Policy and Criminology, The University of Liverpool*

SCHOOLS OUT!

The Hidden History of Britain's School Student Strikes

Steve Cunningham
Michael Lavalette

Bookmarks  Publications

Schools Out!
The Hidden History of Britain's School Student Strikes
Steve Cunningham and Michael Lavalette
Published by Bookmarks Publications
c/o 1 Bloomsbury Street
London WC1B 3QE
Designed and typeset by Peter Robinson
Printed by Melita Press
ISBN 978-1-910885-17-8 (pbk)
978-1-910885-18-5 (Kindle)
978-1-910885-19-2 (ePub)
978-1-910885-16-1 (PDF)

Contents

About the authors

STEVE CUNNINGHAM is a Senior Lecturer in Social Policy at the University of Central Lancashire. He jointly authored *Social Policy and Social Work* (Sage) and *Sociology and Social Work* (Sage). His research interests are focused on welfare history, poverty and social security, the sociology of welfare, asylum and immigration policy, child labour and children's rights.

MICHAEL LAVALETTE is Professor of Social Work at Liverpool Hope University and national coordinator of the Social Work Action Network. He is the author of *Capitalism and Sport: Politics, Protest, People and Play* (Bookmarks), *Radical Social Work Today* (Policy Press), *Race, Racism and Social Work* (Policy Press) and *Adult Social Care: Critical and Radical Debates in Social Work* (Policy Press). He is a member of the Socialist Workers Party.

Acknowledgements

We HAVE been collecting material on student school strikes, on and off, for 15 years. We published our first piece on this just as the 2003 strikes against the Iraq war began. We suddenly found ourselves being interviewed in the press and radio—our 15 minutes of fame. But quickly interest in the subject dissipated and we were once again ploughing a lonely furrow.

We would like to thank various people who, over the years, have offered support, help and various sources. Thanks to Jo Cunningham, Laura Penketh, Ron Lavalette, John Charlton, John Newsinger, Stephen Wagg, Barry Goldson, Jim McKechnie, Sally Campbell, Tony Staunton, Rahul Patel, Sandy Hobbs, Judith Orr and Charlie Kimber at the SWP national office and Hannah Sell at the Socialist Party national office. Particular thanks to Lina Nicolli at Bookmarks and Eileen Short, Peter Robinson and Carol Williams who were all involved on the production side.

We would particularly like to thank those who gave their time to talk to us and share their memories of their time as school student activists. Thanks to Steve Marsh, Rehad Desai, Erika Laredo, Dave Kersey, Chris Fuller, Angela McCormick, James Doleman, Keir McKechnie, Tom Kay, Nancy Taaffe, Lois Austin, Hannah Sell, Henna Malik, Mike Morris, Weyman Bennett and Dave Gibson. In 2003 a number of school strikers agreed to be interviewed. Their insights inform chapter 8. We would like to thank each of them (identified by their first names only in the chapter) for giving their time and talking to us in the midst of those heady days. Finally, Jimmy Ross and Jock Morris talked to us about their experiences as activists in the teachers' union and their relationship with school student strikers.

Socialist Worker gave us access to their photo-library; thanks to Judith Orr and Ken Ollende for their help with this. Both Sam Ziesler at the Salford Working Class Movement Library and Darren Treadwell at the People's History Museum, Manchester were very helpful in directing us to key sources.

Finally we'd like to thank the University of Central Lancashire and Liverpool Hope University for small grants allowing us to travel, to access archives and carry out interviews with former school student rebels.

Our title has similarities to the campaign group Schools OUT UK. After discussion with the group we both decided there was no clash but we asked them to write a few words to describe their excellent work. We are grateful to Sue Sanders, chair of Schools OUT UK, for the following:

Schools OUT UK is a charity that has been working for over 40 years to Educate OUT prejudice by making LGBT people in all their diversity visible and safe. We have to that end initiated www.the-classrom.org. uk which has over 50 lesson plans for all ages across the curriculum and that usualises LGBT themes, Embedded February as www.lgbthistory-month.org.uk and introduced The LGBT National History Festival.

1

Introduction: Working class childhood, politics and school strikes

On 11 September 2014 thousands of young people from across Scotland got onto school buses and travelled to the SSE Hydro centre in Glasgow to take part in "The Big, Big Debate". The event was organised by the BBC and brought 16 and 17 year olds together to discuss Scottish independence. The students were preparing to take part in the referendum and were about to become the youngest ever voters in British electoral history.

The debate was remarkable for a number of reasons.

First, the interest it generated. Between 7,000 and 8,000 young people took part in the event directly;[1] an indicator of a quite remarkable political engagement. In England this would be equivalent to 16 and 17 year olds packing Wembley football stadium to take part in *Question Time*, for example. Further, as the event went on, the hash tag #bigbigdebate trended number 1 in the UK for four hours.

Second, the mismatch in the sides. The Yes Alliance sent the SNP's Deputy Leader (now Scotland's First Minister) Nicola Sturgeon and Green MSP Patrick Harvey. These were two of the Yes side's big hitters from the two-year referendum campaign. Both were identified with the left and, during the campaign, both had repeatedly spoken out about issues of social justice, inequality, climate change and war. Both argued that the referendum offered people hope; that an alternative to Westminster driven neo-liberalism was possible; that a different Scotland could be won.

Representing the No side were Scottish Tory leader Ruth Davidson and Respect MP George Galloway. This was a strange combination. Over the campaign Davidson had been kept in the background because the Labour leadership of "Better Together" argued any association with the Tories would push people into the Yes camp. So why was she rolled out here? There is no doubt that Galloway is a very able debater. Yet the "Better Together" leadership had kept their distance from him during the campaign. He had been marginalised to such an extent that he had to organise his own speaking tour to defend the union, called "Just say naw".

This choice of speakers for the union, whatever their individual merits, seemed to indicate that, for the leadership of the No side, this debate was less significant than the other televised ones. Maybe the audience were "just kids"?

If this was the attitude of the leadership of "Better Together" the debate emphasised how completely out of touch the Westminster Labour machine had become.

The debate was remarkable for a third reason. We are constantly told that people are no longer interested in politics—and that young people in particular are totally disengaged from political debate and the political process. James Sloam, co-director of the Centre for European Politics at Royal Holloway, University of London has argued that:

> One of the prominent features of recent general elections has been decreasing rates of turnout among young voters. Turnout among young people (here, 18-24 year olds) has fallen from over 60 percent in the early 1990s to an average of 40 percent over the previous three general elections (2001, 2005 and 2010)... [T]he youth turnout rate in the UK is the lowest of all the 15 members of the old European Union. Voters aged 18 to 24 in Sweden turn out to vote at double the rate of their peers in the UK... This disillusionment extends to public policy.[2]

The whole premise of this argument was dealt a deadly blow during the run up to the Indy vote. Public engagement in politics was remarkable. People registered to vote, attended public meetings in large numbers and many joined marches and flash mob gatherings and took part in canvassing. The engagement of young people in the campaign was particularly marked and indicated their willingness to get involved when the debate—and the vote—could make a real difference.

The suggestion that young people are not interested in politics is based on their lack of engagement with the bland Westminster political game. It is certainly the case that the main Westminster parties hold little attraction for young people. The various youth organisations of the main Westminster parties have collapsed. The Labour Party Young Socialists no longer exists and their student organisation is a rump—populated by young career politicians looking for a safe seat. But to extrapolate from this to suggest that young people are not interested in politics is to ignore the diversity of young people's involvement in a range of social movements.

Over the last two decades young people have continued to take part in, and organise, a range of movement and protest campaigns. These have ranged from movements against climate change and fracking, global poverty and global justice campaigns, anti-war movements, campaigns against racism and fascism, Occupy and democracy movements and a range of other national and local activities.

The campaign to elect Jeremy Corbyn to the Labour Party leadership also brought significant numbers of young people onto Labour's radar, with many joining, either as supporters or members, because Corbyn seemed to offer a different politics to the mainstream. His supporters around the Momentum group have, in many cases, tried to encourage political engagement with young people and offer them a political home within the Labour Party.

The suggestion that young people are now apolitical was always overstated. Any claim that young people were not interested in, or knew little about, the issues surrounding the Scottish Independence referendum was completely dispelled by the 2014 debate. Young people in the audience asked a range of challenging questions. They wanted to know about currency union and/or replacement. How an enhanced welfare system would be paid for. At what level any new tax rates would be set and how we could ensure that those in ordinary jobs would not see their tax rates go up. They asked about student fees, funding the NHS, their own job prospects and apprenticeships. They asked how it was possible that one of the richest countries in the world, Scotland (and by extension Britain), could harbour some of the highest child poverty rates in the European Union? And they wanted to know why Trident submarines were housed on the Clyde and, in the post Cold War era, why the Government was even considering replacing them.

The level of debate from the audience was incredibly high. And if they didn't like the response the politicians gave, they were not slow to let them know about it. On a number of occasions George Galloway's answers were roundly, and noisily, booed. The boos reached a crescendo when he, bizarrely, tried to draw an analogy between the SNP and German Nazis (though, when the programme was broadcast in England and Wales a day after the debate took place, the audience reactions had all been replaced with polite canned clapping).

The debate was an indication of what was to come. One week later young people—like the population of Scotland as a whole—turned out in their hundreds of thousands to vote. And young people were among the most enthusiastic Yes voters. An estimated 75 per cent of 16 and 17 year olds voted to break up the British state!

This book is not about the Independence referendum. But it is about young people and politics and, in particular, their involvement in one form of youthful collective action: the school student strike.

The school student strike has been in existence for as long as we have had compulsory education. In England the education system can be dated from the Elementary Education Acts of 1870 and 1880. Initially children were required to go to school between the ages of 5 and 10. The school leaving age then gradually increased to 11 (1893), 12 (1899), 14 (1918), 15 (1944) and 16 (1972). Up until 1918 there were exceptions allowed in areas where child labour was deemed economically significant (such as agriculture and textiles) and children could get out of schooling with an appropriate exemption certificate.[3]

This also meant that, at times, school student strikers were playing and mixing with other children, of the same age, who were working and engaged in more traditional forms of strike activity. Thus, in earlier periods young people who would today be school students were active in some important strikes and conflicts. Let's consider some examples.

In the earliest phase of capitalist development, the pre-industrial crowd would protest against a range of grievances, from the price of bread to political corruption, by gathering in urban centres to confront local sources of power and authority. Crowds would gather, often riot and, in the process, confront the yeomanry, army or police. The crowds were made up of skilled and unskilled workers, men and women, old and young.[4] For example, in June 1792 in Edinburgh a crowd gathered outside the home of the hated Henry Dundas. Dundas was:

> Home Secretary, president of the Board of Control for India, treasurer of the navy, and political manager for the nobles of Scotland and most of their forty-five subservient members of parliament at Westminster.[5]

Dundas lived in George Square in the New Town area of the city. The Square included the homes of many of his extended family, who had gained their wealth and positions of influence through their powerful patriarch. Robert McQueen (Lord Braxfield) the chief judge in Scotland also lived on the Square. As the crowd grew the garrison was turned out and opened fire on the protestors. One of those killed was Robert Ritchie, described as "no more than a boy".[6]

Louise Raw's excellent history of the Bryant and May matchwomen's strike of 1888[7] provides an important corrective to accounts which portray the workforce as being led into strike action by "outside agitators" like Annie Beasant. Beasant was an active socialist and great supporter of the matchwomen but she did not lead the strike. As Raw shows the strike leadership came from within the workforce itself. As John Charlton notes there were 1,400 workers at Bryant and May "predominantly under the age of 15".[8]

The employers identified five "ring leaders" of the strike. One of those was Mary Driscoll. Mary was 14 at the time and took on a leading role as a striker. She subsequently became a committee member of the Union of Women Match-makers formed out of the strike. Her sister Mog (Margaret) was two years older and also active in the strike. Both Mary and Mog were well versed in politics, came from a strong Irish republican household and held strong political opinions.[9] Raw also discusses the life of striker Martha Robertson. Martha worked as a box maker inside the factory; she was six when she joined the strike.[10]

Paul Ryan[11] has produced interesting and important material on the history of apprentice strikes in Britain. Young workers launched nine unofficial strike movements in engineering and shipbuilding between 1910 and 1970. On average the disputes lasted more than five weeks and involved over 15,000 young workers at a time. Many of those 14 and 15 year olds on strike would, today, be stuck in the classroom.

Dave Lyddon[12] has recently added to the literature about the Great Unrest in Britain 1910-14, and has argued that "one feature of the period of the labour unrest that stands out, but has not been generally commented upon, is the involvement of young people in strikes and strike movements".[13]

As well as the school student strikes of the period, which we discuss in chapter 3, there were, Lyddon says, significant apprentice strikes in the summer and autumn of 1912, especially in shipbuilding. There were also significant strikes throughout the early twentieth century by pit boys. Lyddon quotes data suggesting that there were, on average, two strikes a year by pit boys in the north east coalfield alone between 1889-1907. But it wasn't just in the pits that lads went on strike: young boys and girls in the tin and iron industries were regular strikers. And during the Great Unrest non-traditional workers including newspaper boys, golf caddies and young boys employed in the banking industry all came out.[14]

And it's not just children in Britain who engaged in politics and rebellion.

Young people have often played a leading role in revolutions and struggles against oppression round the globe. Detlev Peukert,[15] in his social history of life in the Third Reich, includes discussion of young people's resistance to the Nazi regime. He argues there were two significant groups of young people engaged in acts of resistance.

First there were groups of Edelweiss Pirates who started to appear in the late 1930s. There were a number of groups across Germany, the Travelling Dudes from Essen, the Kittelbach Pirates from Oberhausen and Düsseldorf and the Navajos from Cologne. All of them considered themselves Edelweiss Pirates.

The Pirate groups were made up of people aged between 14 and 18. They had clearly identifiable dress codes, wore identifying badges and used the weekends to drink, mix with the opposite sex, travel and confront the Hitler Youth. As Peukert notes

> For the Edelweiss Pirates... Dissociating themselves and emphasising differences [between themselves and the Hitler Youth] involved, in addition, taking positive action of their own in order to provoke their Nazi opponents... Reports of brawls with members of the Hitler Youth... Of assaults on uniformed personnel, and of jeers and insults directed at Nazi dignitaries, are legion.[16]

In addition to the Pirates were the Meuten, a significant gang of working class youth based in Leipzig. According to Peukert the Meuten were much more politically self-conscious than the Pirates. They drew on deeper communist and social democratic traditions of organising and resisting in Leipzig and were matched by similar groups in Dresden, Halle, Erfurt, Hamburg and Munich.[17]

The Meuten and the Pirates were subject to all manner of repression. They were rounded up, imprisoned and some of their leaders were executed. Yet they continued to resist and fight up until the end of the war.

As the Second World War battles on the Eastern Front came to their conclusion, the people of Warsaw rose up against the German occupation. The Warsaw Uprising started on 1 August 1944 and lasted 63 days. Under immense pressure, with few arms and little support from the Soviet and Allied Forces, the people of Warsaw launched their magnificent, defiant rebellion. Many children were involved in the campaign. The boy scouts delivered mail and instructions to fighters across the city. They helped put out fires and were involved in various forms of civil resistance. Young girls got involved with nursing and emergency services. But many young boys and girls also got directly involved in fighting. Warsaw's most poignant memorial to the uprising commemorates the hundreds of children killed. The memorial statue, called *The Little Insurgent*, depicts Antek Rozpylacz (Antek the flame-thrower) a 13 year old boy-soldier dressed in oversized army fatigues and holding a machine gun. Antek was killed near the Old City at the height of the fighting.[18]

Perhaps the most inspiring example of school students throwing themselves into battle for their rights took place in Birmingham, Alabama in 1963. The civil rights movement faced a monumental struggle to break segregation in the city. The city leaders were determined to face down the challenge and police chief Eugene "Bull" Connor was vicious in responding to any civil rights protests. Martin Luther King called for his supporters to challenge city prohibition orders banning demonstrations by marching, getting arrested, filling the prisons and bringing the system to a grinding halt. But the trickle of volunteers threatened the strategy. King himself was arrested and wrote his famous Letter from Birmingham Jail decrying the meek support for the struggle given by white establishment liberals. Something needed to change—and it did on what was called D-Day, Thursday 2 May.

Despite a ban on marching, D-Day was a march by high school students against segregation. At 1 pm on 2 May 50 teenagers walked out of the Sixteenth Street Baptist Church singing "We shall overcome". As the police started to make arrests another group of students joined the march, and then another and another. And they weren't only high school students; elementary students joined as well: "Asked her age as she climbed into a paddy wagon, a tiny girl called out that she was six".[19]

The cops started to run out of paddy wagons, so they brought up school buses to ship the students to jail. Over 600 students were arrested that first day and, as one of the movement leaders Fred Shuttlesworth said, "The whole world [was] watching Birmingham".[20]

The following day even more students arrived to support the struggle. The cops' intention was to stop any march, but not to make arrests because the jails were full. As the students came out of the churches Bull Connor responded by turning high powered water cannon on the children. The water pressure was so great that children were knocked off their feet and sent tumbling down the street. Still the children kept coming. Now the cops began arresting them again and school buses were brought up to cart them off to prisons that were already overcrowded.

Connor responded by bringing in his K9 teams. Officers with German Shepherd dogs were let loose on the children. The images of dogs attacking and biting children were beamed across the United States and across the globe.

> Striking photographs of the snarling dogs and the high-pressure hoses appeared everywhere... News reports stated that three people had been treated at hospital for dog bites, that five black children had been injured by the fire hoses or police clubs.[21]

That evening King announced the marches would continue over the weekend and that Saturday 4 May would be Double D-Day.

On the Saturday the movement resorted to guerrilla tactics. The cops expected the marchers to start, as usual, at the Sixteenth Street Baptist Church but the children started marching out of churches across the city. And so it continued. On the Monday the first 19 children arrested danced their way into the wagon singing: "I ain't scared of your jail/ 'cause I want my freedom/ want my freedom/ want my freedom".[22]

On the Tuesday groups of children managed to avoid the cops and invaded the shopping and commercial district—without any arrests. Now the economic pressure on the city elites grew steadily. A group representing the city and business interests met with representatives of the movement, and after two days a negotiated settlement was reached. On Friday an historic agreement was announced that effectively broke segregation in the city: the catalyst for change had been the thousands of young people—school students—determined to fight for their rights, no matter the personal cost.

These magnificent examples and others since, including Paris 68, the Soweto uprising and the Arab Spring, should immediately lead us to reject the notion that young people are not able to engage in politics or grasp the complexities of contested and contentious political action. But these examples are all of young people involved in general political and social movements.

The school student strike is specific to children and presents evidence of young people, in difficult and restricted circumstances, engaging in political action to improve their conditions within the education system or to raise political issues within the school setting. The school strike represents an example of a significant consciously political action. It is a frontal challenge to school authority, to the position of students in the education system and within society as a whole.

What jars about the school strike is that it confronts and confounds the dominant ideological conception of children and childhood and of educational processes as a benign benefit.

Dominant understandings of childhood often treat it as a fixed life stage that has been recognised by all societies across time and place. This is a period in life, so we are led to believe, where children are recognised as having particular developmental needs. They are recognised as not being fully adult, as being dependent and in need of protection. And thus, childhood is also portrayed as a period free from worries, devoted to play and learning.

Of course humans do have a relatively long period of dependence and, compared to most animals, a much longer period of psychological and biological maturation. But these developmental facts do not determine young people's social experiences, their childhood.

The notion of childhood has changed significantly though history. Historically, the further back we go the more unrecognisable childhood becomes.

In pre-capitalist societies there was not such a rigid divide between young people and older members of their communities. Unlike today, people would wear the same types of clothes, eat the same foods and engage in the same range of activities regardless of age. Things like storytelling and play, which we tend to associate with childhood, were communal activities for all.

In agricultural societies young people mixed play with a gradual introduction to work within the family economy. Sometimes things like hunting rabbits straddled both fun, play and leisure activity while also providing food for the family.[23]

In his journal documenting his tour through Britain in the 1740s, author and novelist Daniel Defoe[24] made frequent comments about children working alongside their families in a range of cottage industries. Defoe's account is shaped by the ruling ideas of his epoch. To our eyes his report reveals the horror of child labour exploitation, but he quoted positively examples of children "as young as four" at work and being "independent" and "self-reliant".

As these young independent working children were labouring in cottage industries or, slightly later, being exploited in mills and factories, their betters were leading a rather different life.

In the 19th century:

> The children of the well-to-do were better housed, clothed and fed. But the difference was ideological as well as economic... It was assumed by adults of the middle and upper classes that children were dependent on adults and subservient to them. They did not work; they played and learned... Whether at home or school, children were segregated from the adult world.[25]

The male offspring of the wealthy had their life plotted out for them. Soon after birth they were deposited with a wet nurse. They spent long days in the nursery away from their parents before being sent away to preparatory school. This was followed by boarding school, university and then, for many, a career in the army, clergy or city.

Young girls were also handed over to a wet nurse. They would spend a much longer time in the nursery before coming under the tutelage of a governess. They would be taught reading, embroidery, house management skills, painting and the arts. When judged ready they would "come out" to attend debutante balls. The aim of these events was to find a husband, meaning the young women would leave the confines of their father's home and replace it with that of their husband's.

While these cosseted children had long childhoods, though often brutal and brutalising, their working class counterparts were climbing chimneys to clean the flues and put out fires, working in mines, mills and factories or struggling to survive without paid employment.

Outside of work, working class young people lived on the streets, watched out for their younger siblings and actively engaged in the life of their community.

> The industrial urban working-class household, like its rural predecessor, was one where children lived huggermugger[26] with adults; segregation was neither possible nor expected. In the 1850s, and often still in the 1900s, it was also an economic unit in which all members but the very youngest played a part, contributing unpaid labour and any earnings... They were prepared for the adult life through participation, and their experiences equipped them for responsibility and independence at an age when their "betters" were still in school.[27]

During the 18th and 19th centuries working class young people did not have a childhood as we would understand it today. They were young working members of their families, with "responsibilities" and a degree of independence that was significantly different from that of their so-called betters.

But during the last two decades of the 19th century a more recognisable working class childhood was carved out. Working class childhood is a social construct that was formed in a particular historical context.

There were several elements involved in this process.

First, there was working class agitation against the exploitation of child labour. Children had always worked and played a role within the family productive unit. In the pre-capitalist world work could be hard and taxing. But the rhythms of work were fixed by the seasons and children worked and were guided under parental supervision. Parents often pushed children to work hard. But there is no evidence of general parental brutality.[28] Within the family economy:

> Different work would be expected of different individuals: children's work was more auxiliary and recognised as having a learning component... How far children were divided by gender depended on their age and availability. Between children and adult status there was a continuum.[29]

This started to change with the development of capitalism. In the cottage industries in the early phase of capitalist development the imposition of the market onto productive life meant that the rate and level of exploitation of the family's labour resources intensified—including that of children.[30] With the development of industrial capitalism, the expansion of factories and mills during the latter part of the 18th century, life for the child labourer became much more extreme. Child workers were no longer under the direct authority of their parents but were subject to the whims of the overseer and foreman. The intensity of work was not controlled by parents but was set by the relentless pace of the machines.

> Although factory children sometimes worked under other relatives, including parents, the work rhythm and discipline were set from above, by overlookers determined to keep up pace and production. Parents had effectively lost control over how their children were trained, and on the demands made on their health and strength.[31]

During the 19th century there were increasing demands from working class organisations to regulate and control children's labour and to protect children from long hours of arduous factory employment. Often these demands were taken up by landed Tory philanthropists (famously including Lord Shaftesbury) who were motivated by a mixture of hostility to Whig manufacturers, commitment to religious notions of child innocence and bourgeois ideals of family life. During the 19th century legislation slowly brought more areas of child work under some degree of regulation.[32] A process was unlocked which started to treat working class children as children, rather than workers, and opened up a space for working class childhood to develop.

A second element leading to a focus on working class young people arose from changes to the employment structure. In contrast to the above, as the 19th century progressed changes to the labour market meant there was a growing problem of child unemployment and underemployment.[33]

The new industries being establish at the end of the 19th century had less space for child workers. This led to increasing numbers of unemployed working class young people hanging around on the streets during the day. In contemporary debates these "street arabs", as they were known, drifted around the city and were viewed as a potential threat to the established order. Journalists, social commentators and politicians increasingly raised their voices against the problem of unruly youth—and openly debated what measures were needed to control them.[34]

The problem of controlling unemployed and unruly working class youth took place during a more generalised period of crisis for the ruling class.

Economically, Britain remained the foremost global economic powerhouse, but growth rates were sluggish and newly industrialising countries led by the USA and Germany were catching up and starting to challenge the dominance of British capital.[35]

Politically, the gradual expansion of the vote and the birth of a number of working class political parties, alongside the rise of new unionism and unemployed agitation, further fuelled the growing sense of disorder and potential challenge to the existing order.[36]

Socially, there was growing concern about the living conditions in which the outcast population of the inner cities lived.[37]

A range of voluntary organisations committed to "child saving" emerged in the second half of the 19th century. Organisations such as Barnardos (1867), the Girls' Friendly Society (1874), the Church of England Waifs and Strays Society (1881), the Children's Society (1881), the Church of England Purity Society (1883), the White Cross Army (1883) and the NSPCC (1889) were committed to saving children from a life of vice, misery, crime and danger.

In part these organisations were shaped by a set of ideas that argued that if poor working class children were not saved from danger, they would themselves become dangerous.

There was anxiety that the conditions of urban living were fuelling opposition to government and state. Such fears prompted a number of investigations into working class living conditions. Perhaps most famous were the poverty studies of Booth and Rowntree.

Booth was a Liverpool industrialist and arch Conservative. He wanted to study poverty to disprove the "outrageous claims" made by the Marxist organisation the Social Democratic Federation (SDF) that poverty was rife in the inner cities. A study by the SDF had suggested that 25 percent of the population of London was living in poverty.[38] Booth set out to attack the SDF for: "Putting such erroneous... 'Incendiary' statements [about the extent of poverty], before the people".[39]

Rowntree was a Quaker and, impressed by Booth's study of poverty in London, he decided to do something similar in York. At the start of his study he thought the poor were poor because they drank too much.

Both Booth and Rowntree undertook their studies with a set of assumptions about poverty based on very traditional notions of what was termed "less eligibility"[40] and the personal failings of the poor themselves. But the results of their studies emphasised that there was a deeper structural problem: poor wages and employment conditions were the root cause of poverty.[41]

These findings seemed to point to an even greater problem. Poverty, ill health and nutritional deficiencies led to recruitment problems experienced by the British army during the Boer Wars. In 1900 56.5 percent of the men who were measured at army recruitment offices were under 5 foot 6 inches; in 1845 only 10.5 percent of potential recruits had been under this height.[42] During the Boer War between 40-60 percent of potential recruits were deemed unfit to serve.[43]

As worrying for the defenders of Empire was the decline in the birth rate, from 35.5 per 1,000 between 1871-75 to 29.3 per 1,000 between 1896-1900, alongside the increase in infant mortality, from 146 per 1,000 live births in 1876 to 156 per 1,000 live births in 1897.[44]

In 1903 the government set up an Inter-Departmental Committee on Physical Deterioration, which made a number of recommendations including demands for improvement to the standard of food and drink, regulation of overcrowding, control of air pollution, training of young girls in cookery and "home economics", provision of school meals for underfed children and school medical inspections.

This coincided with the formation of a National Efficiency movement, which focused on working class children and aimed to improve their education, health and morality. It also led to the growth of organisations like the Boys' Brigade, Boy (and then Girl) Scouts, Lads' Clubs and a range of sporting clubs shaped by notions of "muscular Christianity", all promoting "healthy living" for working class young people.

The message was clear. British capitalism and the British Empire needed a fit and healthy workforce and army if it was to fend off competition from its economic and military rivals. This meant focusing on working class children, as "Children of the Nation",[45] and women as "mothers of Empire".[46]

The consequence was an increase in state legislation and activity in the area of child protection and regulation. State activity was shaped by a relationship of both "care" and "control" and both these drivers were embedded within the growing state welfare activity unleashed from the end of the 19th century. According to Hendricks what we witnessed was:

a consciously designed pursuit of the national interest, which included all-round efficiency, public health, education, racial hygiene, responsible parenthood and social purity.[47]

There was substantial legislation passed relating to child welfare and protection at the turn of the 20th century. The Prevention of Cruelty to Children Act (1889), the Poor Law Adoption Act (1889), the Custody of Children Act (1891) and the Children Acts (1872, 1897, 1908) laid "the ground for the removal of children from parents on the grounds of "unreasonable" treatment.

Through such legislation state welfare professionals started to carve out their roles. Midwives, doctors and social workers started to gain a role as regulators of children's lives, of appropriate family relationships and of what was acceptable within the home.

As part of these processes the school, and the education system, became established as central features in children's lives. Education seemed to address a number of the problems that contemporary commentators identified.

For those concerned about the growing economic competition from the US and Germany, education would allow the basic numeracy and literacy skills required in the new industries. This was "education for work"—and remains a central driver for some aspects of the education system today.

Interestingly while some sections of capital wanted a more educated workforce to keep up with global competitors others, like textile manufacturers, were opposed to the schooling system because it would deprive them of a source of cheap labour. On this issue an initial compromise was reached where "half time working" was allowed up until 1918.[48]

For those concerned about unruly street arabs the school system offered an institutional location for young people which would require them to spend the main part of the day "locked in the classroom".

The schooling system was based on hierarchy, complete subservience to the teacher, rote learning and obedience. These were thought to be the ideal values that would train young minds to be obedient workers in the factories in later life. This was viewed as a positive counter to the trade unionism, socialism and all forms of anti-capitalist values that were seemingly growing among the working population.

Gender roles and the importance of the family could be taught via home economics, commitment to the Empire instilled via the annual Empire Day celebrations (where pupils were encouraged to dress as "natives" of conquered lands), and health and nutritional issues addressed via school medical inspections and even free school meals (both established after legislation was passed in 1906, enabling school meal provision, and 1908, establishing compulsory medical inspections).

Education was also supported by significant sections of the working class. Education was valued as a way of lifting people out of poverty and ignorance. Of course support for the idea of education was not the same as support for the kind of education that was established. Conflict over the form and content of education has always been a feature of educational debates. Free school meals may have been driven by a mix of eugenicist and national efficiency concerns, but they also brought a very real material benefit for working class children and their families, and were supported for this reason.

As it developed, therefore, the education system contained a number of contradictory elements and drivers. But this leaves one aspect out of the discussion: the attitudes of young people now required to attend school.

Stephen Humphries[49] argues that the response of working class young people to the "regulatory invasion" of their lives was a rebellious anti-authoritarianism which brought them into conflict with teachers, schools, park keepers, police and a range of "authority figures".

As the editorial in the *Educational News* in 1889 argued in the face of that year's school strikes:

> Schoolboy strikers... are simply rebels. Obedience is the first rule of school life... School strikes are therefore not merely acts of disobedience but a reversal of the primary purpose of schools. They are on a par with strikes in the army or navy.[50]

Working class childhood, then, was forged in a particular socio-economic context, out of the conflicts between state institutions, policy makers, welfare agencies and professionals and the responses of working class young people to these processes.

In the school setting young people are subject to rules that dictate everything from the clothes they wear to how they should conduct themselves in the classroom. The school regime regulates their activities, their interactions with teachers and those in authority and delineates their learning schedule. In all these aspects of schooling students are denied a significant voice. Schooling has, in part, also been about teaching us to accept authority and know our place: today the authority of the teacher, tomorrow that of the foreman or office manager.[51]

The school strike challenges all of this.

School strikes have been far from uncommon in Britain; indeed we will argue that hardly a year goes by without a school strike somewhere in the country, though generally the strikes are not reported and remain hidden from history. As Robert Adams notes:

> Collective protests by pupils have received scant attention from researchers... Pupil protest has been largely ignored by commentators over the years, despite the fact that schools...have a long history of pupil protest.[52]

In the second decade of the 21st century in Britain school students have taken strike action on a range of issues: changes to school hours and holidays, petty rules about dress codes, school privatisation, and, perhaps most memorably, against changes to student fees, funding and maintenance support in 2010.

In November and December 2010 young students left their schools and sixth form colleges to join mass demonstrations against cuts and student fees.[53]

The student Day X protests were a response to the Conservative-Liberal Democrat government's austerity measures. The focus was the implications of draconian cuts to education and their impact on students. The government was rushing ahead to implement changes to student funding which would see students paying full fees of up to £9,000 a year for their higher education; the most expensive fees in Europe.

As the student movement developed, more grievances were raised. In particular the government's intention to scrap the means-tested Educational Maintenance Allowance (EMA), affecting some of the poorest students in post-16 education, became a central mobiliser. Almost 600,000 young people qualified for the EMA, which offered payments of up to £30 a week to students from poorer backgrounds enabling them to attend post-compulsory education.

The movement of 2010 was led by university students. They occupied universities, colleges, politicians' offices, banks, shops and offices owned by tax avoiding firms and turned out in large numbers for many local and national demonstrations. The demonstration on 10 November, organised by the National Union of Students and the lecturers' union the UCU, saw over 50,000 students lay siege to Tory party HQ in Milbank.

The Millbank siege galvanised opposition to austerity. It also gave confidence to others to join the battle.

On three massive days of protest, Day X (24 November), Day X2 (30 November) and Day X3 (9 December), university students were joined by significant numbers of school and sixth form students:

> It was precisely the youngest school and college students who were to become the cutting edge of the movement... Most major cities saw several thousand school and college students walk out on Day X, with hundreds in even some of the smallest towns. Pupils went from classroom to classroom chanting "Strike, strike" and pulled out whole schools. Town halls and Lib Dem offices were occupied. In Brighton protesters took over four buildings.[54]

The 24 November day of action saw considerable numbers of school students take action across the country. There were school strikes recorded across London, Liverpool, Newcastle, Manchester, Nottingham, Oxford, Cambridge, Leeds, Sheffield, Birmingham, Barnsley, Bristol, Brighton, Milton Keynes, Cardiff, Bury, Blackburn and Winchester.[55] The school students were involved in a range of actions. According to the BBC:

> Up to 3,000 students paraded through Brighton city centre as eggs and fireworks were thrown.
>
> In Manchester, around 3,000 protesters gathered outside the town hall, disrupting city centre traffic.
>
> In Oxford, hundreds of students and school pupils protested in the town centre.
>
> In Cambridge, more than 200 students scaled scaffolding to erect banners at the Senate House and protested in the grounds of King's College.
>
> In Liverpool, more than 2,000 students marched, with about 300 of them blocking three major city centre roads to traffic.
>
> In Sheffield, 2,000 students and secondary school pupils marched to the town hall.[56]

The centre of the protest was London. Laurie Penny, writing from the demonstration for the *Guardian*'s rolling coverage of the events, captured the excitement and dynamism of what was happening:

There are no leaders here: the thousands of schoolchildren and young people who streamed into Whitehall three hours ago in protest at the government's attacks on further and higher education were working completely off script.

A wordless cry went up somewhere in the crowd and they were off, moving as one, with no instructions, towards parliament.

But just because there are no leaders here doesn't mean there is no purpose. These kids—and most of them are just kids, with no experience of direct action, who walked simultaneously out of lessons across the country just before morning break—want to be heard. "Our votes don't count," says one nice young man in a school tie.[57]

The BBC reported:

[T]here were a disproportionate number of younger pupils who had bunked off school for the day. Some were as young as 13—although that particular pupil insisted his mother knew where he was… Three teenage boys from a St John's Wood school—none of them older than 17—told me why they had turned up. "I want to study medicine," said the first one who was in his first year of A Levels. "What the [expletive] am I supposed to do to pay the fees I'm now going to face?"

Another 16 year old, describing himself as "Kieran from Camden", had been reading up on Marx. He gave every journalist who would listen a passable essay on the theory of class.[58]

Similar stories were heard across the country:

Jamil Keating led a walkout of over 400 students from Xaverian Catholic Sixth Form College in Manchester. "We feel like the rich have been completely let off the hook. It's the poor that are being made to pay. We have to fight, we have no choice."

Samir Hinks from Bury College echoed this: "We're the ones who will have all our rights taken away. The Lib Dems have lied. The first demo on 10 November was a spark, now it's turned into a roaring inferno. There is a huge sense of unfairness at the system—it's two-tier. We have to fight tooth and nail for everything while the rich get it handed to them on a plate. This isn't just about the cuts to education—it's about being young and working class and not having a future."

Arnie was one of 1,100 who walked out of Chiswick Community School, in west London. He said, "I was expecting a handful of people but suddenly there were hundreds, then a thousand."

"Our school wouldn't let us hold a sit-in," said Shona, a year 11 student at Chorlton High School [Manchester]. "They said we had to do it in break time. We didn't feel like this would make the point strongly enough so we organised a walkout".[59]

On Day X2 (30 November) there was, again, significant school and college student involvement across the country with school and college walkouts in London, Manchester, Leeds, Birmingham, Colchester, Cardiff, Belfast, Newcastle, Bath and Liverpool.[60]

In Twickenham school students from Orleans Park School demonstrated outside Lib Dem Cabinet Minister Vince Cable's office. Many were as young as 14. Joe Rogers (aged 15) said:

I want to go to university, so does everyone here but we can't afford it. We just want to be heard.

Charlie Pellow (14), added:

I want to get a job but I'm worried I won't be able to afford university.

While Sophie Mann (15) said she feared the cost of higher education would rise even more in the coming years:

We're worried that when we go to university it's going to be even worse.[61]

In Wiltshire, school and sixth form students from Hardenhuish and Sheldon schools met up in Chippenham town centre. Chris King, aged 17, said:

The [fee] rises are totally unjust and unfair when you consider that most of the people in the cabinet either went to Uni for free or are millionaires... The government are continuing our involvement with Afghanistan and Iraq, but they are unwilling to put money behind the education of young people in this country.[62]

On Day X3 (9 December) the protests culminated in a blockade of Parliament as MPs voted on the issue inside. Once again there were protests across the country, but the focus was on Westminster and the vote.

The day was notable for three things.

First, the resilience of the young protestors who had been protesting for a month and created a massive political problem for the Coalition, especially the "junior partners" the Liberal Democrats, who had stood in the election in May 2010 on a platform of "no fees".[63]

Second, the brutality of the police. Mounted police with truncheons and on foot snatch squads picked off small groups of students. Others were kettled for hours in freezing cold conditions. Many were beaten. Many were arrested.

Finally, on the evening of 9 December some demonstrators got close to Prince Charles—an action that caused apoplexy in the popular press the following day.[64] That the royal family should actually be confronted by young working class people demanding their rights made the establishment froth at the mouth.

Over the month-long protest movement the school students were dismissed, and slightly ridiculed, in the press as "copy cat" strikers. This suggests they were unthinking and easily led; out for a bit of fun and a bit of disruption—but not serious about the issues. They were, after all, kids. And as kids they were, apparently, vulnerable to the influence of outside agitators, mischievous university students and assorted radicals.

For example, in Liverpool Head Teacher Sister Brigid Halligan of Sefton Park secondary said schools across the city would be "anxious" that students walking out of lessons would affect attendance rates and exam preparation for 14 to 18 year olds:

> I don't think compulsory school age students should be encouraged to join such a protest. We have a responsibility for them. Even for sixth form students I would prefer them to be in school, their exams are coming up... The danger is some very young children will think this is a really good idea without really understanding what they are doing it for.[65]

Other head teachers noted their general support for the issues, but not the form of protest:

> Litherland High's headteacher Jim Donnelly said: "I share their concerns over the cuts" but as all his pupils were 16 or under he was forced to mark them truant for skipping class.

Dr David Dennison, headmaster at Aigburth's St Margaret's CE Technology and Language College said while students should register their concerns over the "bitter blow" of a rise in tuition fees it should be "done in a manner that would not be detrimental to their present courses".[66]

This led to those in authority trying to treat the strikes as examples of truancy, not political action. In Sheffield Police Supt Martin Scothern was reported as saying:

I am disappointed that large numbers of schoolchildren joined the demonstrations. We are working with local education authorities to deal with truancy issues.[67]

As we will see in the chapters that follow, dismissing the political meaning of strikes is far from uncommon (although the quotes from school strikers above indicate quite a clear political understanding of what was happening). But as the following examples show, such dismissal completely misunderstands the rapid political learning that can take place during strike waves.

In Sheffield, on 7 December 2010, 250 students from King Edward VII School marched on the town hall.

The school students tried to get into the town hall but were stopped by police, so they marched off down the main road. They then went into Topshop—run by tax avoider Sir Phillip Green.

About 50 students got inside Topshop which closed down. They then went on to Boots—which moved its HQ to a Swiss post office box to avoid paying some £86 million a year in UK taxes.[68]

The young students were drawing political conclusions and linking education cuts to tax avoidance. In practice their actions were posing a serious alternative to the government's austerity agenda—they were asserting that cuts and austerity were not inevitable, the deficit could be funded by making the tax avoiders pay their due.

Similar views were expressed by young students who occupied their school in Camden. The students from Camden School for Girls occupied their school for 24 hours. They explained why they were occupying to journalist Sadie Robinson:

"It came about after two of us went to visit the student occupation at University College London (UCL)," said Jen. "It was very inspiring.

We were glad that university students were doing things, but we thought that sixth form students should take action too—because we'll be the ones paying higher fees... The younger kids all support us too. They all walked out last time—and they will again tomorrow."

Cathryn explained that the students had three goals. "We want the school to agree not to penalise students for taking part and to issue a press statement against fee rises," she said. "We also want the school to confirm that it supports the right to protest."

[The] Students [were] against plans to raise fees but also many other Tory proposals. "The Tories say that they want ex-soldiers to be able to train up quickly to become teachers," said Cathryn. "But our teachers have years of training and are committed to teaching. The Tories just want to discipline the working class."

Jen added, "We're against Michael Gove's white paper. I'm fine with discipline from trained teachers—but not from a bloody military commander!"

They also question other aspects of the coalition government. "The government says there are too many people on benefits," said Nikki. "But if they stop people being able to get degrees, how are they supposed to get jobs? I want to go to university—but I won't be able to afford it if they raise fees. Then what?"

Students reject the idea that cuts are inevitable and necessary. "A lot of people used to think that there's not much else the government can do but make cuts," said Jen. "But after we had a couple of UCL students and a South Bank student came to talk to us, people think differently. It was a mind-opening meeting".[69]

The protests of 2010 came close to defeating the government's plans for education. They opened up fissures in a weak government and damned the Liberal Democrats, who plunged in the opinion polls and following elections as a result.

The student radicalisation didn't simply end with the passing of the legislation introducing increased fees. Indeed many of the young activists returned to the streets a year later to join trade unionists fighting to defend public sector pensions.[70]

Through their actions the young students dismissed notions of student apathy and provided an example of the energy, drive and huge potential young people have to challenge the political status quo when they act together to assert their rights.

As we show in the chapters that follow, this energy and enthusiasm for change is common to all school student strikes, it is what makes them vibrant and exciting—and a challenge to the dominant order.

Tom Kay (Sheffield, 2010)
"The strike was very mixed... It emphasised that the EMA was a class issue"

In 2010 I was 17 in the second year of Langley Park sixth form college in Sheffield. The college is in the north of the city, in one of the poorest wards in the country.

The atmosphere in the college had been quite political since the election. A lot of students relied on the EMA and others were nervous about what the Coalition's plans for higher education funding would mean.

The college itself had made a submission to the government against cuts to the EMA and the impact it would have on students from our part of the city. But though they spoke out against the cuts in this way, in the days before the 24 November strike the senior management tried to stop us talking about any walkout.

For a few days before the planned strike I leafletted the college. I also had a stall outside. I was arguing people should come out at 2pm and join the protest in the city centre.

The college authorities said I couldn't have a stall. The Principal and Vice Principal came outside and said "If we let you have a stall, what happens if the BNP turn up tomorrow? We wouldn't be able to stop them".

I told them this was a stupid argument and if the BNP turned up there would be loads of students out to stop them. Langley Park is the most multicultural sixth form in the city, there is no danger of the BNP turning up!

I refused to take the stall down. When I went back into the school they took me to the administration section. Normally students weren't allowed in here, but I was kept for two hours. I was told I had an "inherent problem with authority" and my actions were a "danger to other students"!

The day before the strike I was called out of class again. This time there were two cops waiting for me. They questioned me and demanded to know if I knew of any plans for violence at the demo!

On the day of the strike 63 students came out. That was pretty good. We are miles from the city centre—about an hour and a half walk.

We commandeered a bus—all 63 of us piled on. We were chanting and singing. One of the students had brought a Palestinian flag—which is interesting because it emphasises, I think, that it was political and the politics were quite generalised.

Then the bus got stopped by the cops. A copper asked me what we were doing, told us to stop chanting and when I asked him about this he told me to "fuck off"!

When we got to the city centre we joined the demo. There were about 2,000 school students there. The crowd was very mixed. There were a lot of Somali kids there and poor white working class students as well. The EMA issue was really significant and the demo showed, I think, that this was a class issue.

When we got back to school the following day there were loads of debates about the strike. One of the senior managers tried to stop me talking to other students in the canteen and we had a stand up row about this. In the school I was known to be quite political and people were coming and asking me about what was happening next and I think the school wanted to isolate me.

There were two significant outcomes. First, when I told mum and dad about being taken out of school to talk to the cops, they went ballistic. They demanded to see the Principal. The outcome was that we got a formal apology from them and a guarantee it wouldn't happen again!

Second, the UCU branch in the college put out a statement saying there should be no victimisation of students. This was important and meant the college backed off from that. Instead they moved to be much more open in their criticism of what the government was doing.

Our school didn't join the remaining Day X events. It had started snowing and the college actually shut down for a fortnight! But that meant I was free to join the university occupation—and that's what I did.

I had been planning to take a gap year after college. But after my experiences I decided to go straight to uni. I wanted to keep up my political activity—and that's what I did. This was a great learning experience for me. It was an exciting time and it helped convince me that we can fight for and achieve a better world.

2

The hidden history of school student strikes

In his history of the movements of the late 1960s and 1970s, Chris Harman discusses the ebb and flow of the class struggle and identifies a number of protest waves that shaped the 20th century.[71] Protest waves are periods of generalised upturn in social conflict. The American sociologist of social movements Sidney Tarrow describes what happens during a typical upturn in a protest wave:

> [These periods] are characterised by heightened conflict: not only in industrial relations, but in the streets; not only there, but in villages and schools. In such periods, the magnitude of conflictual collective action of many kinds rises appreciably above what is typical both before and after. Particular groups recur with regularity in the vanguard of waves of social protest (for example, miners, students); but they are frequently joined during the peak of the cycle by groups that are not generally known for their insurgent tendencies.[72]

School students would be a group "not generally known for their insurgent tendencies". For the most part schools are places where sustained discontent is hard to organise. The school regime makes it relatively easy for students to be isolated, disciplined and potentially expelled for misdemeanours and infringement of often arcane rules.

Yet despite this, school students resist and engage in a range of protest activities. Booth and Coulby[73] draw attention to the variety of ways individual students resist school regimentation and fight against the school experience: carrying on, mouthing off, challenging dress codes, attacking teachers and bunking off are just some of the ways some students reject authority.[74]

Occasionally rejection of school authority takes a collective form:

the school student strike. As Stephen Humphries suggests, "The most dramatic and subversive act of resistance to schooling…[is] the pupils' strike… [It is]…essentially a defiant gesture of protest by working-class children and their parents against the authoritarian, bureaucratic and centralised structure of schooling".[75]

In the limited academic writing about school strikes, they are often portrayed as an example of what the sociologist Rubel calls a "disruption". A disruption:

> is some kind of organised group [behaviour]…specifically characterised as an activity designed to accomplish a planned goal or establish a point of contention…[which] must additionally have the effect of interfering with the education of other students.[76]

Yet seeing school strikes as disruptions decontextualises the actions. The political focus and nature of the strikes are lost.

School student strikes dispute the generally held view that schooling and education somehow exist in a social vacuum, detached from the iniquities and class relations of capitalist society. They question the dominant notion that children, locked within modern notions of childhood, are unable to comprehend social injustice, inequality or oppression. They suddenly involve young people in politics and protest as active social agents—rather than as mere passive objects who should "do what they are told". And thus they also challenge the marginal social position of children within family, school and society.

And neither, of course, are they a peculiarly British phenomenon. Table 1, opposite, presents the findings of a review of the main British papers concerning school strikes by students in a range of countries during the twentieth century.

Let's look at some high profile international school strikes in more detail.

Perhaps the most famous school strike in history took place in 1976 in apartheid South Africa. School students in Soweto struck because they refused to be taught in Afrikaans, the language of the oppressor.

Education under apartheid was based on the Bantu Education Act (1953). It produced an overcrowded, under-resourced system of schooling for black young people. Between 1955-1967 the staff-student ratio went up from 46:1 to 58:1 and the per capita spending differential was

Table 1: British reports of school strikes across the globe 1931-1966

Year	Location	Numbers/Scale	Grievance	Source
1931	Berlin, Germany	More than 1,000 students	Cuts, school closures and teacher redundancies	"School children on strike against Berlin economies", *Guardian*, 30 September
1935	Cuba	Joint teacher student strike across island. Other unions threaten to join.	Removal of maintenance grants	"Cuban Unrest", *Times*, 2 March
1936	Cairo, Egypt	Schools and universities closed. Four killed	British rule	"Boy shot dead in new riots", *Daily Mail*, 29 January
1937	Achill Island, Ireland	13-week long strike led by, what's described as a "Soviet gang"	Removal of school meals	"'Soviet gang' in school strike" *Daily Mail*, 11 March
1940	Lillehammer, Norway	"hundreds"	Imposition of Nazi teaching by Quisling Government	"School strikes in Norway", *Daily Worker*, 21 November
1941	Oslo, Bertgen, Aker, Norway	"hundreds"	Against the brutal activities of Quisling "youth guards" and attempts to impose Nazi teaching	"School strike in Norway", *Guardian*, 2 March; "Nazis beat up pupils in Norway" *Yorkshire Post* and *Leeds Mercury*, 3 March
1955	Cyprus	"large numbers"	Fights with police; demands for freedom of political prisoners	"Protest strike by children", *Guardian*, 9 April
1956	Singapore	500 girls—part of the 3,000 strong "Chinese Middle School Students Union"	Strike against banning of the union and arrest of two communist teachers by the British	"'Children's Union' is banned as subversive", *Daily Mail*, 25 September
1956	Algeria	Particularly strong in Algiers, Oran, Moroccan Border	Response to a call for a school strike by the National Liberation Front	"Trial of rebel's strength: Moslem school strike", *Guardian*, 2 October
1963	Boston	3,000 black students strike against segregation	Called by Civil Rights leaders. School students attend "freedom centres" to hear lectures on civil rights	"Negroes stage new school strike", *Daily Mail*, 19 June
1966	Stockholm, Sweden	1,000 pupils	In support of teachers' strike.	"Pupils defy board in teachers' strike", 27 October

stark. In 1976 the Government spent R644 per pupil annually on white children's education compared to R42 for black children.[77]

Overcrowded classrooms were often used on a rota basis and in Soweto, the large township just outside Johannesburg, no schools were built between 1962 and 1971. The government's intention was that black children would return "home" to their homelands to attend school. But by the 1970s South African industry wanted a better trained and educated workforce and there was growing pressure on the government to improve the system in the economic interests of South African capital. In Soweto alone 40 new schools were built and the number of school students rose from 12,656 to 34,656 between 1972 and 1976.[78]

The expansion of schools had an impact on black youth culture. The schools created a social space where young people could talk about apartheid and the liberation struggle. When in 1974 the Education Board announced that Afrikaans should be taught alongside English, the seeds of revolt were planted.

School strikes started in the Transvaal in 1975. In Soweto students organised themselves into the Soweto Student Representative Council. On 16 June 1976 the school students marched peacefully against the Afrikaans decree and against the poor conditions in schools. The crowd quickly grew until there were an estimated 10,000 students marching to the Orlando football stadium.[79]

As the march progressed they were confronted by the police. The officers first launched tear gas before firing live ammunition into the crowd. Two students, Hastings Ndlovu and Hector Pieterson, were murdered, hundreds more were injured. The shootings sparked an uprising that soon spread across the country.[80]

The school strike led to a massive confrontation at a time when the liberation movements were banned in the country. For the previous decade the liberation struggle had been subjected to significant government repression. The school strikes confronted the police, closed the schools and occupied the town centres. The students re-lit the fuse of rebellion, raising the banner of the anti-apartheid struggle across the country—and indeed across the globe.[81]

But South Africa is not the only example.

In 1951 in Virginia, at the heart of the Jim Crow system that operated in the southern states of the US, young black school students struck for better school provision.

At the time the US Constitution upheld the right for states to provide "separate but equal" facilities for people from different "races". This was enshrined in a Supreme Court ruling (known as Plessy v Ferguson) made in 1896. The ruling institutionalised and legalised segregation: separate and unequal facilities.

The school strike at the Robert Russa Moton High School in Prince Edward County, Virginia took place four years before Rosa Parks refused to give her seat up to a white passenger in Montgomery, Alabama and six years before nine black students were enrolled at the Central High School in Little Rock, Arkansas. This was a strike about the conditions of black schooling and a demand for investment in high schools for black kids. Yet this is a story that is little known.

The strike started on Monday 23 April and was incredibly well planned and organised.[82] As the 450 students marched out of school they screamed:

> Two bits—four bits—six bits—a dollar—all for this strike stand up and holler.[83]

The students then mounted a checkpoint picket to ensure there were no strike breakers going to school over the next few days.

The strike started with the demand for a new high school, equal to that available to local white students. By day three their demand had changed: they demanded desegregated schooling. The students drew in support from parents, the black community in the county, from national civil rights organisations including the NAACP,[84] from the black churches and even from sections of the local white community. They held rallies in local Baptist churches, managed the media and got widespread coverage.

On 3 May the students submitted a lawsuit demanding desegregation. There were large protests against the strikers' demands from the racist right. But instead of being intimidated the school students called a mass rally of their supporters—the largest black political meeting ever held in the county up till that point.

The students returned to school on 7 May. They soon got a new state of the art school building to replace the previous ramshackle structure. The case Davis v County School Board of Prince Edward County was lost in the Richmond District Court (partly because a new building was now in place so the authorities claimed they had fulfilled the separate but equal clause enshrined in Plessy v Ferguson). But the students didn't give up. They combined with three other law suits and in 1954, took their case to the Supreme Court, which led to a formal decree against school segregation![85]

An incredibly well organised and brave struggle by school students was central to the early phase of the 1950s civil rights movement in the US. Though perhaps because these were school students, their role has been underplayed.

Anti-racism was also a mobiliser for school student strikes in the US in 1968. Mexican-American students in East Los Angeles staged a walkout in their high schools to protest against school conditions and institutionalised discrimination.

Students were forbidden from speaking Spanish in class or from using the toilets during lunchtime. The school curriculum largely ignored or denied Mexican-American history and students were pushed towards menial jobs rather than moving to college or university.

In March the students decided to take a stand against the injustice and staged walkouts in schools across LA. Around 20,000 students took part.[86]

In the same year in France school students joined university students in the massive protest wave that rocked the country. The students struck, joined marches and demanded greater democratisation of the schooling system. In some cases this included the right to determine what subjects were taught in the classroom. This was the birth of the "pupil power" movement, whose manifestation in Britain we discuss in chapters 5 and 6.

In Australia there were school student protests against Australian involvement in the Vietnam war. In 1970 school students struck and joined a large anti-war rally in Sydney.[87]

In Kenya and Uganda there was a major wave of school student strikes in 1973 and 1974. The students were protesting against the poor quality of education, teaching methods and lack of resources. The national media blamed the strikes on students "copying" events in Europe and the US led by a minority of political activists. As we will see, suggesting strikes are copycat activities and that most students are duped into activity by radical activists is a common refrain during school student protests.[88]

In Italy school student strikes are far from uncommon. Almost every autumn some students go out on strike! The protests are often over national issues, such as opposition to government education reforms or the impact of austerity measures. Students also strike over local issues such as the inadequacy of school heating, or defence of victimised colleagues. As Chris Roseshows:

> All over [Italy, students] go on strike, they have demonstrations in the street, they occupy their schools, they have lots of meetings and sometimes they try and run the schools themselves...setting up their own lessons and courses.[89]

More recently across Europe and North America there are numerous examples of school students engaging in strikes against the impact of austerity in the aftermath of the 2007 bank crash.

In 2008 there were significant school student protests in Italy, Spain, Greece and Germany. The protests were about cuts and privatisation of education.[90] The main demands of the students included smaller classes, more teachers and an end to privatisation measures.

On 24 April 2009 an estimated 60,000 school students in Austria struck—the third strike in as many weeks.[91] The students were protesting about the impact of austerity measures.

In April 2010 hundreds of high school students in New Jersey, USA went on strike against proposed cuts to their school's budget.[92] And 2010 was the year of the university and school student demonstrations and strikes against cuts and fees in Britain (see pp25-34).

There were further school student protests in Spain[93] and New York in 2012[94] against cuts in education, both heavily influenced by the Indignados and Occupy movements taking hold in the respective countries.

In December 2013 around 5,000 school students in Hamburg, Germany organised a mass school strike. Students from over 30 high schools in the city struck and marched in defence of refugee rights.[95] At the same time thousands of students in Austria were on strike against changes to the final school exam system.[96] And school occupations played a prominent role in the struggle against austerity in Greece in 2014.

In September 2015 Arab students in Israel (both Muslim and Christian) joined forces in a strike against discriminatory cuts to funding that affected their education and their access to school trips. An

Table 2: "Sporadic" school strikes in Britain 1913-1962

Year	Location	Numbers involved	Grievance/demands	Source
1913	Bentley, Doncaster	300	Distance of school from pit village	*Daily Mail*, 29 November
1914	Herefordshire	"hundreds"	Teachers went on strike for more pay, children came out in support	*Daily Mail*, 3 February
1914	Bedworth, Warwickshire	"hundreds"	Warwickshire County Council decision to raise school leaving age from 13 to 14	*Guardian*, 5 March; *Daily Mail*, 5 March; *Daily Mail*, 6 March; *Times*, 5 March
1914	Buckie, Aberdeenshire	45	Demands for a shorter day, weekly half-holiday and "no strapping"	*Times*, 5 March
1915	Haverfordwest, Pembrokeshire	Unknown	Excessive punishment	*Guardian*, 19 July
1916	Monmouthshire	20 schools, including "even toddling infants"	A teacher was reported as saying: "It was...the most impudent strike I have ever heard of, and the most successful"	*Daily Mail*, 14 June
1920	Tonna (near Neath), Glamorganshire	Whole school. Lasted several days and older pupils "acted like pickets"	Against the appointment of a new head (who was replacing local teacher who had been acting head for four years)	*Times*, 27 February; *Guardian*, 29 February; *Times*, 2 March; *Daily Mail*, 3 March
1920	Hevingham, Norfolk	"whole school village"	Demanding reinstatement of local teacher. Children had "daily parades with banners and flags"	*Daily Mail*, 19 April
1920	Orpington, Kent	380	Demanding re-instatement of pre-war head rather than ex-officer of the army corps	*Daily Mail*, 5 May
1920	Llanelli	500	Students claim "the school is dirty" because no cleaner appointed	*Guardian*, 21 September
1921	Wrexham	300	Against the "appointment of an outside man" over a local	*Guardian*, 27 January
1921	Stirlingshire	175	Miners' children were refused free school meals, so strike and picket demanding to be fed	*Daily Mail*, 21 April
1923	Gloucester	Unknown	Demanding the reinstatement of the head	*Guardian*, 28 March

1924	Maids Moreton, Buckinghamshire	Whole school	Demanding the removal and then celebrating the dismissal of a "caning teacher"	*Daily Mail*, 16 February
1924	Ebbw Vale	280	Reinstatement of local head. Pickets used	*Guardian*, 6 March
1924	Buckton Vale, Stalybridge	Whole school strike, lasted four and a half months	Against local education board decision that those over age 11 should complete their schooling at a different school in neighbouring village	*Guardian*, 28 August
1926	Manchester	No reliable figures	Five young communists arrested for holding a "reds meeting" where the pamphlet "Stand with the miners" was available. The pamphlet included the line "we must mobilise school children by mass refusal to attend school", which was quoted at the trial	*Guardian*, 18 May
1926	Bromley	Unknown	Against inadequate school provision on Dawnham estate. Parents summoned to court	*Guardian*, 7 December
1927	Bredgar, Kent	Nine senior pupils	Against a "spy" who reports bad behaviour	*Daily Mail*, 30 November
1929	Watford and East Ham	Pupils "locked out"	Against reorganisation of education, making children walk further to their new schools	*Times*, 10 September
1929	Rowley Regis, Staffordshire	50 percent of pupils in village	Against reorganisation of education, making children walk further to their new schools	*Guardian*, 2 October
1929	Winsford	Unknown	Reorganisation of schools; transfer of pupils	*Guardian*, 14 November
1932	Edinburgh	300	Reorganisation of schools; lasted several weeks	*Guardian*, 7 September
1932	Blaina, Monmouthshire	50 percent of local pupils	Against changes to local "relief" (benefits) regulations	*Times*, 6 December
1935	Lenzie, Dunbartonshire	300	Teacher transfer	*Daily Mail*, 8 June
1935	Hyde Heath, Bucks	Unknown (lasted several weeks)	School reorganisation and pupil transfers	*Daily Mail*, 8 June
1937	Wallsend-on-Tyne	250	Poor condition of school	*Guardian*, 24 September
1937	Bedford	800 pupils out for 14 days	Reorganisation of local schools and pupil transfers	*Times*, 20 April
1938	Willsden	90 percent of pupils at two schools	Demanding speed limits after a fatality on the road outside school	*Times*, 4 May

1948	Crewe	500 pupils; three days	Reorganisation of schools and pupil transfers	*Guardian*, 5 August
1959	Rutherford	283	Overcrowded classes	*Guardian*, 17 November
1960	Altrincham	150	Overcrowding	*Guardian*, 15 March
1960	Kidlington	Unknown	Delay in starting GCE course	*Daily Mail*, 15 March
1960	Markgate	Unknown	School closure	*Daily Mail*, 9 September
1961	Widnes	Unknown	Poor quality of school meals	*Guardian*, 28 September
1961	Reading	72	Road crossings	*Daily Mail*, 1 November
1962	High Wycombe	Unknown	Lack of heating in snow conditions	*Daily Mail*, 1 March
1962	Midhurst	50 pupils from grammar school, but try to pull others out	Cuban Missile Crisis; demanding an end to US blocade	*Guardian*, 25 October
1962	Banbury, Oxfordshire	20 for three days	Fifth form girls walk out after being forced outside in the cold	*Daily Mail*, 11 December

estimated 33,000 students were on strike[97] and on 7 September "450,000 students from Israeli Arab schools across the country joined the strike in solidarity".[98]

The evidence seems clear: school strikes are a far more common—and global—phenomenon than is often assumed.

There are two general forms of school strike. One is isolated or sporadic, often in response to a specific grievance: the brutality of a head, the sacking of a teacher, the victimisation of a pupil or the privatisation of a school.

Generally sporadic strikes are difficult to document. Because they represent a significant challenge to authority, schools often go out of their way to disguise them in records. The strike can bring embarrassment to teachers, schools and local authorities and so may be recorded not as a strike but as truancy or given some other, more acceptable, label. Nevertheless, in Table 2, above, we present details of school strikes in Britain recorded in the national press in the 50 years between 1913 and 1960. We don't claim this list is exhaustive, but it presents evidence of a form of protest far more common than is often thought.

Typical of these types of strike is the story of Les Kenyon from Bolton, who recalls going on strike in 1914 against teacher brutality:

> I remember going on strike at school... Over Mr Fernhall giving one of the lads [the] stick... He'd had stick, he said, for something, for nothing, so he got us all to go on strike... We went back to school at dinner time, and then when the whistle blew about a dozen of us went to Mere Hall Park, and we stayed there till Mr Fernhall, Mr Smith and Mr Roshill came...and brought us all in, and we all got four raps apiece and our name in the black book.[99]

As Table 2 suggests, sporadic strikes are far more common than generally thought. There are of course many much more recent examples.

In February 2011 students at Villiers High School in West London went on strike to protest against the sacking of one of their teachers. Head teacher Ms Juliet Strang claimed the students had been "wound up" as part of an orchestrated campaign by teachers' representatives. Speaking to the BBC she claimed the protest wasn't a strike and that the school was happy to let pupils "work out their protest".[100]

On 19 March 2014 students at Bilton High School in Rugby went on strike after the head banned them from wearing charity bracelets in support of a classmate who had leukaemia. One hundred students walked out and held a demonstration on the school playing fields. The head, Patsy Weighill, claimed the bracelets breached school uniform policy!

The head teacher suggested that the strike had been organised by "a small minority of students whose actions can be described as anti-social and potentially dangerous" and who "used this as an opportunity to be disruptive". To control the students she called the police, suggesting the strikers were a risk to themselves and others.[101]

On Thursday 27 March 2014 students in Brighton went on strike against changes to their school day and holiday arrangements being implemented by the local authority. The students came from five schools (Hove Park, Varndean, Dorothy Stinger, Blatchington Mill and Cardinal Newman) and congregated in Brighton's central square.

Parents reported that they were informed that their children could face suspension for truancy and criminal records for joining "the so-called strike".[102]

On Friday 4 April 2014 school students at Cowes Enterprise College on the Isle of Wight went on strike against threatened redundancies to teaching and support staff. The redundancy threat came from the Ormiston Academies Trust, due to take over the school.

Shortly after registration at 8.30am hundreds of students walked out of class, waving banners and chanting "save our teachers." As the head teacher tried to address striking students she was met by chants of "Who are you? Who are you?" The head girl Jenny Stokell was quoted as saying the protest showed how strongly students felt about supporting their teachers and support staff:

> It shows how valuable we think the staff are. The restructuring hasn't come from the school, it's come from Ormiston. It's a shame the fantastic staff who've done so much to improve the school...are losing their jobs.[103]

Students on the Isle of Wight were not the only ones to take strike action against the impact of "academisation".

Georgia A was 12 when she led a strike against her school becoming an academy. Georgia launched a petition in the school to garner opposition to the governors' plans and led the strike on 3 June 2014. Georgia was threatened with punishment for truancy, something she said she was "happy to take" if it meant her views would be heard.[104]

Georgia argued, "We don't want the school to become an academy. It'll be privatisation by the back door". Esther, another striker, added, "I'm not happy that we didn't get a say. Less experienced teachers will get hired and we won't get as good an education". Luke added, "The school is fine as it is. They're doing it for the money—they don't care about us".[105]

These three students show a sophisticated level of political analysis about the government's Academy Programme and its impact on students and teachers.

On Wednesday 4 March 2015 students in Lewisham also went on strike against their school becoming an academy. The students at Prendergast Hilly Fields College in Lewisham walked out against the governors' plans.

Year 10 pupil Stevie Johnson said:

> We don't want our school to become an academy and want the governors to change their minds. We don't feel the governors have listened to us and that's why we staged the protest. It's our school, our education and we have a right to voice our opinions as any decision they take on

the future of our education and our school will have a huge impact on us. I am prepared to keep protesting until they listen to us and take our views seriously.

Lili Kramer, year 10, said:

We united to show our governors that we deserve to be listened to, that we are not afraid to voice our opinions and that we will not be silenced. This is our future, our education. The battle is not over yet.

Year 12 pupil Ella Daley said:

All we are being told is that nothing will change. If that's the case, why do we need to become an academy? It doesn't make sense. They've taken a decision on our behalf without discussing it with us and getting our agreement. I think that's wrong.[106]

As we will see in the chapters that follow, student strikers regularly get full support from their families and wider community. The Lewisham strike was no exception. Jon Johnson, whose daughter Stevie was on strike, said:

I absolutely support her and her decision to protest. I think what the students are doing is inspirational. They have had a lot of pressure put on them not to do this but decided it was really important to them.[107]

These examples show the range of student grievances that can provoke strike action. These are strikes of relatively short duration. On the whole they are confined to a specific school (though the Brighton example is a more generalised response to imposed changes to school hours by a local authority). They are conceived as strikes and are examples of contentious political action. Yet in most of the cases above they have not been officially recorded as strikes by the authorities.

There are exceptions to this pattern, of course. The "Burston Rebellion"[108] is one of the most famous school student strikes in British history. It was a sporadic strike in the sense that it was confined to one school. But it was a dispute that gained huge publicity and became a cause célèbre, lasting from 1914 to 1939.

In April 1914, in response to the sacking of their teachers Tom and Anne Higdon, school students at the Burston village Church of England School went on strike. Sixty-six of the school's 72 students marched through the village, went on strike and attended an alternative school set up by the Higdon's and supported by funds from the labour movement nationally. The strike, and alternative school, continued until 1939 and thus this was a movement that involved several generations of children, their parents and their community in a struggle against Church interference and control of schools and education.

School student' strikes to defend "good" school teachers are not uncommon. The vignette from Jock Morris at the end of this chapter gives an example. Another was the case in 1971 when school students at John Cass Foundation and Red Coat School in Stepney went on strike after their teacher Chris Searle was sacked. His crime was to publish a small book of poetry written by pupils. The book initially got the full support of the school governing authorities, but when they saw the content of the poems they quickly backed off. Searle published and the governors sacked him. One hundred local head teachers made a public statement saying they would not employ him. But the school students saw things differently and went on strike.

> They marched to Trafalgar Square in their uniforms demanding that Mr Searle got his job back. "Thank you God from high above, For sending Searle for us to love," they chanted at the school gates. On the walls, slogans in purple paint proclaimed: "If Mr Searle goes—we go".[109]

The school students stayed out for three days, but it took two years for Searle to win his job back. Nevertheless, the support of the school students was, he claimed, very important to him and the campaign.[110]

In addition to these sporadic strikes there have also been periods of more generalised protest, when school students have collectively challenged the authority of schools, governors, head teachers and local authorities for a sustained period and drawn others into the conflict. During these strike waves school students express their collective anger at injustice and present an organised form of opposition to schooling. Though, as we will see, they are often subjected to ridicule by political and media commentators keen to dismiss their "childish" actions.

During these generalised periods of protest there is a clear relationship between school strikes and more general contentious political action. In the chapters that follow we look at the six major school student strike waves in Britain: 1889, 1911, 1968-1974, 1978-80, 1985 and 2003. These were all significant and sustained periods of generalised protest.

1889 was the year of the mass movement which established New Unionism. It was the year of the great dock strike, the gas workers' strike and a series of disputes that spread to engulf the whole country.[111] School attendance was only made compulsory in England in 1880 when the Elementary Education Act was passed. Technically local authorities were meant to ensure attendance up until the age of 13 (though there were a range of exemptions, including provision for "half-time working" in textile towns), which meant that in reality schooling was compulsory until the age of 10. At the ages of 11, 12, 13 and 14 the demarcation between scholar and worker was often blurred. The great rebellion of the unskilled and unorganised in 1889, perhaps not surprisingly, had an influence on school students who took to the streets in the first school strikes in Britain.

The school strikes of 1911 occurred in the midst of the Great Unrest[112] of 1910-1914. This was a period of monumental class struggle across much of Europe. Many of the strikes took on near revolutionary characteristics. In London, South Wales, Liverpool, Manchester, Newcastle and across the Clyde these were years of intense struggle. In 1911 school students joined the affray.[113]

One of the first schools to join the strike was Bigyn School in Llanelli, South Wales.[114] The location is significant. On 19 August 1911, during the first national rail strike, the town of Llanelli witnessed mass picketing and the killing of two strikers by soldiers. Rather than being cowed the working class districts of the town rose up and took part in a furious confrontation with the authorities.[115]

The school strikes took place just after the national railway strike. On 5 September students marched out of Bigyn School to protest against caning and corporal punishment. The strike spread. During September 1911 there were strikes by schoolchildren in at least 62 towns and cities showing the huge impact the rail strike had within working class communities.[116]

1968 was the "year of the barricade".[117] From Vietnam to the United States, across Europe, east and west, through Africa and China, 1968 saw the start of a protest wave that lasted until the mid-1970s. As part of the protests students, and school students, in France occupied their institutions and demanded greater control over the curriculum. Some of that anger was seen in a series of student disputes in Britain. Over the next few years school students formed their own organisations: the Schools Action Union (SAU) and the National Union of School Students (NUSS), which was affiliated to the National Union of Students. Both the SAU and the NUSS were involved in a range of student protests and strikes—which led to considerable surveillance of young activists by the state.

Between 1978 and 1980 there was a significant mobilisation against the far-right in Britain. This was primarily coordinated by the Anti Nazi League (ANL). The far-right grew against a back drop of growing youth unemployment, cuts in government social spending under a Labour government and declining real terms wages. The far-right blamed these ills on Britain's Black and Asian population.

The ANL mobilised to counter the Nazis on the streets, in workplaces, communities and schools. The group School Kids Against the Nazis (SKAN) was formed and drew large numbers of young people into politics. SKAN utilised music and fanzines to create a broad anti-Nazi youth culture. The increasing politicisation of some young people fed into other campaigns like the Right to Work Campaign and the campaign against the Corrie Bill (the move by Tory MP John Corrie to restrict abortion rights). In this atmosphere there was a burst of school student strikes and a re-activation of the NUSS.

1985 marked the end, and the defeat, of the Great Miners' Strike.[118] For the previous year Britain had been thrown into turmoil and the reality of class conflict dominated the television screens. During the year-long dispute there were a number of school student strikes in the South Yorkshire coalfield as school students came out in solidarity with their mining friends and families. As the miners' dispute ended a series of school walkouts took place as school students protested against youth unemployment and, in particular, the threat of the compulsory imposition of the Youth Training Scheme (YTS) on unemployed working class youth.

Finally, 2003 saw the creation of a global mass movement against war. This developed out of the anti-capitalist movement that had germinated at the protests in Seattle at the WTO Third Ministerial in 1999. As the US government and its acolytes in the "coalition of the willing" (including the Blair government in Britain) launched their attacks on Afghanistan, the movement developed to become one against capitalism, war and imperialism. By 2003, as war with Iraq loomed, the mass movement organised some of the largest demonstrations ever held in Britain.[119] An important part of that protest movement was a series of school walkouts against Blair's war.

In these periods the school strikes did not occur in isolation or appear out of the blue. They were not mere disruptions to school routine but a serious challenge to the political establishment. They were each located within broader waves of social protest as young people gained confidence from the activities of (sometimes only slightly) older peers. In these episodes young students joined protests and raised their own demands about conditions in schools, corporal punishment, payment for school prefects, unemployment and youth "training" schemes and, in the case of the 2003 strike wave, against the horrors of war.

The interrelationship between the school strikes and the more generalised confrontations can be viewed as one aspect of mass protest captured by Rosa Luxemburg in her writing on the mass strike:

> The mass strike...is such a changeable phenomenon that it reflects all phases of the political and economic struggle, all stages and factors of its origin are constantly changing... It flows now like a broad billow over the whole kingdom, and now divides into a gigantic network of narrow streams; now it bubbles forth from under the ground like a fresh spring and is now completely lost under the earth. Political and economic strikes, general strikes of individual branches of industry and general strikes in individual towns, peaceful wage struggles and street massacres, barricade fighting—all these run through one another, run side by side, cross one another, flow in and over one another—and it is a ceaselessly moving changing sea of phenomena... Every new onset and every fresh victory of the political struggle is transformed into a powerful impetus for the economic struggle... After every foaming wave of political action a fructifying deposit remains behind from which a thousand stalks of economic struggle shoot forth. And conversely... ceaseless economic struggle...keeps their fighting energy alive in every political interval.[120]

Large economic and political confrontations generate confidence within the working class that collective action can win. This confidence can spread to the most marginalised sections—including school students—who start to fight for their rights. In this sense school strikes are not mere disruptions to the school regime, but an important component part of a more generalised period of contentious political conflict.

As we will show, the school strikes are also based on genuine grievances. In the early period strikes were motivated by anger against rote teaching methods, corporal punishment, brutal teachers, overcrowded classrooms and non-payment of prefects. These were real issues—despite the attempt to portray the strikes as mindless, copycat acts by rogue children.

In the late 1960s and 1970s corporal punishment and school uniform dress codes continued to act as sparks to school student revolt, but now new demands were made by the "pupil power movement", including greater democracy in schools and the right to pupil representation in decision-making processes. Interestingly, in 1889 and 1911 teachers were often the object of student hostility, but by the late 1960s things were less clear cut.

The gradual expansion of higher education in the post war period meant a larger number of working and lower middle class students could go to university. As Harman points out:

> In 1900 the total university population was only 20,000, with another 5,000 students training as teachers...at the outbreak of the second world war there were still only 69,000 students... But with the post-war boom...the number of students nearly doubled by 1954; and doubled again to 294,000 by 1964; and it reached more than twice this figure by 1972 [15 percent of the age group].[121]

Many of those who had lived through the student radicalisation of the 1960s went into teaching with a commitment to make the system better, and the move towards comprehensive education in the 1960s seemed to offer greater hope of achieving a more democratic schooling. Many of the new teachers defined themselves not as middle class professionals but as workers, and joined the growing teaching unions. And for some this changed their relationship to school students and fostered their support for aspects of the pupil power movement.

Nevertheless the focus of school student activity up to the late 1970s remained concerned, overwhelmingly, with the "organisation and structure" of schooling. But from the late 1970s this started to shift. The anti-Nazi movement and demands for the right to work began to impact on school politics and events in the outside world started to shape the demands of school student protestors. In 1985 the massive school strike of that year was little concerned with matters of schooling. Its focus was the Youth Training Scheme and the Tory government's plans to make it compulsory for all 16-18 year old school leavers, while in 2003 school students struck and took to the streets in a massive wave of protest against the threat of war in Iraq. Thus as we come closer to the present there is evidence of school students taking strike action over much more political issues as well as specific issues associated with schooling.

Dave Kersey (Sheffield, 1978-1980)
"You *can* say no to authority"

I was 13 in 1978. I started to get involved in politics around the anti-Nazi struggle. In Sheffield the NF started leafleting schools and it created a lot of debate. I remember one poster they put up that said: "Handsworth 1973, Your Street sometime soon".

In my class there were two Rasta kids. They were well known for being able to look after themselves, and also for challenging school uniform rules. So they had quite a lot of respect. They basically polarised things in my class by saying you're either with us against racism and the Nazis or you're with them.

I started to get involved with SKAN. We distributed leaflets and material and created an anti-Nazi pole of attraction for kids in the area. The SKAN and ANL badges were very popular and soon there was a group of us who were clear that we were not going to let the NF leaflet our school.

In 1979 I was deeply affected by the murder of Blair Peach. I was 14 at the time and went to meetings about what had happened. In a really dramatic way it helped teach me about the role of the state.

Some of us now started to argue that we needed to move on to address other issues as well as anti-Nazi work and so we set up a branch of NUSS.

There were three key issues we worked around: uniforms, corporal punishment and the authoritarianism of the school.

My school was High Storrs Comprehensive. It drew students from across the city, including relatively affluent suburbs and much more deprived inner city areas. But up until 1969 it had been a grammar school and many of the older teachers struggled to teach the comprehensive intake. Many of these teachers could be brutal. But there were other teachers who were more open and left wing in orientation. So the teachers were a divided group.

We started to put leaflets into the school. We managed to tap into the built up tension. We called a meeting in the school about uniforms and corporal punishment. The school gave us a room. I think they thought it would be a small meeting and we would be incorporated into the school council. But about 30-40 kids turned up.

We marched around the school corridors chanting against school uniforms. The old grammar school teachers went ballistic. Some were dragging kids across the playground.

We then had a "We're not wearing school uniform" day. This led to some of us getting suspended. I got one day. But the school didn't formalise this because they said they "didn't want to create martyrs".

Then we organised a city wide day of protest involving people from a number of schools. We had a rally in the centre on the town hall steps. It was great fun and I remember the cops trying to control us!

The NUSS was very good at drawing disaffected kids into action.

The schools were authoritarian places. There was growing youth unemployment. There were cuts in services under Labour. In that atmosphere some could have been drawn to the NF. But SKAN and the NUSS were able to draw these kids over to our side. In Sheffield a group of skinheads came over to us.

In 1979 I went to NUSS conference. It was very serious. There was lots of discussion about perspectives and strategy. There was a lot of fun as well, but it was a very serious conference. It resulted in the Young Communist League losing control of the union and the main positions being taken by members of the International Marxist Group and Socialist Workers Party (SWP).

I wasn't a member of any organisation, but I felt the debate on perspectives was very important and I was impressed with the debate and what was being argued. I would eventually join the SWP in 1980 during the steel strike.

Looking back I think my involvement in school student politics taught me some important lessons. First, you can say no to authority. The school is a difficult place to speak out in. But it is possible and once you learn that lesson you can take it with you through life.

Second, you can change things, but to succeed you need to do things collectively. For me this enforced a commitment to self activity as the means to bring about change.

Third, young people involved in politics are serious and should be treated as such. You hear people dismiss young people, or school strikes, as "flash in the pan" acts, or some form of larking about. But school strikes are not entered into easily; they are difficult to organise and they involve a very significant challenge to authority. They are serious political events and the participants deserve to be respected.

Jock Morris (Glasgow, 1981)
The teacher's story

In 1981 I worked as an English teacher at Possilpark Secondary School in the north of Glasgow.

Unemployment in the west of Scotland was rocketing—and youth unemployment in particular was very high. During 1980 the TUC organised a number of events against unemployment. There was a demonstration in London (in March) and a day of action in May. The Labour Party also organised a massive demonstration in Liverpool in November. At the start of 1981 the next big event was the Labour Party and STUC organised demo on 24 February in Glasgow, led off by the recently elected Labour leader Michael Foot.

In one of my classes I wrote the name "Margaret Thatcher" on the board. The purpose was for the students to write what they felt as part of a creative writing exercise. The students wrote all sorts of stuff, but given the time and the location their pieces were full of anger at what Thatcher and her government were doing to the local community and to student job prospects.

As the demo approached some journalists from *Socialist Worker* asked me if they could reproduce some of these comments. The purpose was to look at what young people thought of Thatcher. The piece appeared, anonymously, in the paper the week of the demonstration.

However, about three weeks later the Tory MP for East Renfrewshire, Allan Stewart, raised the issue in Parliament. Stewart would later gain notoriety when he was forced to resign his ministerial position after brandishing a pickaxe at demonstrators protesting against the building of the M77 extension!

Stewart's intervention led to a media frenzy. It was assumed that it was a Modern Studies teacher who had set the task and this was used as evidence that it was a politically charged subject. Stewart had made a number of interventions in Parliament raising "concerns" about the subject during 1980 and 1981. One of the Modern Studies teachers at my school was a Communist Party member and some journalists initially suspected him of setting the task.

However, I was soon identified as the culprit. I was disciplined and given a final written warning. One of the conditions was that I couldn't talk to the press, but this meant I couldn't respond to the lies and distortions that the press were turning out.

The press camped outside the school. They were offering money to local residents so they could go into their houses and take photos of classes through the school windows and some students were offered money if the journalists could look at their jotters and see what they were being taught! The stories lasted for about seven days, though the *Evening Times* kept up the coverage for three weeks.

However, the week when there was most press speculation coincided with me being ill and off school. In the school a rumour started that I wasn't in because I'd been sacked. The students got organised and on the Friday they went on strike. They marched around the school and refused to go into classes. I was told they were chanting "Morris in, Thatcher out!" When I returned to school the following week the students were excited and talking about what they had done and their right to take action.

I both really appreciated what they did, but was also a bit worried that this would be used against me again—it was a very stressful time. But their support and solidarity was really important and significant to me.

I also got a lot of support from many other teachers, from the students and many of their parents and from the union, the EIS, with the General Secretary John Pollock saying there would be "no witch hunt" on his watch. Mind you, the final written warning continued to be pretty oppressive for a number of years.

3

The children's rebellion of 1889

We are all on strike,
And we are as happy as we can be;
We mean to keep it up,
For we've got the £ s d.[122]

IN HIS history of the second wave of unionisation, John Charlton[123] describes the rapid birth and spread of New Unionism. Conservative craft-based trade societies were eclipsed by the emergence and consolidation of new, general trade unions that were more prepared to take militant industrial action in the pursuit of their members' interests.

In March 1889 Will Thorne led his newly organised union of gasworkers in London to a historic victory, securing a reduction in the basic working day from 12 to 8 hours. Encouraged by this success Ben Tillet, Tom Mann and John Burns led London's dockworkers to victory in a bitter dispute over pay and conditions. Throughout Britain—in Clydeside, Teeside, Humberside, Merseyside and South Wales—dockers, gasworkers, miners and other sections of the working class sought to replicate the success of their counterparts in the capital. 1889 was, in short, a year of intense industrial conflict.

1889 was also the year of another, unusual and original, form of strike activity—the school student strike. In the early autumn contemporaries witnessed what has been described as the first nationwide "children's rebellion" as the country witnessed a series of pupil protests.[124]

The first strike took place in Hawick, in the Scottish Borders, on 25 September. According to an account of the dispute in the *Times* children from two board schools "marched out of their classrooms" demanding "shorter hours, lighter work…and better teachers", demands the paper considered "very shocking".[125]

The pupils marched through the streets of the town between the two schools in what the *Times* saw as a worrying "breakdown in discipline". Not surprisingly the report was entirely bereft of sympathy for the children's cause. But it also located the blame for the dispute with their parents' "hot-headed" and "irresponsible" embrace of militant New Unionism:

> Of course, the whole thing is frivolous, and a speedy collapse is inevitable; but the incident, though ludicrous enough, may serve to show the parents of the strikers how dangerous is the example which they set their own children.[126]

The *Times'* portrayal of the strike as "frivolous" and "ludicrous" was part of a much wider tendency to seek to trivialise the protests, undermine the rationale for the children's actions, and to dismiss the very notion that they could form or articulate legitimate political demands. However, the "speedy collapse" predicted by the *Times* failed to materialise. On 30 September children in Greenock were reported to have "openly revolted". Their demands were based around much the same concerns as their Hawick counterparts—the need to address long school hours and excessive homework. But in addition there was also a call for the abolition of school fees.

The strike rapidly spread across the town as pupils sent out flying pickets.

> Forming themselves into procession and singing, shouting and cheering, they proceeded to the Board school nearest their own, in the hope that they would get the scholars of the higher standards to join their ranks.[127]

Teachers at nearby schools locked the gates and sent urgent requests for police to be dispatched, but this did little to deter other children from joining the strike as they day wore on.

On 2 October the *Manchester Guardian* reported that the strike movement was gathering momentum in Scotland:

> The remarkable strike of schoolboys reported from Greenock on Monday is spreading. We now hear of two hundred boys parading through the streets of Glasgow in character of "strikers" and at Govan and Port Glasgow the ranks of the disaffected have been swelled by large contingents.[128]

Glasgow's striking children added an end to the cane to their demands, but as in Greenock they also called for the abolition of homework and the introduction of free education.

On 2 October pupils in Aberdeen joined in when a "large body of scholars paraded the streets of the town", demanding "free education and the abolition of certain tasks and grievances". The *Times* expressed its surprise at the level of organisation and discipline shown by children. "A feature of the demonstration", it noted, "was the use of roughly improvised banners. The youngsters discuss the situation with great gravity and speak of calling a meeting to ventilate their 'grievances'".[129] In the days that followed the scope of the protest widened. On 4 October children in Paisley and Irvine walked out of school.[130]

> In Paisley...a large number of children left the schools to take part in the agitation... A body of children, estimated at about 400, assembled at the New Town and thence marched through the principal streets and visited schools. The processionists amused themselves by crying out, "Free education for all", "Shorter hours", and "No home tasks".[131]

By now newspapers were reporting support for the pupil protest movement in England.[132] Barnet's children were the first to announce their intention to strike, during a lunchtime protest on Thursday 3 October. Children attending Christ Church schools devised a manifesto which demanded "Abolition of the cane, less hours in school, less parsing[133] and no home lessons". The following day between 80 and 100 children initiated a protest during their dinner hour, though most returned to school in the afternoon. According to the *Pall Mall Gazette* they "paraded the streets of West Barnet...declared their determination to strike, and created a great uproar by shouting, cheering and beating tin kettles".[134] The same week saw protests in the centre of London, including Kings Cross, where "The spectacle of around 50 children parading...with banners, protesting against home lessons and long hours, caused some local excitement".[135]

A sketch which appeared in the *Graphic*[136] was accompanied by text which highlighted the extent to which participants in the children's rebellion embraced the tactics and symbols of the dock strikers:

> Thus, they formed themselves into a column, to the number of several hundreds; they carried banners specially prepared for them; they had a

band composed of most discordant instruments, and they had a score or more of boys who carried collecting boxes fastened by chords round their necks. The tallest boy in the column walked at the head of the procession carrying a pole, at the top of which was fastened a doll. Behind him came a band, composed of about a score of lads beating trays, kettles and triangles, and a few blowing flutes or playing jews harps. Then came the lads carrying banners made of paper, on which were printed in ink such phrases as "Shorter Hours", "More Holidays", "No Cane", "No Home Lessons".[137]

Now newspapers were carrying reports of strikes breaking out across the country, some of which involved very large numbers of children. The strike in Dundee, for instance, is said to have involved "thousands", who, in the process of parading through the city's Esplanade, were accused of, among other things, damaging at least 40 heavy tree branches and entirely destroying another.[138]

Humphries estimates that at least 36 towns and cities across Britain were affected by what turned out to be a three-week long period of resistance.[139] In each case the demands were broadly similar—free education, no homework, less rote learning and the abolition of corporal punishment. Most of the strikers articulated a deep antipathy towards their education. As one of the strikers from Hull succinctly put it, "We pay 3d. per week and get slugged for it".[140]

As the protest movement grew, a discernible shift occurred in the tone of reporting. Acts which had initially been portrayed by correspondents as largely amusing if somewhat disobedient forms of rebellion were quickly re-interpreted as having more serious, sinister connotations. The protest movement, it was alleged, was being "infiltrated" by "louts" and "hoodlums", as this report on the dinner hour demonstration by Barnet children illustrates:

The demonstration of schoolboys at Barnet, though undoubtedly prompted by a spirit of fun, turned out to be a more serious matter than was at first supposed. The lads were joined in their parade of the streets on Friday afternoon by a number of rough youths who had either outgrown their school days or belonged to the class which rarely attends school at all... The roughs thought that the calling in of the boys justified them in throwing stones at the school windows and insulting the teachers and it was found necessary to obtain the assistance of the police.[141]

The press reports were now increasingly filled with all manner of class based stereotypes about working class kids. In West and East Hartlepool it was reported that "gangs of unwashed urchins" were congregating in the back streets, "many of them armed with sticks, and apparently ripe for mischief".[142]

London's *Lloyd's Weekly* sought to link the disruption to a wider moral malaise that it claimed was gripping sections of working class youth, cautioning against the notion that the protests should be viewed with some amusement; "when windows are broken, and innocent, well-conducted children are injured...by mischievous and impish urchins, the thing ceases to be a joke". We certainly cannot afford, it lamented, "to have the police running round in all directions after idle boys".[143] The *Dundee Advertiser* saw the strikes as "evidence of a deep conspiracy against social order". "The doom of Empire", it gravely stated, "must be near at hand if the country is honeycombed...with secret societies of schoolchildren".[144] Even Thomas Hughes, the author of *Tom Brown's Schooldays*, felt compelled to enter the fray. Commenting on the pupil protests, he expressed his dismay that "the spirit of disobedience which was being manifested in various ways at the present time would, in the long run, prove a very great danger and evil to the country":

> If the schoolboy strikes which were taking place now had occurred when he was a boy, the lads would have been summarily dealt with, and in a way, too, which the boys of this generation would be astonished at.[145]

For Hughes, the strikes were yet another example of the "vitiation" and "demoralisation" of English boys that threatened the ability of the nation to defend its "magnificent" Empire.

The *Educational News* continued with this dystopian theme, claiming that the strikes were "manifestations of a serious deterioration in the moral fibre of the rising generation", and were "on par with a strike in the army or navy". Unless immediately identified and expelled, the ringleaders would, the journal argued, prove to be "dangerous centres of moral contamination".[146] The tone of commentary around the strikes had, therefore, become far more hostile. There was a demand for a return to an idealised pre-strike normality, where the authority of the teacher was sacrosanct and working class children "knew their place".[147]

The response to the strikes was part of a broader set of concerns about what was happening in British society and within working class communities. The end of the 19th century marked a period of crisis for the British state. The economy was facing new problems. The American economist David Ames Wells, writing in 1891, argued that the previous 20 years had been marked by "unpredicted disturbance and depression of trade...[engulfing] old communities like England and Germany, and equally...Australia, South Africa and California, which represent the new".[148]

Though Britain was still the predominant global economic power-house in the last quarter of the 19th century, Germany and the USA were gradually catching up, especially in the new industries like steel making where they soon became dominant.[149] Relative economic decline caused all manner of anxieties about the role of the education system in providing the skills necessary for workers in the new industries,[150] about the failings of lazy and immoral workers[151] and about the lives being led among the "outcast" population of the cities.[152]

The contemporary response to the strikes, however, failed to acknowledge the legitimacy of many of the children's demands and grievances.

The schooling system in 1889 was brutal. Discipline was severe and even minor misdemeanours were met with the cane. Learning was tedious, based on rote methods of instruction, and imposed upon students by badly trained teachers who had little or no connection to the lives led by their pupils.

The call for free education was a key issue for the labour movement across Britain. The Trades Union Congress had been committed to the introduction of a free national system of education since 1885.[153] At that year's TUC Conference its president, T R Thelfall, railed against the injustice of school fees for elementary school children:

> As our Education Acts are now framed they inflict great privation upon vast multitudes of the poorest parents, because the school pence, paltry as it may be to the well-to-do, is a considerable sum when taken from a family whose weekly income amounts to less than a pound a week... There has to be a limitation of food or clothing to supply the requisite pence for education.[154]

The children's protests received broader trade union support in some areas. For instance, the Honorary Secretary of the Street Masons, Paviors and Stone Dressers' Amalgamated Union wrote to the London

School Board in support of the strikers' demands, an action that received widespread condemnation in many sections of the press.[155]

The campaign for the abolition of fees was particularly strong in Scotland, where, as we have seen, the pupil protests originated. As the *Times* noted on 10 September, just two weeks prior to the outbreak of the Hawick strike, "Free education is the question of the hour in Scotland". It went on that it was "quite plain that the current of opinion and of desire runs strongly in the direction of making education entirely free in all the standards of all elementary schools".[156]

In Hawick fees had already been abolished for junior scholars, but the failure to extend free education to older children had generated widespread dissatisfaction among parents and children.[157]

The issue of school fees had also generated particular controversy in Glasgow, and it was hardly surprising to see strikers in that city calling for their abolition. There, charges for children studying up to the fifth standard had been abolished in 55 of the city's schools, but they continued to be levied in ten others. As the Tory *London Standard*[158] noted in its discussion of growing support for the pupil protests, this had generated considerable animosity among Glasgow's parents, and the striking children were evidently aware of the hardship and inequity that the continued imposition of school fees had generated. The *Leeds Mercury* drew attention to the fact that a similar inconsistency had been the principal cause of the school pupil strikes in Dundee.[159]

It is therefore hardly surprising to find significant parental support for the children's protests.

This situation was true in England as well as Scotland. For instance, in East and West Hartlepool it was reported that "parents of the young truants [sic] seemed to look upon these demonstrations with an eye of favour".[160] The authorities were similarly dismayed to find parental support in Darlington. There, the authorities issued a statement warning that "where sympathy is shown by parents of the action of their boys in striking, summonses will be promptly issued against them for not sending their offspring regularly to school".[161]

That school fees were widely seen as a major and genuine concern was confirmed by a prominent London head teacher. When asked by the *Pall Mall Gazette* (at an early stage in the protests) whether it was likely that the strike movement might spread throughout London, he replied:

Not if things remain as they are now. The catch words of "no cane", "no grammar", "shorter hours" &c, do not greatly appeal to the parents, but if one were to set up the cries of "no fees", they would soon catch at that and back up the children.[162]

In fact, within days the provision of free or more affordable and better education had become a key demand of London's pupil protesters. Indeed, the mass walkout at Sancroft Street Board School was prompted by widespread dissatisfaction at the costs of schooling, as well as the school's poor resources. The strikers called for their school fees to be reduced from 4d to 1d and for the school to ensure that all their books were purchased for them. For this widely "insubordinate" act, the children were branded "malcontents".[163] In addition, at the New-Road Board School on Wandsworth Road, where the atmosphere was described as "menacing", it was "believed that some of the parents are encouraging their children merely for the purpose of getting off paying the school fees and obtaining free school meals".[164]

While the demand for free education was gaining popular support, opposition to fee abolition remained significant. In 1888 the Cross Commission examined the administration of the Elementary Education Acts, including hearing evidence from witnesses in favour of abolition. Yet despite the evidence its commissioners flatly refused to support the demand for free education. It was, they insisted, the moral responsibility of parents, not the state, to fund their children's schooling. "Many persons", the Commission noted approvingly, believe that, "the assumption by the State of duties primarily belonging to its individual members not only violates sound principles of political economy, but also tends to sap...independence of character." The Commission's view was that the "provision of the due necessaries of education, as well as the necessaries of life, is part of the responsibility incumbent upon parents" and that "the balance of advantage is greatly in favour of maintaining the present system".[165]

The demand for the abolition of corporal punishment was based on genuine complaints. As Thompson has shown, "one of the most recurrent themes from the late 19th and early 20th century childhoods is that of the savagery of school teachers towards their pupils". He goes on:

In innumerable schools...children were regularly caned, not only for being late or for talking in class, but for not getting their answers right, for not speaking correctly, even for coughing. And besides caning, teachers would slap, pull hair, throw books or slates, or use the tawse [a leather strap]. Others preferred slow torture, such as making a girl stand all day holding her petticoat over her head, or tying a truant boy to a radiator.[166]

As the strikes gathered momentum, some contemporaries publicly acknowledged the legitimacy of children's demands for an end to corporal punishment. Edith Lupton, a member of the Bradford School Board and a prominent figure in the women's suffrage movement, wrote to the *Daily News* defending the children's stance. She argued that "much lasting good will result" from "the abandonment of the idea that the cane is an educational instrument, and an appreciation of the fact that a child's mind will no more develop under blows and unkindness than arose will unclose its petals under the same conditions".[167]

However, Lupton was an exception within the educational establishment and most newspaper accounts of the strike showed little sympathy for the protesters' demands in this regard. Indeed, the portrayal of the rebellion by journalists as an outbreak of infantile foolishness and frivolity served to reinforce the belief that rigid and severe discipline was a necessary feature of working class schooling. The *Times* stated that the disruption showed that "without the enforcement of discipline the work of the schools would be impossible",[168] while the *Lancashire Evening Post* derisively commented that it hoped "the 'striking' part of the business" would "not...be at an end" once the dispute was brought to a conclusion.[169] The latter newspaper subsequently noted with some satisfaction that the ringleaders of a strike at a school in Liverpool had received "a sound birching while stripped" for the part they played in the protest.[170]

Children's complaints about the excessive use of rote learning methods and homework were also well founded. As Simon[171] points out, the regimes found in the schools that catered for working class children were stultifying and deadening. Indeed, elementary school teachers themselves openly acknowledged that this was the case in their union's submission of evidence to the 1888 Cross Commission.

The National Union of Elementary Teachers' memorandum to the Commission was particularly critical of the system of payment by results, which had "debased educational ideals and debased all who had come under its influence". It was "a constant and fruitful source of over-pressure upon scholars and teachers" and had "forced upon the schools a miserable system of 'cram' which secures but few lasting educational results, and gives the scholars little taste or desire to continue their education".[172] Of course, this aspect of elementary schooling was not incidental; as R H Tawney put it, elementary schools "were intended in the main to produce an orderly, civil obedient population, with sufficient education to understand a command".[173] To this end the school curriculum, with its emphasis on "drill" and reading, writing and arithmetic, was designed to crush rather than enhance initiative, and to develop habits of obedience, docility and passivity.[174]

Connected to the strikers' calls for the introduction of a more stimulating, interesting curriculum was the demand for less homework (or home lessons). On this particular issue the protesters managed to elicit a good deal of support—in some cases from surprising quarters. For instance, while the *Journal of Education* dismissed the strike itself as "absurd", it acknowledged that some "very reputable authorities" concurred with the children when it came to the question of "home lessons".[175] One such authority was Bennett Williams, the head teacher of Islington's Gifford Street Board School, one of the largest in London. When asked by a *Pall Mall Gazette* correspondent whether this particular grievance was justified, his reply was that this was "decid-edly" the case:

> Many of the children's homes consist in one room, which is inhabited by the whole family. It is absolutely impossible for a child to collect its thoughts when several other people are talking in the room, and the plea which they bring to school—that they have no place where to do their homework—is very often quite justified... You can't punish the children for not knowing their lessons when you know the conditions under which they live.[176]

Another school master made many of the same points:

> Now the chief cry of the boys...has been "no home lessons". Is this a grievance? I confess, as a school manager of more than ten years' stand-ing, that I think it is, and a serious one".[177]

The 1889 children's protests were based on a genuine set of grievances about the nature and content of working class education. But by striking, the children were challenging the authority of schools, local government and, indeed, some central pillars of bourgeois thought about the role of children in society. What was the response to the strikes?

Initially the authorities responded by isolating and administering *ad hoc* beatings to children considered to be directing the protests. For example, a number of Berwick strikers were flogged before the town's mayor and the school's managers. Two of them were also expelled.[178] In Darlington, the organisers of a 70 name petition, which had demanded shorter school hours, were administered a "sound thrashing". In London, a Thames Police Court Magistrate decided that two boys "deserved a good whipping" for their role in organising "a ridiculous parody of a strike" and announced "if brought up again he would imprison the delinquents".[179] In Liverpool a "sound birching" was administered, a punishment that was widely supported in the press:

> The ringleaders of the strike at Beaufort Street (Liverpool) Board School were yesterday severely lectured by the headmaster, and subsequently, in the presence of the Committee, severely birched after being stripped. Two or three bore their punishment defiantly, but others, judging by their yells, felt somewhat galling the humiliating punishment induced for striking against home-lessons and reduced fees.[180]

However, in many cases, teachers' threats of physical punishment failed to act as a sufficient deterrent. Indeed, such tactics frequently appeared to strengthen the resolve of the strikers, and led to teachers themselves being targeted.

For example, a teacher in Liverpool who attempted to return a striker to school forcibly, "was speedily surrounded by a crowd of threatening boys" and only saved by the intervention of a policeman. In Holyhead "some of the teachers were...subjected to rough treatment by their pupils, who armed themselves with sticks and cabbage stalks".[181]

In Leith a number of children were apprehended by police after bombarding schools with stones, with one of their number ultimately being convicted of "striking the janitor and a lad with a stick".[182]

In Middlesbrough "malcontent lads were prowling about the streets in groups" prior to attacking St John's School, where they smashed five or six panes of glass before being chased off by the police,[183] while in Finsbury a school janitor who refused to allow strikers to picket the school gates and encourage others to join them was repeatedly "pelted with stones".[184] At Stockton-on-Tees 200 strikers were said to have conducted themselves in a "very disorderly" manner, surrounding Bowesfield Lane School, whereupon they "bespattered the windows with mud and any of the teachers who appeared". They also "chalked" their demands, along with other slogans, on the school doors, a practice that seemed to be fairly commonplace in other areas affected by the protests. The following day, two police officers were stationed at the school gates in Stockton-on-Tees in an attempt to subdue the "malcontents".[185]

Meanwhile in Cardiff 200 children laid siege to a number of schools, including St John's National, where a running battle took place between the demonstrators and pupil teachers. Here, the strikers, who had made banners from hedge sticks and scarves, were driven forward by a pupil with a milkman's horn. The siege was only interrupted after the arrival of a police inspector and a number of constables, "though not before some considerable damage was done" to the school.[186]

Some of the more serious confrontations occurred in the capital. In one such incident involving around 600 children from three schools in the Thames area of London, one of the constables called to quell the disturbance expressed his shock at the violence he witnessed. "The scene", he stated, "was an extraordinary one, and was in reality worse than the dock strike".[187]

The school students used a range of tactics during their actions. In Berwick strikers "obtained possession of the key of the school during the dinner hour, locked the door, filled the keyhole with gravel, played truant during the afternoon, and assaulted some companions who refused to join them".[188] In other places pupils drew up petitions and wrote leaflets encouraging others to join them. The *Glasgow Herald* published an account of the "capture" of a "ringleader, who had in his possession a document, containing a number of signatures, which read:

Schoolboys' Strike. Strikers meet at 9am at Dalry Park to-morrow. Strike for short hours and no home lessons, and free education for the whole school.[189]

As we saw, school buildings and teachers were a principal target of the protesters, but those who refused to join the strikes also found themselves confronted by school student pickets. In Clerkenwell a "very riotous" group of up to 300 strikers "armed with sticks and stones...molested the scholars as they came out".[190] In Islington 500 children armed with sticks and stones laid siege to St Mathias's School, informing "blacklegs" that they would "bash their heads in" if they refused to join the strike.[191] In Woolwich, Charlton and Plumstead several hundred strikers "went about, many armed with sticks, to induce the lads of other schools to come out, and when they refused the malcontents broke the windows".[192]

Faced with the flying pickets the school authorities invariably turned to the police. The following request for police help, made by the head teacher of Single-Street School in London on 9 October, was far from unique:

> I write to report an interference with our scholars by the boys of some neighbouring schools, and to ask your protection. At midday a crowd of boys armed with sticks and stones came to the schools and called upon our boys to "come out on strike". Those that refused to do so were called "blacklegs" and had brickbats and stones flung at them. Many of the boys were hurt, and one has gone to hospital.[193]

Following the head teacher's plea, two policemen were posted to "protect...children and entrances, and prevent brutal intimidation".[194]

But there were numerous instances of children failing to be intimidated by the police. The police struggled to cope with a 300 "very riotous" group, who besieged St Luke's School in London. The children were, police informed Clerkenwell magistrates, "armed with sticks and stones" and "One of the attacking party was armed with a knife".[195] As the *Times* noted, it "was only with some difficulty that the police dispersed them".[196]

In another instance, a 13 year old boy was hauled before Govan Police Court charged "with throwing potatoes or other missiles at the police...or otherwise having shouted, bawled, and made a great deal of noise".[197]

In other cases police attempts to contain and capture the strikers in order to return them to school were frustrated by the children's greater agility and better geographical knowledge. In one case in London the police were involved in a fruitless chase involving "100 urchins scampering in front of the police, and dodging into every bye-street of the main thoroughfares through which they passed".[198]

While the presence of police at school gates may, to an extent, have curtailed the effect of picketing, it could do little to ensure that those involved in the strike returned to school. Here, the education authorities turned to the courts for support.

In West Hartlepool the School Board applied for and obtained summonses against the parents of 250 children who were absenting themselves from school.[199] In other towns and cities, children were dragged before the courts. In some cases, children were released after being severely chastised by magistrates and lectured upon the "folly" of their conduct. In other instances children were punished more severely. Thus, Lambeth Police Court ignored the pleas for clemency made by 14 year old Elijah Goodey's father and remanded the boy to the workhouse for one week. According to the magistrate the sentence would "act as an example to the other disorderly lads, who appear to have joined together to defy the school authorities and the police".[200]

More commonly strikers coming before the courts faced fines and/or binding over orders. The latter invariably stipulated that any future misconduct would result in either a flogging or imprisonment. This was the fate that befell six boys in Leith who stood accused of battering the door of North Ford Street School with stones. Although the magistrate had "a good mind to order them to be flogged", he ordered them to pay a fine of 2s6d, or face the prospect of 24 hours imprisonment.[201] Likewise, Thomas Street, a nine year old boy who was accused of being part of a 500 strong gang caught "molesting" blacklegs at London's St Mathias' School was fined 5s "as a deterrent to others".[202]

Thus the state responded with brutality directed especially against local leaders of the movement. The coercion gradually worked with the return to school after a three-week period of resistance. The children's rebellion, it seemed, had been defeated, without any of the demands being met.

How then should we gauge the significance of the children's rebellion of 1889? As we have seen, many contemporary commentators alleged that it represented little more than a short one-off outbreak of child lawlessness and indiscretion. According to this interpretation gullible misled children merely imitated the "irresponsible" behaviour of their parents, engaging in a "copycat" "parody" of the dock strike and new unionist activism. Certainly, as we have seen, the strikes did erupt in areas such as Clydeside, Merseyside, South Wales and London's East End, where New Unionism was gaining strength and where there had been recent strike activity. As Taylor notes, there was "a clear correlation between the location of major school strikes and areas of militant 'New Union' activity".[203] Moreover, the child protesters, such as the 500 or so who marched through Bethnal Green wearing scarlet liberty caps and waving red flags, did embrace the political symbols of their older counterparts.[204]

However, the children's rebellion was a much more meaningful event in the history of childhood activism than contemporaries were prepared to admit. The school strikes were not, as publications such as the *Times* frequently alleged, isolated acts of copycat hooliganism. Nor were they, as one magistrate alleged, simply a result of children being "led away by reading in the newspapers things which they did not understand".[205] Rather those participating in the rebellion were "not merely playing at strike", they were striking "in dead earnest".[206] The young strikers did imitate many of the tactics of the New Union movement—wildcat strikes, demonstrations, picketing, processions, streamers and banners— because they were actively learning from the tactics being deployed by their communities, their families and their friends. And they did so in the pursuit of a range of genuine grievances.

The strikes were also successful in so far as they further increased the pressure for change within the schooling system. They focused attention on the question of free schooling and within two years a significant step towards the implementation of one of the protesters' key demands— free education for all—had been made. In 1891 the Conservative government reversed its previous implacable opposition to free schooling and passed the Free Education Act. Although this did not introduce universal free education (this was not achieved until 1902), it was "permissive" and allowed School Boards to admit children to their schools without payment.

The strikes of 1889 were the first concerted collective actions by school students in Britain and they were an important element in the drive towards free education. The strike wave of 1889 was soon to be followed by an even greater rebellion in 1911.

4

Children and the great unrest: The 1911 school strikes

Blame not the "elementary" boy
Who joins the latest agitation
His stolen leisure to employ
In warring against castigation
He only seeks a milder rule,
Why should the little chap be chided,
For no one loathed the cane at school
More than you or I did?

Do you recall the fearful hiss
Of blows outside the range of vision
Which, though we prayed they might miss,
Came down with hideous precision?
How hateful then the tyrant seemed
Who smote a cuticle abraded
And yet, 'twas only he who screamed
Who felt himself degraded[207]

ANY DISCUSSION of the 1911 school strike movement must begin with an acknowledgment of the remarkable parallels between the political and industrial climates of 1889 and 1911. The year 1911 was also marked by a period of militant industrial unrest. The number of disputes reported to the Labour Department of the Board of Trade had increased from 399 in 1908 to 903 in 1911. In 1909 the number of people directly involved in industrial disputes was only 170,000; by 1911 this had risen to 831,000. The number of strike days during the same period increased from 2,560,000 to 38,142,000.[208] Trade union membership grew by 600,000 during the year.[209] As Newsinger has pointed out:

1911...was one of the most important years in British working class history... It saw an unprecedented level of class conflict sweep over much of Britain. It was a year of mass strikes with what amounted to local general strikes being called in Hull, Cardiff, Salford and Liverpool... In many places, school children emulated their parents and walked out on strike.[210]

The statistics alone fail to convey the revolutionary fervour gripping Britain. French historian Elie Halevy[211] has used the term domestic anarchy to describe the events of 1911, while the British historian George Dangerfield argued that the Workers Rebellion of that year marked the beginning of the "death of Liberal England".[212]

The summer of 1911 saw troops dispatched to 27 towns and cities and general officers commanding Britain's army garrisons were instructed by the Home Office to use their own discretion in deciding whether to use firepower to maintain law and order.[213] Across Britain fierce battles erupted between strikers, their families and the police and armed forces. In Liverpool on 15 August barricades and street bonfires were used to hamper the progress of police and soldiers and, according to one contemporary source, "the whole area was for a time in a state of siege". Two days later, when the War Office had finally managed to gain control of the city, two strikers were shot dead by the army.[214]

On 18 August two more strikers were killed by troops in Llanelli, South Wales[215] and four more died there later in the day (and many more were injured) when railway trucks that had been set on fire exploded.[216] Against this background, school strikes burst onto the scene once more.

It is perhaps no coincidence that the first two areas to be affected by the school strike movement of September 1911 were Llanelli and Liverpool. The strikes started in Llanelli on 5 September, when boys at Bigyn Council School walked out after one of their number had been beaten by an assistant teacher for passing a piece of paper around in class.[217]

The children were aggrieved not just at the beating, but also the fact that it had been carried out without the authority of the head teacher, who was absent on the day.[218] This relatively orderly protest was concluded with the help of the intervention of an ex-chairman of the local Education Committee who appealed to the good nature of children and parents.[219]

On 8 September children in Liverpool struck, "parading the district and calling upon other schools, asking the scholars to come out in sympathy".[220] The strikers put forward a range of grievances and demands: the abolition of the cane, the abolition of home lessons, an extra half-day holiday and the payment of monitors (elder children chosen by head teachers to deliver basic instruction to younger pupils).

By 11 September the strike wave had reached Manchester, where "thousands of school children came out on strike":

> Meetings were held and pickets were appointed... Asked what their grievances were, one of the youthful leaders said, "No cane, shorter hours, and lunch time at eleven, our most important demand being the first one"... At a meeting of the boys held at Taylor-Street School one of the scholars carried a great card with the legend: "Please teacher don't be offended. We shan't go back till the strike is ended".[221]

The strike hit the capital on the same day. Children from at least six schools in the Shoreditch and Islington districts of London walked out of school, demanding much the same terms as their Liverpool and Manchester counterparts. These demands became common to the strikes in 60 towns and cities recorded in the following three weeks.

As in 1889, the possibility that the protesters' grievances were genuine was rejected outright in contemporary accounts of the strike. Once again, blame for the disruption was placed on the "hot-headed" and "foolish" example set by militant mothers and fathers.

This claim was invariably substantiated by an acknowledgement of the fact that many of the strikes occurred in areas most affected by other strike activity, and by references to the "astonishing similarity" of the tactics used by child and adult strikers.

Hence, the *Llanelly Advertiser* was quick to accuse children of mindlessly mimicking the behaviour of their parents. "The strike epidemic now prevalent", it said, "has infected the rising generation at Llanelly, and, in order to be in the 'fashion', the schoolboys decided on a 'down tool' policy".[222] One head teacher in Grimsby described the strikes as a "kind of imitative hysteria", predicting that "the little beggars will be in their places tomorrow—all innocence".[223]

Wider educational opinion reflected this interpretation of the strikes. The *Educational News* believed the strikes were caused by an "ignorant", "ill-informed" class of children, using their over-elaborate powers of imitation; "strikes, being the fashion with adults", had "become likewise that of the juveniles".[224]

The Labour Party leadership were not slow to reflect similar views. J R Clynes, a Manchester MP and vice chair of the Labour Party, described the children's behaviour and their demands "as nothing more than a freakish imitation of their elders". Further, he asserted that the demands were baseless and there was little evidence of excessive use of corporal punishment by teachers:

> He understood that some of the boys struck against the use of the cane, but figures showed that there was not very much punishment in schools. It had come to be realised that education could not be thrashed into a child, and it was impossible to teach by fear. A little correction might be necessary at times, but it ought never be carried to making a child feel degraded, disgraced, sullen and dissatisfied, and so far as he knew, that was the general opinion of teachers.[225]

We will examine later whether Clynes underestimated the degree of "correction" via the cane in elementary schools. For now, though, we will focus upon claims that children were merely imitating the behaviour of their "reckless" elders.

There can be little doubt that many of the children participating in the strike wave will have been influenced by the wider industrial conflict occurring at the time. In addition, commentators were quite right to point to the close correspondence between the tactics used by child and adult strikers. It is well established that social movements learn from each other and expand the "repertoire of contention" available to protest movements.[226]

But there is another more direct reason why the children were adopting the tactics used in the industrial disputes in their areas. The children themselves had sometimes played an important, albeit hidden, part in adult disputes. It was through their participation, and not through "childhood imitation", that they learned and internalised strategies of working class resistance.

For example, children's involvement in the year-long miners' strike that affected the Rhondda valley between 1910-11 was significant. A flurry of telegrams and letters between the Home Office and its representatives in South Wales show that children were frequently involved, alongside their parents, in violent attacks on the police and armed forces. As the following communiqué from the Home Office official J F Moylon to his superiors in London highlights, children also played a significant part in the intimidation of strikebreakers. Moylon says the children's action was "more serious" than the illegal harassment of blacklegs by adult strikers outside pit gates:

> More serious still [than illegal picketing] are assaults on officials and "blacklegs" and their families and attacks on their houses. Cases of actual assault are, so far, not numerous, but window smashing is common. The procedure is for a crowd largely composed of women and children to gather round the official's house and stone it. The men in the crowd usually stand by and look on... During the last two days a new plan of painting "B" or "Bl" or "Scab" on a "blackleg's" house has been adopted.[227]

Contemporary newspaper accounts also contain numerous references to children playing a key role in the protests associated with the Workers Rebellion of 1911. In some instances this resistance was non-violent, involving children helping to ensure their families' subsistence needs were met at what was obviously a time of severe hardship.

The *Daily Mail*, for instance, provides us with an account of an incident involving around 40 Cardiff children who swooped on the city's railway station in an attempt to procure milk for their families. The account suggests they "swarmed onto the milk carts and endeavoured to remove the lids from the churns". "They were eventually driven off," but not before they had "helped themselves to about five and a half gallons of milk".[228]

But in other instances, children were directly involved in more violent confrontations, often witnessing and being subjected to the most extreme forms of state brutality. The *Daily Mail* and the *Manchester Guardian* accounts of the riots in Llanelli in the aftermath of shootings on 18 August clearly situate children at the centre of violent protests.

The *Daily Mail* account notes the presence of children in the attack on a store owned by the JP who had read the Riot Act to protesters earlier in the afternoon. Unperturbed by his demands for the restoration of law and order a "mob", including women, girls and small children, destroyed every window in his shop before besieging and looting another nearby store.[229] In response, the police made "continual baton charges" and "the military also made at least half a dozen charges with fixed bayonets", causing multiple casualties. "Numerous men, women and children were seriously injured...many being carried away by their friends".[230]

Children also played a central role in the industrial unrest in Liverpool. Indeed, the General tasked with quelling the protests in the city claimed the children's presence among rioters as one the principal reasons why troops from the Yorkshire Regiment refrained from opening fire in Homer Street on 15 August, despite being encouraged by a local magistrate to do so.[231]

The following day troops from the 18 Hussars showed no such hesitancy. Children were among the first who rushed to the aid of a Liverpool man fatally shot in the head during that day's confrontations.[232] He was one of two men killed by troops during an ill-fated attempt to secure the release of arrested fellow-strikers from prison vans tentatively making their way through the city. The subsequent inquest into the two men's deaths heard how children had played a key part in the riot, replenishing the missiles used by assailants to attack the police and troops guarding the prisoners. As the testimony of one of the soldiers to the inquest made clear, the fact that children were in the direct firing line of the Hussars did little to deter them from discharging their weapons at the crowd.[233]

Like their counterparts in Liverpool and Llanelli, children in other parts of the country had supported their parents in their struggles against employers and the state during 1911, often finding themselves at the forefront of the battle lines. As *Justice*, the official journal of the Marxist Social Democratic Party acknowledged in its account of the national disturbances, "men, women and children have been brutally bludgeoned in the streets of London, Liverpool, Hull, Cardiff and other places".[234] It is therefore not surprising that protesters involved in the school strike movement sometimes resorted to similar tactics.

Indeed, as contemporary newspaper reports of the school strikes illustrate, participation in the Workers Rebellion had acted as a political apprenticeship for some of the children involved in the school strikes. In Birkenhead, where around 400 boys were said to have "come out", the "leader addressed them in one of the streets...telling them to do like their fathers, who 'got their rights' a few weeks ago". Likewise in Colchester, children "armed with sticks and singing 'Britons shall never be slaves', marched to the school...to intimidate the 'blacklegs'".[235]

Not all the protests were violent. The initial school strike in Llanelli was a peaceful, disciplined protest. A contemporary report claimed the children had "not...shown any inclination to destroy property".[236] The same was true of many of the school strikes that occurred in September 1911.

However, on a number of occasions the strikes led to significant confrontations and disruptions. In West Hartlepool a storage room at the rear of a hotel was looted and strikers helped themselves to stout, whiskey and boxes of cigars. Suitably refreshed the children then proceeded to throw stones at houses occupied by teachers.[237]

In most cases the strikers focused their protests at school buildings, teachers and the police. In Birkenhead police protection was needed for teachers, and School Board officers were "stoned and compelled to abandon their work".[238] In Liverpool gangs of strikers smashed street lamps and school windows, and "loyal scholars were beaten with sticks".[239] Similar scenes occurred in Manchester, where "Some of the truants carried big sticks in an attempt to terrorise the weaker spirits".[240] Here, in addition to attacks on schools and "blacklegs", a fruitier's van was ambushed and overturned when the half-time student in charge of it refused to join the strike.[241] In Dundee on the evening of 14 September, around 1,500 children were involved in an assault on up to nine school buildings, attacking teachers and breaking at least 100 windows.[242]

Such scenes were replicated across Britain's towns and cities. As in 1889 the police were stationed at school gates and this led to further confrontation, as this report from London highlights:

> Many [strikers] were provided with ammunition in the shape of stones and other missiles. So boisterously did the boys behave that the assistance of the police was sought, and for some hours constables kept the strikers from gaining entrance to the schools, although in one case it was reported that the boys effected an entrance into one of the playgrounds and smashed several windows.[243]

Hull's schools were described as being "besieged" by gangs of pickets, demanding that non-striking scholars "come out":

> [S]everal schools' policemen were stationed, as there had been some stone-throwing and the pickets had attacked schoolboys whom they

had caught in the playground... Whenever a schoolmaster made his appearance he was hooted by the boys.[244]

Here, plain clothes policemen were on duty in an attempt to combat the strikers' tactics, though this was insufficient to prevent the Vicar of St Mark's church being struck in the face with a lump of coke.

At the Payne-street School in Islington the constable stationed on the gates was faced with strikers:

> armed with sticks, stones, bits of iron and similar weapons. One small boy had no fewer than three half bricks tucked under one arm as he marched through the streets. They [the strikers] threw stones at the school windows and the policeman on guard had a difficult task in quelling the disturbance.[245]

In Stoke-on-Trent numerous schools were attacked and damaged. The police struggled to maintain control, leading to the Chief Constable being called before the city's Watch Committee to provide a briefing. Several of his probationary officers were due to have accompanied him to the meeting to have their appointment as constables confirmed. They were unable to do so because they were guarding school gates![246]

As in 1899, contemporary reports blamed the strike on the "irresponsible" actions of their parents. According to the *Northern Daily Telegraph*, the "mad conduct" displayed by the strikers showed "how well the lessons of the late labour troubles have been imparted to the younger generation".[247] Others apportioned the violence to the "perverse" and "wilful" nature of delinquent working class children.

However, attacks on teachers, school buildings, pupil-blacklegs and the police had an instrumental value. They helped in the recruitment of children to the strike, helped maintain pupil solidarity and were necessary to counter the strike-breaking attempts of the school authorities and the police.[248]

The fact that the strike was driven by political motives rather than hooliganism is evident from the comments and slogans of the protesters. As one Liverpool boy stated, "Our fathers starved to get what they wanted; what our fathers have done we can do".[249]

It is also clear that the demands made by strikers were justified. Complaints about the excessive use of corporal punishment were well founded. Canings—and in many cases floggings—were common. In elementary schools punishment was often handed out for minor "offences" such as "going unwashed", "untidiness" and "dirty habits".[250]

In London's West Lambeth elementary schools alone there were 55,297 recorded instances of corporal punishment in the 12 months up to 31 October 1908; 6,069 of these involved infants. In adjacent East Lambeth's schools there were 63,169 such incidents, 5,567 inflicted on infants.[251]

The brutality of the regime led to some horrific treatment of children. The case of Rose Dean, a 12 year old Manchester girl, was, unfortunately, not unusual. Rose was punched, pushed against the corner of a desk, physically thrown out of her class and into a wall whereupon she repeatedly vomited. Her crime was to have sung out of tune in a music lesson. For this "heinous" misdemeanour she would spend three weeks in hospital and four weeks in a convalescent home.[252]

Occasionally, the most horrific cases of abuse would prompt questions in Parliament, as with the Peterborough head teacher who was convicted of flogging an eight year old boy "with great and unreasonable severity". This particular head teacher already had one conviction for physically assaulting a child in his charge, and the case prompted backbench calls for greater oversight and restraint of corporal punishment.[253]

Contemporary Parliamentary exchanges also highlight the abject failure of the Board of Education to punish those found guilty of violent acts against school students. Three years after the school strikes the president of the Board of Education was forced to admit that the Board was "not aware of any precedent in regard to the withdrawal of a teacher's certificate for abuse of powers in connection with corporal punishment".[254]

In the absence of any official forms of redress for such extreme, acknowledged acts of violence and cruelty, the children took matters into their own hands in 1911. They did so in the full knowledge of the risks they faced if they were unsuccessful, a testimony to their determination and sense of purpose.

The demands for the abolition of homework and for additional holidays were also reasonable. Working class homes were often gloomy and overcrowded, not ideal conditions for study. There was also pressure on working class children to contribute to the family purse by working outside school hours.[255]

Calls for the payment of monitors were also justifiable. In under-staffed, overcrowded elementary schools, the assistance of monitors was crucial for the instruction of younger children and the "maintenance of discipline". From the perspective of the present we may wonder at the hierarchy embodied in the use of monitors. But in the context of 1911 and the demands placed on monitors, the demand for a penny per week "compensation" for carrying out their duties was hardly unreasonable.

Finally, that the children's strike movement was not simply an expression of delinquent-led, anti-social adolescent rebelliousness is evident from the active support of parents in many areas. In Ashton-under-Lyne, "masters complained that some women were encouraging the boys, and one master said that a women had called the school and threatened him with what she would do to him if he thrashes her boy, who was among the strikers".[256] In Hull "women incited the children to follow the "strikers" example",[257] and in Leeds "Some of the mothers... showed open sympathy".[258] In Birkenhead pupils had "the open conniv-ance at least of their parents".[259]

Such examples of adult solidarity with the children's cause were not universal, and in some areas parents cooperated with school authori-ties in securing an end to some of the strikes. However, such support *was* commonplace. As well as supporting their children and families, many of the parents had in the previous months been on strike and subjected to the most extreme forms of state coercion and brutality. Given this it is hardly surprising that many of them supported their children's demands.

The authorities encouraged parents to stop their children from participating in the strikes. Most commonly, parents were informed that their children would face physical punishments and they were threatened with police intervention and court action. In Llanelli the education authority appealed directly to the financial interests of par-ents, stating that pupil absences would "greatly affect" the town's government education grant, the costs of which would ultimately be borne by parents themselves one way or another.[260]

Where these appeals failed other tactics were contemplated. In Liverpool the possibility of calling upon a company of "loyal" Boy Scouts to "put down" the protests was raised.[261] However, even the loyalty of Scout troops could not be guaranteed, as evidenced by a plea made by one Scoutmaster to striking scouts to return to school:

One of the most important of the Scout promises made on joining is: "To be loyal to God, the King, my parents, officers and employers". This clause embraces schoolmasters. If any Scouts have gone on "strike" I would urge them to remember their oath and return immediately to school, taking any punishment that may be meted out to them cheerfully, as a Scout should.[262]

Although such appeals were largely unsuccessful the strike wave started to recede after three weeks. Many of those who had participated in the strikes faced a brutal return to the classroom. The schools argued that the strikers had participated in a flagrant abuse of authority that could not be tolerated. Future generations of working class children needed to be taught through the "restoration" of the iron rod of discipline to "know their place".

A correspondent to the *Lancashire Daily Post* argued that the disruption had been caused by the proliferation of "humane methods" of teaching and "ridiculous restrictions concerning the use of the cane", a view that was widely shared within the educational establishment, particularly among teachers. There was a need, therefore, not only for the "guilty" children to be physically punished, but for there to be a strengthening of school discipline and a wider, not more limited, use of corporal punishment. As he went on:

This is the time for parents to place more confidence in school teachers and to replace in their hands the discretionary powers that were vested in them years before the so-called humanitarian cranks alerted their puerile crusade against corporal punishment.[263]

The *Times*, in a lengthy editorial on the strikes, also expressed its hope that a reassertion of discipline would be one positive outcome of the protests. "For the moment", it acknowledged, "the position is serious", but "these school strikes might serve a purpose if they induce parents to realise the limits of peaceful persuasion as an educative force".[264]

The school authorities showed a determination to inflict harsh discipline upon strikers. In Lancaster "severe punishment [was] inflicted by the masters" while in Sunderland so-called truants returning to school were "soundly birched".[265] The same fate was said to have befallen one of the "ringleaders" of the strike in Liverpool, who on returning to school "learnt that the use of the cane is still in operation".[266] In

Manchester the local press congratulated the school masters on their authoritarian reaction following the end of the strike there. "The boys returned to their lessons humble and penitent and the injunction 'down with the cane' was interpreted by the masters in a fashion which did not appeal to the truants".[267]

How should we assess the impact or success of the school strike wave of 1911?

In the short term the strikers failed to achieve their principal demands, including the abolition of the cane. However, the strikes helped create a national debate on the uses and abuses of corporal punishment within the school system. Less than five months after the strikes, Cheshire's Education Committee adopted a new disciplinary code for its elementary schools which stipulated that "head teachers should use every endeavour to reduce all forms of punishment to a minimum compatible with the welfare of children and the school, and should not in any case inflict corporal punishment (except for grave offences) until all other methods have been tried and failed".[268] In other areas school authorities began to restrict the use of the cane to head teachers. This was one of the key demands of the school strikes in some areas, and it was a restriction that was deeply resented by some teachers.[269] On a national level although unacceptable abuses continued to occur, evidence suggests that the incidence of corporal punishment in schools fell and continued to fall in the years following the strike.[270]

But the strike was a success in another important sense. It represented a welcome "expression of the resistance of the local working class community to the abuse of fundamental rights by the authoritarian and bureaucratic organisation of state schooling".[271] As in 1889, children showed they had not been overwhelmed by the stultifying, sometimes brutalising regimes found in elementary schools and that they were prepared to engage in collective acts of resistance in an attempt to improve their educational environment.

JIMMY STEWART (Newcastle, 1911)[i]
Strike, strike, strike a blow for freedom[ii]

Jimmy went to Sandyford school in the North East. He was involved in the school strike wave of 1911. In his recollections Jimmy talked about home, school and the 1911 strike.

CONDITIONS IN working class communities in the North East were difficult. There was little money to go around. And in 1911 there was a real sense of rebellion with a whole series of strikes.

The schools were brutal places. It was based on rote learning and was very boring.

Each class had about 52 scholars in it and we were divided into tables of four (so there was always 48, 52 or 56 in a class, but 52 was the most common). The teachers further set the class. Those they had given up on sat at the front, where they could be controlled but ignored in terms of education. The brightest sat at the back, and they were left to get on with it themselves. The teachers focussed on the group in the middle.

Each day we started with a prayer. Once a week we had hymns and an assembly. But then the rest of the day was academic lessons.

Discipline was severe. You could get beaten for not wearing the right clothes, for not knowing the answer to mental arithmetic or for breaching one of the many rules.

As school students we saw all the strikes locally—and, of course, our families were all involved. So we started to raise our own demands for improvements to school. We wanted free pens and paper, heating in classrooms, a reduced school week, payment for monitors and abolition of the cane and the strap.

By the first week in September the school strike had started. At first there were only 30 of us, but the numbers rapidly grew. The large numbers participating made it easier for us, it gave us protection from the authorities.

i   Unlike other life stories in the book this is not from a direct interview with the authors. It is based on an interview carried out by Ray Challinor—and the focus was slightly different. This is our summation of Jimmy's contribution to the taped interview. Thanks to John Charlton for making this tape available to us.

ii   This chant was sung by the strikers to the tune of an old hymn, *Jesus loves the little children, all the little children of the world.*

We started to receive delegations from other schools. They came and asked us about the strike and our demands. Then they went back to their schools and went on strike as well.

Our parents were threatened by the "school Board men" (truancy officers). They could fine families for their children's "truancy" and this was a big deal when there wasn't much money around. Working class families were strict. Being a good scholar was something families were proud of and education was viewed as a way of getting on in life.

So there was a lot of pressure on us. After a week our strike finished and we returned back to school.

Jimmy remained active in politics and went on to be a founder member of the Communist Party.

5

Children of the revolution:
Organising for pupil power

"A SPECTRE is haunting the citadels of power...the spectre of revolutionary youth".[272]

In 1889 and 1911 the contemporary press attempted to explain the school strikes as a "quirk", the result of children "imitating" adult protests. Similar notions were developed to dismiss the first great school strike wave of 1968-72. Such explanations were inadequate in both 1889 and 1911, but they are even less applicable to these strikes. The events of this period cannot be fully understood without locating them within the emergence of a confident, organised and militant pupil power movement during the late 1960s.

In the following two chapters we look at this episode in some detail. In this chapter we focus on the growth of the pupil power movement and its roots in the student unrest that erupted in Paris in 1968.

The year 1968 is usually associated with university student protests but school students were not insulated from the radicalism generated by those in the universities. Pupils became actively involved in a whole range of protest campaigns but within the school setting the focus was the demand for greater school democracy and opposition to the authoritarian, sometimes brutalising, nature of state schooling.

The pupil protests of the late 1960s and early 1970s witnessed far greater levels of organisation and coordination than the earlier strike waves. Taking their cue from the wider student movement, the protests were much more overtly political. The range of issues discussed and campaigned over were far broader than in either 1889 or 1911.

This did not go unnoticed by the UK political establishment. Indeed, it generated a significant level of concern within the higher echelons of the state apparatus. This culminated in May 1972 with Prime Minister

Edward Heath instructing his private secretary Robert Armstrong to contact the head of the security service, with a view to establishing the risk that pupil power posed to the foundations of the British state!

For anyone who cared to look, signs of pupil disaffection, politicisation and unrest in Britain's schools were evident in the late 1960s.[273] Demands for greater levels of pupil power were embraced and promoted by the youth wings of political movements of the left including the Young Communist League (YCL) and the Labour Party Young Socialists (LPYS)—which itself was a host to a range of far-left political groupings including International Socialists, orthodox Trotskyists and Maoists.

In 1966 the YCL launched a recruitment drive which tried to relate to a wider layer of working class young people. Under the campaign slogan "The Trend—Communism" they engaged with the contemporary music scene. For a period Pete Townsend of The Who became a prominent, though short-lived, member.[274] YCL full time organisers targeted coffee bars, and the 1967 YCL National Congress changed from a relatively dry political conference to a much more "cultural event" with competitions in a range of the arts. These included:

> painting, poetry, short-story writing, plays, photography, cartooning, song competitions, even a beat group contest. Among the judges were the journalist Malcolm Muggeridge, Arnold Wesker the playwright and Adrian Mitchell the poet.[275]

The YCL in Manchester managed to get a team onto the BBC television programme *Juke Box Jury*, and YCL branches opened up dialogue and debate with the LPYS, Christian groups and even the Young Liberals. The result was that the YCL grew to somewhere in the region of 6,000 members in 1967.[276]

Such growth led the YCL into a range of political campaigns. They were at the forefront of early attempts to organise and coordinate school children's protests. In May 1968 the YCL Midlands District announced plans to set up Sixth Formers' Committees and by the end of the year the YCL had announced its intention to run a national campaign in schools.[277]

Calls for greater levels of school democracy were not the sole preserve of the left. In January 1968 the Young Liberals published a school campaign guide, which the *Guardian* described as a "strike guide for school children". Citing Yugoslavian experiments in classroom democracy as the ideal, the guide demanded that pupils "be given as big a say as is practicably feasible in the running of their own lives". It exhorted pupils to demand representation on school governing boards and offered advice on how to fight any resistance they might face. In such circumstances, pupils should "organise a one day strike or ban on homework", before moving to the ultimate sanction of a "full strike".[278]

The involvement of the Young Liberals illustrates the broader appeal of the pupil power movement at the time, and also both the slightly confused and dynamic nature of politics and youth cultural movements in the late 1960s.

The "problems" of pupil power were a key point of discussion at the 1968 independent schools' Headmasters' Conference, an illustration of the extent to which the "dangers" of school democracy exercised the minds of senior figures in the educational establishment.[279]

Growing levels of pupil activism were seen in several developments in 1968.

The Leeds Schools Socialist Federation was set up. Dave Gibson was one of the early joiners:

> I was a student at Leeds Grammar School, and one of my fellow students was a member of the International Socialists, a guy called John Bradbrooke, and he was a big influence in the school. We were angry about the way the school was—the petty rules, the discipline, corporal punishment etc—but there was also a lot of concern and interest in things like racism, Vietnam, Czechoslovakia, the student revolt and what was happening in Paris. These were all blending together. At Christmas 1967 we produced a magazine in the school called *More in Sorrow than in Anger* that we sold outside the school gates. It caused absolute uproar in the school and there were threats of expulsions. The school decided to let us set up an "alternative" school magazine, really as a way of trying to incorporate us. But the magazine gave us a space and it covered articles about all the issues—the Kenyan Asian crisis, racism, Vietnam, Paris, Czechoslovakia—that were important at the time... At Leeds Modern John Dyson was in the IS and we got to know one or two others across the city. So in 1968 we set up the Leeds Schools Socialist Federation... I think, certainly if I look back at what we were writing, this was the first Schools' Action Union in the country at the time.[280]

Leeds Schools Socialist Federation brought out a regular cross-city magazine called *Handful of Dust*—shortened by the second edition to *HOD*. The first edition included a clear statement of what "We stand for" which was made up of eight demands on school organisation, education and more general issues in society:

> Democratic school councils of pupils, staff and other workers involved, which would have real authority. Prefects would have to go.
>
> No compulsory religious services or instruction, all games to be voluntary.
>
> A general attack on petty regulations and school uniforms, all of which are designed to increase the conformity of school pupils.
>
> Abolition of the 11 plus; exams should not decide a person's whole future in the way they do at present.
>
> Abolition of corporal punishment.
>
> No discrimination or inequality due to race, sex or class.
>
> Freedom of speech, assembly and the right to organise inside schools; no censorship of magazines, clubs and societies.
>
> Opposition to education cuts as an attack on the working class.[281]

The accompanying paragraph gives a brief introduction to the group and their view on education:

> In our view, education should not be considered in isolation, it plays a vital part in conditioning people to accept their place in society. "Do what you're told—or else" is something which under capitalism you will be hearing for the rest of your life... This is what we are trying to break down. As far as general politics go, we are libertarian socialists, which means, among other things, that we are as opposed to the Russians in Czechoslovakia as to the Americans in Vietnam. In our opinion society can only be transformed into true democracy and socialism from below by the conscious action of ordinary people.[282]

The first six issues of the magazine included some fairly long essays on politics and education, music and gig reviews, cartoons and poems, features on the arts and the local Leeds scene as well as a smattering of pieces on sex, love and relationships. But the magazine was also an "organiser" advertising fund-raising gigs, identifying up-coming protests and demonstrations and keeping readers informed of local issues in the city's schools.[283]

In Cardiff school students produced a magazine called *Ashes and Grapes*. It led to a city wide conference attended by 200 school students and the formation of the Cardiff Union of School Students.

December saw the creation of the Manchester Union of Secondary School Students, which in its first month was said to have around 120 members drawn from 35 different schools. The spark in Manchester was a strike by 200 students at the Miles Platting School against the use of the leather tawse as an implement of punishment.[284]

Anxious about the union's foundation, the Cheshire Association of Divisional Executives dispatched its vice president to a teach-in organised by the union, where he pleaded with pupils to act "responsibly" and not to "go out on a limb".[285]

Similar attempts to organise secondary school pupils into locally-based unions were already occurring in London, Oxford, Swansea, Bristol, Hertfordshire and Surrey.[286] The *Daily Mail* expressed its outrage at what it estimated were the 17 different groups and unions scattered around the country, each seeking "to infiltrate schools with extreme left wing propaganda and achieve 'pupil power'".[287]

There were now efforts to coordinate these different groups into a national federation. At a meeting at Holborn library in January 1969 there was a proposal to set up a national union called Unison. The meeting was addressed by a representative from the French pupil power organisation, the Comites d'Action Lyceens.[288]

The proposed union failed to materialise but in March a national school students union, the Schools Action Union (SAU), was formerly set up. The SAU was initially founded by a small group of London sixth formers who had been inspired by the success of the student unrest in France and Italy a year earlier, but it soon became a focus for the wider national pupil power movement.

The YCL and other groups on the left (most of whom existed within and around the LPYS) were actively engaged in promoting the SAU, something that its media and political detractors were keen to emphasise. The bulk of the SAU's activists were young school students and sixth formers motivated by a profound desire to fight injustice in the school system and wider society. Sheila Rowbotham recalls being impressed by the commitment shown by the "lively" young SAU activists from London's Camden School for Girls whom she met while she was helping organise the London School of Economics (LSE) "Living

School" experiment.[289] The Living School was a three day conference at Conway Hall. Dave Gibson remembers the conference bringing SAU activists together. "The Leeds group had quite a lot of credibility among the SAU because we had been around for a time".[290]

It was this "lively", youthful edge to the SAU which gave it its appeal, and explains why its calls for school democracy and pupil involvement found a ready audience among pupils of all ages and backgrounds. Ultimately, the SAU would prove to be a very effective campaigning body. Through its well circulated pamphlets and newsletters, it articulated (and organised protests around) a number of basic demands, including an end to corporal punishment and detentions, greater children's participation in the running of schools, the abolition of school uniforms, better school meals and the reintroduction of free school milk (which had been stopped for primary children by Education Secretary Margaret Thatcher[291] in 1970).[292] The degree of interest that would ultimately be shown in the organisation by the Department for Education and Sciences, the Home Office and the security services (see below) remains a testament to the organisational skills of its members and its impact on the national stage.

The SAU's first major protest was in March 1969, when around 400 children, along with some sympathetic teachers, marched through London to County Hall and the Department for Education and Science, where they presented a petition setting out six key demands: control of schools by all students and staff, freedom of speech and assembly, an end to corporal punishment, abolition of school uniforms, co-educational comprehensive schools, and more pay for teachers.[293] On the same day, Dave Gibson recalls, a march took place in Manchester around the slogans "Free speech in schools" and "No victimisation" because "Manchester activists had been threatened with expulsion from school".[294]

By the end of March 1969, 50 London schools were said to have affiliated, with provincial branches in Dover, Fife, Leeds, Leicester, Reigate, Stevenage, Stoke on Trent, Tunbridge Wells, Swansea, Bristol and Cardiff.[295]

In June 1969 the SAU organised a demonstration to Dulwich College. This was a selective school in south London and was targeted by the SAU because of their commitment to comprehensive education. The protestors arrived in the middle of the school's Open Day, much to the annoyance of the school head.[296]

By July 1969 the SAU was estimated to have around 15,000 members and the print run of its newspaper, *Vanguard*, had increased from 500 to 4,500 in the space of six months.[297] In interviews with the press SAU activists sought to emphasise the moderate nature of their demands for greater school democracy. As one argued, "If every factory manager made every employee attend morning service, wear a cap, and be beaten for trivial things, there would soon be a general strike".[298]

Support for the SAU's activities was found in some surprising quarters. In July, following a discussion with SAU activists, 22 boys from exclusive fee-paying Harrow School signed up, prompting its head teacher to dismiss SAU members as a bunch of "long-haired children under the aegis of the Communist party".[299] In the same month, an SAU branch was constituted at Eton. Much to the dismay of head teacher Anthony Chenevix-Trench, the young Etonian activists complained to the *Times* about the school's "dictatorial system" and "19th century dress and school government".[300]

The SAU's appeal to pupils at Harrow and Eton serves to demonstrate the growing influence and strength of the pupil power movement, but it should not detract from the essentially class-based character of the union's activities. Its association with the "left" was self-evident; in this, the head teacher of Harrow was at least partially correct. It rented its first national headquarters, a one room office in Bloomsbury, from Agit Prop, an organisation that specialised in the distribution of revolutionary propaganda.[301] The SAU's newspaper, *Vanguard*, was published by the Socialist Review Publishing Company, and its columns had a distinctly Marxist hue. A 1969 editorial emphasises the range of issues the paper wanted SAU activists to engage with:

> This issue includes articles on such apparently diverse topics as student politics, religious teaching and alleged racism in education plans. But are such topics really so estranged? Not really, education is not an isolated issue—it is intrinsically interlinked with many, many aspects of the society in which we live—it must be if it is to have relevance to that society. Therefore as we fight to change education we are also engaged in changing the society that this education is part of. If we fail to see this link, we miss the dynamic of the schools movement. The call for democratic control of schools is an echo of a feeling current in many sectors of society at the moment.[302]

The SAU, the editorial went on, was "seeking to turn the course of education", but it also intended to be "part of the struggle for a radical social change in this country".[303] Journalists who covered the SAU's activities were also struck by its "leftist" leanings:

> Its membership is packed with teenage revolutionaries—Maoists, Trotskyists, Young Communists, and International Socialists. Their rhetoric is filled with Lenin's slogans and Marxist clichés. Bourgeois is the omnipresent adjective; imperialism the arch enemy; and the working class the means of salvation. The goal is the transformation of the capitalist State; the path is revolution... But the SAU is not all strident adolescent militancy... Young Socialists [ie Labour Party supporters]... are pressing the SAU to be more realistic; to forget revolution for the moment and be content with reform.[304]

Certainly, as we will see, there were elements within the pupil power movement who were advocating a more "moderate" approach, but it was the SAU's militant politics that was responsible for the growing notoriety and profile of the pupil power movement.

As Malcolm Dean of the *Guardian* wrote, "For those trying to promote a paranoid style of politics the SAU is tailored to their needs".[305] In a sense he was right; from its inception, the SAU's activities engendered a heightened state of paranoia within not only the press, but also the educational establishment and the political classes. The response of the educational authorities was, predictably, one of overt hostility. As the following contemporary account illustrates, SAU activists faced harassment and victimisation within their schools:

> In London, during the spring term, a number of leading members of the movement who had made no particular secret of their efforts to democratise schools were summoned by their head teachers and forbidden to belong to the SAU or to distribute its magazine *Vanguard*. In more than one case head masters threatened [that] hints of their allegiance to revolutionary groups might appear on their university admissions forms.[306]

In this particular instance, the SAU alleged that the Inner London Education Authority (ILEA) had conspired with secondary school heads in an attempt to intimidate activists and quash the union. At the time, the SAU's allegations of spiked university references were impossible to prove, but other contemporary accounts lent support to the allegation that school and college heads were making it clear that SAU activism would jeopardise university applications and grants.[307] Less than a year later this would be confirmed when a student occupation at Warwick University uncovered files showing that sixth form heads were surreptitiously informing universities of the "political activities" of applicants. Michael Wolf, an SAU activist and former pupil at William Ellis School, Highgate, was one of a number of applicants whose "militant" views would cost them a place at Warwick after he was "outed" by his head teacher, Sidney Baxter.[308]

In other instances head teachers used the threat of expulsion to deter SAU activism. At Dulwich's Kingsdale School in south London, a number of pupils heeded the SAU's call to strike and demonstrate on the final day of term in December 1969. Here, although many pupils had participated in the action, only the five SAU activists who had picketed the school gates were expelled. Their expulsion was confirmed after the children, with the support of their parents, had refused to accept a period of "academic probation". Malcolm Dean covered the story for the *Guardian*. The school's managers had informed him that militant agitators and "professional troublemakers" lay behind the children's decision to strike, yet he found no such evidence when he interviewed the pupils concerned:

> Yesterday I talked to four of the children, when it became obvious they needed little guidance. Two of the students particularly, Jerry Balcombe, aged 14, and Clare Robinson, aged 15, handle political concepts with an ease that would win the admiration of an LSE student. Clare is honest and straightforward; Jerry is guileful; but both, although having politically committed parents, are clearly in control of their SAU activities.

Dean found the children's arguments "both cogent and convincing" and hinted that the head, a Mr Rees, who also happened to be chair of the London Comprehensive Heads Committee, may have "made his biggest mistake in suspending them by making them 'martyrs'".[309] A month later Dean was more forthright in his assessment of the head's actions: "Blunt reactions, like the expulsion of the Kingsdale students who went on strike unites the members. A better way would be to meet their realistic demands".[310]

As we will see, Dean was by no means alone in expressing sympathy for the SAU's cause. Indeed, a small number of commentators did acknowledge the reasonableness of the SAU's manifesto for change, noting that many of its demands had already been conceded by school authorities in other countries.[311]

However, the bulk of the initial press reaction to demands for pupil power was overtly hostile, a trend which would continue well into the 1970s. On the one hand the SAU's activities were portrayed as undisciplined, childish immaturity, albeit immaturity that had the potential to harm children and society itself. SAU activities were sometimes discussed in a tone of amused irritation. "Before the end of winter", one commentator wrote, "they will probably start demanding pay for the work they do at school. And the first nursery walkout over compulsory school milk cannot be far off".[312] Others, meanwhile, depicted its members as a sinister threat to the moral, social and political order. The *Daily Mail*'s Lynda Lee-Potter's piece, based upon an interview with a young woman SAU activist, was fairly typical of this genre of reporting:

> Eve has a flat, unemotional voice, a rather frightening ruthlessness, no sense of humour and an attitude of mild indulgence toward her permissive parents, who allow her to use their home and telephone as an extension of the union office. She sounds in conversation rather like a trades union manifesto. She is quite shatteringly self-possessed and fanatically devoted to the cause.[313]

Elements of the political establishment seemed to be rocked by the SAU's activities. Among the correspondence unearthed by students occupying Warwick University was a letter from Enoch Powell advocating an official investigation into the SAU.[314] Tory MP Patrick Wall went further, accusing the SAU of threatening the very basis of democratic governance. He called on Labour's Education Minister Edward Short to "seek powers to prevent the spread of propaganda in secondary schools directed at the overthrow of government" by "Trotskyist and anarchist forces".[315] In fact, contemporary newspaper reports and testimony from SAU activists and teachers themselves suggest that elements within the state apparatus, including special branch, were already beginning to take a close but covert interest in the pupil power movement, a development that would be confirmed some 30 years later with the release of previously secret government documents (see chapter 5).[316] The pupil power movement would also soon face a very public challenge in the courts in the form of Edward Heath's Tory government's attempts to ban the *Little Red Schoolbook*, seen as a manifesto for the movement.

The *Little Red Schoolbook*, or *Den Lille Røde Bog for Skoleelever* was initially published in Denmark by Jesper Jensen and Soren Hansen. Around 100,000 copies were initially sold. In the Forward to the recently republished 2014 edition Hansen explains that the book was intended to be "a protest against the Victorian/authoritarian school system with its robotic discipline".

Some chapters were devoted to providing practical and entirely sensible advice about sex and drug use. It was these that would generate the most notoriety. The bulk of the book provided a concise, accessible, radical critique of schooling in capitalist societies, setting out a strategy for change based on direct action by pupils. As we illustrate below, the extent to which opposition to its publication was motivated by a much wider objection to this political message and its calls for pupil power should not be underestimated.

Information about the original Danish edition of the book had filtered into the UK via articles in the *Times* and the *Guardian* in 1970, which stimulated the interest of the left-leaning independent publisher Richard Handyside. Following a meeting with the Danish authors, he made the decision to release the book in the UK. The UK edition was translated and edited by Handyside, with the help of three school teachers and three sixth form pupils. It is not clear whether the three pupils had direct links with the SAU, but liaison certainly occurred between the SAU and the book's authors, and the organisation was enlisted to help with the distribution of the book, receiving hundreds of free copies. The SAU was also listed among a range of organisations pupils were encouraged to turn to for further advice (others included the National Council for Civil Liberties and the anti-corporal punishment organisation STOPP):[317]

> There is in fact already a small but growing pupils' union in Britain. It's called the Schools Action Union, and their programme calls for proper democracy in schools and for making schools real centres for education rather than industrial training centres. Get in touch with them and find out where their nearest branch is.[318]

The publication of an English translation in Britain was announced (with its standard dose of moral outrage) by the *Sunday Telegraph* on 28 March 1971.[319]

> More than 70,000 copies of a revolutionary handbook for children aged 10 and upwards, which tells them how to defy school discipline, make love, set up shop with contraceptives, get an abortion or indulge in sexual deviations, are to be canvassed to booksellers and offered to pupils outside schools.[320]

The story was inevitably picked up by the tabloid newspapers the following day; they were quick to accuse the authors of engaging in political indoctrination. The design of the book, and the similarity of its title to Mao's *Little Red Book*, inevitably attracted attention:

> The revolution has reached the classroom. So much so that your 11 year old is likely to come home and tell you you're a paper tiger waiting to be overthrown. If he does, take a look in his jacket pocket before you clout him. You might find the *Little Red Schoolbook* there. It's an insidious publication—written as the revolutionaries' schoolroom guide, too obviously designed to look like the thoughts of Chairman Mao—and on sale to the young this week.[321]

In content, the book differed in some minor respects from its Danish equivalent, but the general gist of the analysis in its 208 pages was much the same. Some 20 of its pages were devoted to sex and another 30 to drugs, but the bulk of the book sought to promote the cause of pupil power and school democracy. As one of the teachers responsible for editing the book explained at the time:

> We hope this kind of publication will help to increase the self-confidence of children—particularly working class children. They should feel that if they don't like the system it's not because they are wrong, but because schools and the system are not catering for them properly.[322]

The education system, the book argued, "is controlled by the people who have the money, and directly or indirectly these people decide what you should be taught and how. Whatever teachers and politicians may say, the aim of the education system in Britain is not to give you the best possible opportunity of developing your own talents". Schools "teach you the things our economic system needs you to know" and "to obey authority rather than to question things". The book exhorted students to use all the powers at their disposal to demand and agitate for a "proper education", free from the trammels of bourgeois discipline and control. It provided practical advice on making complaints, and detailed strategies and tactics pupils could use, including leafleting, creating magazines, writing to newspapers, demonstrations, strikes and the formation of school student unions. "Try to form a real pupils' union," the authors advised. "In France in 1968 the pupils' union did organise a large-scale strike and succeeded in getting important changes made".[323]

The publication of the book provoked the interest of the puritanical Tory MP for Worcestershire South, Gerald Nabarro, who vowed to mobilise Conservative MPs and public opinion in a crusade against it. In incensed letters to Tory Minister for Education Margaret Thatcher and Home Secretary Reginald Maudling he denounced the book as "disgraceful, immoral and most harmful", demanding to know "what combined ministerial action" they were taking to "deal with the matter urgently, before the book is allowed to get into circulation".[324]

Senior civil servants in the Department for Education and Sciences initially viewed the publication with amused curiosity. "Can you please get hold of this tomfool publication—from your usual underground newspaper agency!—and think what we are supposed to say about it?", wrote one official to his junior colleague.[325] However, within days the Department was besieged by letters and telegrams from MPs and an eclectic mix of councillors, teachers, clergymen and other "moral entrepreneurs" (mostly, it would seem, *Telegraph* readers) expressing outrage at the book's "seditious" contents.

Nabarro's crusade was joined by the notorious Mary Whitehouse, president of the National Viewers and Listeners' Association. Their combined efforts led to a flood of "outraged" correspondence arriving at the Department for Education and Sciences and prompted officials to treat the "tomfool" publication with more seriousness. Within days of the initial *Sunday Telegraph* report, Thatcher's private secretary wrote to officials stating that, "The Secretary of State has asked for inquires to be made urgently to establish whether the *Little Red Schoolbook* could be construed as obscene and likely to corrupt school children". Thatcher specifically asked for advice over whether, as Nabarro and Whitehouse were demanding, it was "appropriate for her to send a copy to the Director of Public Prosecutions"(DPP), with a view to having the publication banned?[326]

One official wrote back pointing out that Whitehouse had already presented a copy of the book to the DPP the day before.[327] However, this did not deter Thatcher from arranging for another copy of the book to be delivered to the DPP by hand, with a note suggesting that it would be "advantageous" to focus on the sections on sex and drugs.[328]

Within hours the DPP's E MacDermott contacted the Metropolitan Police's Criminal Investigation Department instructing it to act. A search warrant was issued under the 1959 Obscene Publications Act and this was executed on the publisher the following day. One thousand and sixty nine copies of the book were seized, along with related material including distribution lists.

The Met Police were clearly taking their duties seriously; in his account of the raid, C Turvey, the Criminal Investigation Department's deputy chief inspector, triumphantly announced that a further 152 copies of the book were seized at three other addresses following the receipt of "reliable information". Turvey was also keen to convey his impression of the scene, and of the publisher. "From the books seen on the premises", his report stated, "Mr Handyside deals mainly in extreme left wing and anarchist publications written by Marxist black panther movements and the like".[329] What Turvey neglected to mention was that his officers were too late to prevent the distribution and sale of around 17,000 copies of the book.[330]

The succeeding weeks and months were characterised by desperate, almost comical attempts to gather "reliable" witnesses to support the state's case against the publisher of the *Little Red Schoolbook*. A request from the DPP for the Department for Education and Sciences to try and identify "suitable" witnesses from the barrage of complaints it had received about the book proved fruitless. A detailed trawl through the correspondence by one official confirmed that only two seemed to have actually seen copies of the book, and even they may not have read it all. One of the two was Nabarro himself.[331]

In the event a motley collection of individuals were gathered together to defend the state's case against the book, a number of whom had close ties to Whitehouse. Whitehouse herself did not give oral evidence on the day though she was in court, and her written testimony pulled no punches. Like other witnesses she seemed equally offended at the book's political and moral message:

I feel that the aim of the book is to undermine children's confidence in the whole system of education by teachers and parents. It perverts the characters of children in that it encourages them to be dishonest, to spy on teachers, it incites to strike and disruption, and I further feel that they are being used as political pawns. The book attempts to undermine the basic educational principles that a teacher stands in Loco Parentis. It is anti-authority in all its form. The book undermines the character of children in that it encourages pre-marital sex and deliberately stimulates sexual experiments in children who would otherwise not think about these matters. It seeks to use the school to demoralise and subvert them.[332]

It must be said that not all commentators were as hostile. The Advisory Centre for Education (ACE), an organisation well respected by educationalists as well as the Department for Education and Sciences itself, stated that the case the *Little Red Schoolbook* made for greater school democracy, and the advice it gave on drugs and sex education was "presented with simplicity, clarity, cooperativeness, reasonableness and a true feeling of responsibility". It described it as "a lovely little reference book for secondary school age", a decision which prompted the Catholic Archbishop of Liverpool and the Vice Chancellor of York University to resign as honorary vice presidents of the organisation.[333] Representatives of leading publishers, including Faber and Faber, Penguin Books and George Allen and Unwin also rallied behind Handyside, promising to set up a fighting fund to defend the book.[334] In addition, the National Council for Civil Liberties (NCfCL), the Arts Society and the Defence of Literature also supported the book's publication, as did a host of correspondents to newspapers such as the *Times* and the *Guardian*.[335] As one argued, "It is difficult to believe that it was not the "redness" of the *Little Red Schoolbook* which led to its seizure and prosecution; if not, then I assume we may look forward to the prosecution of the vendors of a great deal of disgusting rubbish presently on sale".[336]

The book was banned, ostensibly on the grounds that the 20 pages devoted to "sex" were "obscene" and had the potential to "deprave" children. The NCfCL described the verdict as "an absolutely sickening decision and one of the gravest steps against free expression that we have seen in this country for some time".[337] Handyside, who was fined £50 and ordered to pay 110 guineas costs, felt the judgment reflected a wider desire on the part of the state to silence the pupil power movement. "What is at stake here", he insisted, "is not sex education for young people, but the ability of young people to question authority".[338]

> It is clear to me—and also many more people than the magistrate may realise—that this whole prosecution has been political from the start... The *Little Red Schoolbook* encourages questioning of authority, and this is why Mrs Whitehouse, the police (whom she has been advising in this case) and the government are so determined to get this book banned... The government is trying to stamp out dissent through the Industrial Relations Bill and the Immigration Bill. This prosecution, and the magistrate's verdict, is a further step in this process of repression which is increasing so rapidly.[339]

Comments made by the judge hearing Handyside's appeal against the judgement on 29 October certainly lent weight to his allegations that the decision to prevent the book's publication was politically motivated. Unlike the original magistrate, who steered carefully clear of discussing the book's advocacy of pupil power, appeal judge Gerald Hines QC made his objections to this wider "political" message quite clear. There are, he said, "visualised the possibilities of children who have failed to persuade their teachers to adopt what seem to the pupils to be good ideas, organising demonstrations, indeed strikes". "Here", he insisted, "are mixings of an intolerable head-on collision between the pupils and the headmaster". Such passages within the book were "subversive, not only to the authority but to the influence of the trust between children and teachers," and hence intensified the book's "tendency to deprave and corrupt".[340]

Prohibiting the *Little Red Schoolbook* did little to prevent its circulation. Extracts of the original book were published with a good degree of regularity in pupil power journals including *Vanguard*, *Cherry Red* and *Tolpuddle*. And in a very public show of defiance the Young Liberals distributed around 2,000 extracts from the book outside schools in a number of major cities.[341] Worse still for the DPP, soon after the ban was implemented, 100,000 copies of a revised version of the *Schoolbook* went on sale with the "obscene" section on sex education slightly edited.[342] DPP officials were duly tasked with scouring through the new edition in a search for potentially "obscene" material that was likely to "deprave". Handwritten notes in the margins of the new edition show that the sections on abortion, venereal disease, homosexuality, pornography, menstruation, masturbation, wet dreams, contraception, intercourse, petting and organisms attracted the particular attention of officials. However, even the DPP had begun to realise the futility of its efforts to restrict the book's circulation, and the serialisation of the new edited edition in the *Sun* in November 1971 appears to have signalled the end of the DPP's interest in the affair.[343]

While the DPP was challenging the *Little Red Schoolbook* in the courts, the pupil power movement on the ground began to face its own challenges, as schisms began to emerge within it. Between 1969-1972, SAU continued to put considerable effort into consolidating its support base among school children; SAU activists had organised multiple small-scale demonstrations in London, Manchester, Leeds, Dagenham and elsewhere with the intention of forcing the educational authorities to accept their demands.[344] Though often ostensibly focused on local issues, these demonstrations were organised, coordinated and built around the SAU's national programme. The protests also frequently made national headlines, strengthening the SAU's reputation as the principal, most effective campaigning body for school students. However, the SAU were not the only organisation seeking to establish itself as an organised advocate for the pupil power movement. Ideological divisions began to emerge, and a sizeable body of opinion became convinced that the creation of a school students "branch" within the National Union of Students (NUS) offered the movement the most effective means of achieving its aims.

The NUS had already begun to take an interest in opening its membership to non-university students, through an initiative whereby older school pupils (aged 15 and over) and sixth form students could enrol as associate NUS members. Opened in 1969 the NUS's Scholar Associates Scheme allowed access to NUS travel benefits and other perks for a small subscription fee.[345] It was a largely apolitical affair, without any real trappings of a democratic union, but by 1971 it had around 10,000 members. However, the YCL (and other "fringe" pupil power groups, such as the London based *Cherry Red*), felt that the Scholar Associates Scheme could provide the foundation for the development of a more effective, nationally organised movement of pupils, and calls were made for the SAU leadership to utilise it as the principal vehicle for promoting school democracy.

The SAU viewed suggestions that it should engage with the NUS with suspicion. "There have been suggestions that the SAU should dissolve/affiliate to the NUS", noted a *Vanguard* editorial, "but this... would seriously limit the developing school students' struggle".[346] Quite apart from potential fears about its own future viability, the SAU did not trust the NUS to represent pupils' interests with sufficient vigour. When the NUS issued an open letter to sixth formers setting out its manifesto for schools and colleges, the SAU accused it of being ridden with "pernicious elitism", and of seeking to "dilute" the demands of the pupil power movement.[347] The NUS open letter had been sent to head teachers asking them to send it forward to sixth form students. The Leeds Socialist Schools Federation (the local SAU affiliate) used the magazine *Handful of Dust* to make their position clear:

> It is obvious that this move is in response to the success of the militant schools movement, possibly encouraged by Edward Short, Minister of Education. The NUS is right wing, undemocratic, and in the past almost certain to have received CIA funds. What trade union wanting to move into a new area would write to the employers! The NUS is in effect an instrument of the authorities to channel off and dampen discontent. If you want effective action, ignore the NUS and join the Schools Action Union.[348]

However, the NUS issue continued to dog the SAU during the early 1970s, generating regular "comradely exchanges" in the pages of *Vanguard*.

The YCL's own strategic goals were certainly behind much of the impetus for NUS affiliation. However, also at the heart of the issue were profound ideological disagreements about the direction of the pupil power movement. These disagreements were perhaps most clearly illustrated in an exchange between *Vanguard*'s editorial board and Nic Mitchell, at the time editor of the pupil power magazine, *Cherry Red*:

> We considered the setting up of the SAU as a very positive step, but subsequent events and actions led us to re-examine our views towards the organisation. We believe that the first stage in the Schools Movement must be: to try and organise the mass of school students into a trade union type of organisation. This cannot be done if the

union is putting forward extremely revolutionary demands, like over-throw of society, because the mass of people at school do not agree at present, with such aims and therefore they will not join an organisa-tion, which in reality is not a union but a revolutionary party... A union in the present stage of our struggle must be basically a non-political organisation to which all people can join (right and left)".

In their reply, the SAU leadership defended its revolutionary vision. "How can a union be non-political?" they asked. "Any union that attempts to organise around the aims of equality and democracy...must have a political analysis of the society in which it is organising other-wise it will be crushed". It was necessary for organisations such as the SAU to seek to "raise the general level of political consciousness so as to combat the daily influences of bourgeois ideology". They also reiterated their belief that the efforts of the school student movement should be directed towards organising pupils *within* rather than *outside* schools:

We are organising branches inside schools because we have learned from our past mistakes. We have learned that in order to establish cred-ibility among the school students, in order for them to see that we are a serious, disciplined organisation fighting for their rights and interests... we must organise branches inside schools that are self-reliant and dedi-cated to leading by example.

The SAU stated that it would not oppose comrades who sought to establish an independent section of the NUS that was open to school students, but reiterated its view that the efforts of the movement should focused upon organising pupils *within* schools.[349]

Soon after this public spat, Mitchell was appointed as the YCL's schools organiser, and used the pages of the YCL's new school students' journal *Tolpuddle* to promote the campaign to redirect the efforts of the school student movement towards the NUS. Here, he repeated the themes outlined in his exchange with the SAU in *Vanguard*, emphasis-ing the need for the school student movement to "mature" before pressing forward with radical proposals. "We must wait a little for things are still in their early stages" and "it may be a little over far-sighted to see school students actively engaging in the class fight for socialism against capitalism". The "schools movement", he cautioned "is still very young and...has still to establish close links with the mass of students". Overt references to the SAU were absent, but the whole tenor of the analysis was geared towards highlighting the "failings" of the past, and pointing to a new direction of travel. There were, Mitchell argued, "many weaknesses among the developing schools movement, such as a lack of organisation", and a new, democratic national body was needed to unite students and further their interests. "Such an organisation we believe could be developed out of the National Union of Students (Scholar Associates Scheme)".[350]

By the time the second edition of *Tolpuddle* was published, its editors were able to point to "considerable progress", in particular a motion at that year's NUS conference calling for the Scholar Associates Scheme to be transformed into a democratic schools union.[351] In the event the motion was passed, with the conference voting overwhelmingly to launch a "democratic schools organisation".[352] As Stevenson notes, the fact that the NUS executive member responsible for the scheme, Jeff Staniforth, was a Communist himself doubtless had an influence on proceedings.[353] The *Daily Mail* was predictably outraged at the NUS's decision. "The day of the militant kids is approaching", shrieked the paper in November 1971. "Soon they will have their own union, for all children from primary school up".[354] In one respect the *Daily Mail* was correct—the day of the militant school pupil was fast approaching, and 1972 would witness a wave of school strikes unprecedented in their organisation and impact.

DAVE GIBSON (Leeds, 1967-1968)
"The slogans were 'Head Autocracy Out' and 'Smash the bourgeoisie'!"

IN 1967/8 I was doing my A-levels at Leeds Grammar. It was an incredibly political time with debates and campaigns around the Vietnam war, the French student revolt, the Prague Spring, around racism—especially around the defence of the Kenyan Asians and opposition to Enoch Powell—and over the petty rules and restrictions that dominated the schooling system.

At the school there was a very good activist John Bradbrook, who was in the IS. With his lead we decided to bring out a school bulletin we called *More in Sorrow than in Anger*—which we shortened to *MISTIA*.

The bulletin was political and addressed the big questions of the day as well as being critical of the school. It sold out, but it caused uproar in the school and there were threats of expulsions for those of us that had been involved in putting it together.

Instead, the school decided to let us set up an alternative school magazine. It was clearly an attempt to incorporate us, but at the same time it gave us a space to put across our politics and reflect the excitement of the time.

In 1968 we met up with other school student activists in Leeds, and we set up a network called the Leeds Schools Socialist Federation. It was one of the first organisations of school students in the country, but there were soon similar networks in Manchester, Cardiff and London. By 1969 the various networks were forming into the Schools Action Union.

Our group went to Manchester on 2 March 1969 to take part in a demonstration in support of Manchester students who had been victimised by their schools for their activities. The demands on the demonstration were for free speech in the schools and an end to victimisation, but other slogans I remember were "Head Autocracy Out" and "Smash the bourgeoisie"!

In July 1969 there was a conference called The Living School in Conway Hall, London sponsored by the LSE Socialist Society which we attended. Over the three days we met other activists from SAU groups. The Leeds group had a lot of credibility because we were a long-standing and very active group.

In Leeds we formulated a set of demands which appeared on our leaflets and newsletters. These included:

- For democratic school councils
  (with representatives of students, teachers and workers)
- End the prefect system
- Abolish school uniforms
- Free speech in schools
- End corporal punishment
- No education cuts
- Opposition to racism and oppression

When I've been looking back, I'd forgotten that education cuts was such an issue! This was the era of Labour's pronouncements about "the white heat of the technological revolution" and the rhetoric was about investment in education and technology. It was also the time when there were moves away from grammar schools towards comprehensive schooling—yet on the ground the reality was that the Labour government was making education cuts. In January 1969 we campaigned in support of some school students in Glasgow who marched and occupied the Education Authority buildings against cuts.

The Leeds Schools Socialist Federation (LSSF) produced a magazine called *Handful of Dust*. It was a mixture of politics and culture and we sold it outside schools across Leeds. We had supporters in a number of grammars and comprehensives—but found it much harder to organise in the secondary moderns. In April 1969 the *Yorkshire Post* ran an exposé against what they called the "pupil power magazine". We produced leaflets for mass distribution at school gates in response.

Alongside the LSSF there was a shortlived group called the Leeds Schools Revolutionary Committee set up by one of our group who was Maoist influenced which did some separate leafleting, but we were largely successful in keeping our group united.

Then 11 boys at Leeds Grammar were suspended for having hair that was "too long". The school had about 600 students and we organised a meeting in the school to which about 150 pupils came. After some negotiation the school backed down—students were allowed to have "hair of whatever length" and they also agreed to set up a school council.

These were victories, the result of a lot of agitation in the schools in Leeds over the previous two years and a quite significant and sustained level of school student politics in this period.

6

Pupil power in action:
The 1972 strike wave

THE CHILDREN who walked out of school in 1972 were protesting at authoritarian, stultifying state schooling, as had their predecessors. And there were also parallels between the political and industrial contexts of 1972 and those of the earlier strike waves. 1972 was another year of unprecedented economic trade union militancy.[355] The number of strike days climbed from 10,980,000 in 1970 to 23,909,000 in 1972, higher than for any other year since the General Strike of 1926. According to historian Royden Harrison the labour unrest of 1972 "was far more massive and incomparably more successful" than even the syndicalist-inspired industrial militancy of 1911.[356]

Edward Heath's Conservative government was forced to make a series of humiliating U-turns. First, the Industrial Relations Act (1971), which sought to restrict the ability of trade unions to engage in industrial action, was effectively rendered inoperative by a policy of non-cooperation and a spate of official and unofficial strikes against it. Second, the government's attempt to control public sector wages was shattered when a miners' strike won a 32 percent pay increase.

These successes in the wider field of industrial relations were gradually reflected in the campaigns waged by the pupil power movement.

So in November 1971 pupils from London's Camden School for Girls, where the SAU was particularly active, organised a demonstration in Hyde Park over London Transport's decision to abolish half-fares for children during the rush hour. To galvanise support for their campaign pupils wrote to MPs and trade unions. They also appeared on television to set out their case. A benefit dance they organised to resource their campaign raised £120, a considerable sum in 1971.

On the day of the demonstration the pupils made use of a hired PA system, had 50,000 leaflets and hundreds of printed posters and wore tee shirts with their campaign slogan "Fair Fares for Schoolkids". Upwards of 1,000 people listened to them set out their demands in Hyde Park. The star of the demonstration was nine year old Emma, who even managed to impress the notoriously hostile *Daily Mail*:

> When Emma got up to speak there was a great wave of applause. She stood there with her hands on her hips. Someone lowered the microphone and announced her and she was on. "I think it's stupid", she said. "We are going to have to walk to school if we have to pay full fares. And I just think that's wrong." More applause. And Emma, with a fair eye for a dramatic effect, let the cheers die down with great cool... "I think", she finished, with great scorn, "it's really a stupid idea to make us pay what we haven't got".[357]

The campaign was a success, and the Inner London Education Authority (ILEA) eventually agreed to pay London Transport £40,000 to meet the costs of the half-fare concessions to pupils.[358]

American children attending the private American School in St John's Wood were drawn into the resurgent school student movement. In December 1971 they treated Margaret Thatcher to a dose of pupil power. Sixteen students interrupted her address at the opening of the school's new £2.7m premises, demanding to know why British school children "still had to go to slum schools". As one of the pupils involved explained, they were inspired by a desire to show solidarity with their British counterparts: "We want them to know that we have an interest in their problems and don't want to be connected with Mrs Thatcher".[359]

This new phase of the movement continued into 1972, attracting the interest and support of a number of organisations including the National Council of Civil Liberties (NCCL) and the government-funded School Councils' Moral Education Research Project (SCMERP).

The SCMERP had called for the introduction of non-dictatorial staff/student bodies (in effect, school councils) in secondary schools that would "release and unify the total energies of the school community". In March the NCCL organised a national conference on children's rights, attended by prominent educationalists and child psychologists, as well as representatives of the NUT teachers' trade union and the Schools Action Union.

The NCCL had already expressed sympathy with many of the SAU's demands including the creation of school councils, the right to determine personal appearance and the abolition of corporal punishment. Its 1971 pamphlet *Children Have Rights* called for those involved in formulating policy to scrutinise "the way in which our norms, attitudes, expectations and social institutions (such as schools) contribute to distress among children".[360]

The March conference was over subscribed.[361] Delegates were addressed by Simon Steyne, the 16 year old vice-chair of the SAU, who set out the union's demands for the abolition of school uniforms, an end to racism in schools and a minimum wage for all school leavers of £16.50.[362] Steyne did not disguise the SAU's wider political objectives: "Kids who learn to control schools are not going to take shit from the bosses when they start work. We believe democracy is controlling factories. We're a revolutionary organisation—have been for two or three years".[363]

This was the context for the London school strike movement of May 1972. This was not a premediated, pre-planned series of strikes, but a movement sparked by a series of localised grievances, which were harnessed and developed by the SAU leadership into a more organised, orchestrated campaign of protest.

The catalyst was a strike at Rutherford Comprehensive School on 3 May, spearheaded by Steve Finch, a sixth form pupil at the school and the SAU's information officer—emphasising the link between national leadership and local action.[364]

Pupils demanded the abolition of caning and school uniforms, an end to detentions, the introduction of lunchtime passes and the creation of a pupil/teacher disciplinary panel.[365] The response of Rutherford's school management was relatively positive. The school already had a school council, and the head had made it clear that the issues raised by the pupils were open to negotiation.

The head teacher at the neighbouring Sarah Siddons school for girls had been less accommodating towards a similar set of demands. The following lunchtime (4 May), Finch led a group of 100 pupils from his school to a protest outside Sarah Siddons in a show of solidarity. "Our head's being reasonable", Finch was reported as shouting, "it's that woman over at the girls' school we need to talk to." The Rutherford boys were joined by 80 girls from Sarah Siddons, whereupon they marched to Paddington Green and engaged in a sit down protest. This prompted a swift police response, and Finch was threatened with arrest for inciting a riot.[366]

The *Daily Mail* witnessed the scene and was appalled at the "schoolboy extremist" Finch, seeing his behaviour as symptomatic of the wider tendency among pupils to protest and agitate:

> The antics of the young mob led out of school by Steven Finch are the latest manifestation of the current trend to protest. All over London, fellow Marxist members of the Schools Action Union gather every night outside the gates of grammar and comprehensive schools with arms full of literature. Their message: "If you don't like it, smash it".[367]

What the *Daily Mail* referred to as the "antics" of SAU activists were clearly paying dividends, for the Paddington Green protest was not the only disturbance on 4 May. A momentum was beginning to develop. The same day that Finch was threatened with arrest, children at Quintin Qynaston School in St John's Wood walked out in a protest against school meals, caning and discipline. The pupils claimed that their demands had been ignored, leaving them no other option but to strike. "The staff have ignored our complaints" stated one pupil. "We have tried to approach teachers but they only say they will think about it and nothing is ever done."

The police arrived to marshal the children back into school but the pupils were determined to continue. "Three hundred shouting schoolboys and girls stampeded through the streets, trampling over lawns and hedgerows" wrote the *Daily Mail*. "Squad cars moved in, and police ordered the march to break up".[368] As the *Times* noted, police demands were ignored: "Junior pupils bombarded a police van with cans and stones and smashed a rear light on a sports car".[369]

The SAU leadership sought to capitalise on this growing momentum. Its national committee met on 6 May to discuss strategy, after which the press was informed that strikes would gather pace in the coming weeks. "At least four schools took part in strike action during the past week", announced a member of the SAU's national executive. "Another five have pledged to join us. We also hear that Hampstead and North Paddington may be coming out". Steyne, the SAU's vice-chair, saw the protests as an opportunity to solidify the SAU's position as the "vanguard" of the pupil power movement:

There has been a major breakthrough. It's an incredible political step forward for school students to strike. A major tactic of working people against dictatorial bosses is now being used against dictatorial headmasters... We may have 3,000 school kids demonstrating in London next week. We mustn't let this opportunity slip through our fingers—we must take a leadership position. This is the most advanced stage that the SAU has yet reached in organising mass support.[370]

The timing of the protests could not have been better for the SAU. Just a month earlier the NUS had announced that its new union for pupils, the National Union of School Students (NUSS), would be inaugurated at a conference at University College on 20 May.[371] Clearly this new wave of pupil militancy provided the SAU with an opportunity to consolidate its position in the face of the challenge from the Young Communist League-dominated NUSS. The protests continued and on 8 May Finch was arrested after leading striking pupils from seven different schools through the streets of Paddington. Following clashes with police officers who had been waiting for the demonstrators at Paddington Green, "He was grabbed by police and, against shouts of protest from hundreds of followers, hustled off in a police car".[372] Finch was eventually found guilty of obstructing a police officer and obstructing the highway and fined £15, but his arrest appeared to galvanise rather than subdue the spirits of those present.[373] As one 17 year old activist stated, "nothing can stop us, Steve may have been arrested, but there are a lot of us left—hundreds of us, and soon it will be thousands".[374] The following day (9 May) would indeed see thousands of children take part in an SAU organised mass protest march from Hyde Park to County Hall.

Aware of the SAU's plans to disrupt schooling on 9 May, the ILEA had adopted an uncompromising stance, advising head teachers to treat those who absented themselves from school as truants. It also wrote to at least 3,000 parents reminding them that they were breaking the law if their children failed to attend classes. However, despite these attempts at intimidation, the strike was well supported. According to the *Times*, pupils from around 15 schools were among the children who heeded the SAU's call to strike,[375] whereas the *Daily Mail* reported that children from 20 schools were involved. Precise estimates vary—the *Times* reported around 1,500 children took part; the *Daily Mail* said upwards of 5,000 pupils.[376] After hearing speeches from the SAU leaders, the children marched to London's County Hall where Dr Eric Briault, the ILEA education officer, was handed a letter of protest. It argued:

> For the past five days school students from an increasing number of schools in London have been rising up and saying a determined "no" to being pushed around like dumb animals. The days when they would passively accept being beaten, and locked up on the sole authority of the head was over.[377]

The secretary of the NCCL had accompanied the pupils on the march to County Hall.[378]

The initial ILEA response was not encouraging. Briault met a deputation of 16 pupils and was reported to have done little more than give them "a veiled ticking off for playing truant".[379] Steyne, one of the SAU delegates, stated the "only thing" he learned from the ILEA's dismissive reaction to the SAU's demands was the need to "be more militant".[380] Sixty SAU delegates met to discuss the situation on Sunday 14 May and decided to call a further one-day "general strike" and a march to Trafalgar Square on Wednesday 17 May.[381]

In the meantime, protests continued to break out at other schools. On 10 May the head teacher of Hammersmith's Sacred Heart School responded to a strike by suspending 21 girls, forcing a number of them to miss O Level examinations. The irony of punishing pupils for "missing classes" by forcing them to miss classes and exams seemed lost on the school.

This authoritarian response at Sacred Heart failed to deter several hundred girls at Hurlingham School, Fulham from walking out the following day in protest against school uniforms, detentions and school dinners.[382] In some instances police used repressive strategies to try and contain and control the protests. This was the case with 200 pupils from Netteswell comprehensive school, Harlow who, on the eve of the Trafalgar Square demonstration, had marched to the town hall to lobby education officials against the school's decision to impose a new strict uniform code. Following scuffles outside the town hall, the children were subjected to a form of kettling as police locked them in the council chamber refusing to let them leave. In their frustration some of the protesters climbed onto the roof and hurled milk bottles at the police below.[383]

In some cases the pupil protests met with a measure of success. On 12 May around 100 seven to 11 year olds in Reading struck in protest against the Berkshire education committee's decision to sack 130 teachers. Their campaign slogan, "No Milk, Now No Teachers", was also taken up by parents, and the education committee was subsequently forced to back down.[384] This was not an isolated success. It was mirrored in a significant change in approach by the ILEA towards the planned Trafalgar Square protest on 17 May as Briault opted for a much more conciliatory stance.

In his advice to schools likely to be affected by the demonstration, he recommended they take "a broadly liberal attitude" towards absentees and advised head teachers "to make a clear distinction between taking normal and proper steps to deal with breaches of discipline, including truancy, and giving due consideration to the legitimate views of pupils, some of whom may have been involved in recent events".[385] Briault also hinted at his tacit support for many of the pupils' demands, particularly in relation to school uniforms, school discipline and school councils.[386] This more liberal approach was certainly not shared by many head teachers. C C Kuper, head teacher of Emanuel School in Wandsworth, told the *Times* that Briault's advice was "absolute nonsense". "As far as I am concerned", he stated, "Dr Briault can go and jump in the lake". Kuper had written to the parents of 900 boys at his school stating that he "would suspend any boy who wilfully absented himself from school or, if the boy were a very young and foolish boy, and shows signs of contrition, he would cane him".[387] The head of an anonymous west London comprehensive who spoke to the *Mail* was equally incandescent: "It's telling us to bend over backwards so we can be kicked", he complained. "We need firmness in our schools—not wishy-washy nonsense like this".[388]

Nor did the media share Briault's more liberal attitude towards the pupil protests. The *Daily Mail* was at the forefront of attempts to undermine support for the 17 May demonstration. "Rentacrowd Ltd is recruiting young these days. But its directors have not changed their ways", stormed one dismissive editorial. "The pupil power demos in London follow the same pattern as every revolutionary organisation since Karl Marx was in short pants... The only difference in the case of pupil power is that the slogans are written lower down the wall".[389]

Days later the paper ran a story alleging intimidation of blacklegs by vicious, knife wielding SAU activists. Such tactics, the article claimed, meant that "Even children who enjoy school, and are proud of the uniforms they wear, are being 'persuaded' to tag along with extremist mobs". The *Mail*'s readers were treated to interviews with stunned parents whose children had previously been model pupils and yet had been turned by "half-baked" Marxist militants. The message from the *Mail* was clear—even the most decent, well behaved, docile (and cat loving!) children were in danger of contamination:

> Mr Tobin's daughter Pat was "on strike" for three days. "My wife and I didn't have a clue—we thought she was at school... Pat is proud of her school uniform. She thoroughly enjoys being at school and, academically, she's doing terribly well... It's just not in her character", said Mr Tobin. "We lost our kitten a little while back and she cried for the best part of a week. That's the sort of kid she is—nice and gentle".[390]

On the day of the strike national newspapers stepped up their attempts to undermine support for the demonstration. The *Times* sought to link the agitation to left wing groups who, it alleged, were seeking to turn schools into "seminaries of revolution" by encouraging children into "organised truancy, deliberate breaches of school discipline and possibly of the law".[391] Meanwhile, the *Mail* claimed to have uncovered "the man who is inciting Britain's school kids to revolt":

> The man behind today's biggest pupil power demo—a massive truant march through London—is a 27 year old teacher of maladjusted children. He is tall, bearded Max Hunt, who has been secretly master-minding this climax to three years mounting "revolutions" in schools throughout the country.

The *Mail*'s story was based upon an undercover investigation involving one of its younger reporters posing as an SAU sympathiser and witnessing Maxwell Hunt, a prominent member of the Maoist North London Alliance for the Defence of Workers' Rights (NADWR), chair a meeting of pupil activists. Hunt, the reporter alleged, arrived "in dirty jeans and a floppy shirt" and "set the political tone by addressing fellow members as 'Comrade' and giving a clenched fist salute". As if this was not bad enough, he also helped organise the printing of "pupil power propaganda" and advised the pupils on how to deal with the press:

Max Hunt was obviously in full command. Everyone was calling every-one else Comrade. They were on about Communism and Ho Chi Minh. They had papers and plans scattered all over the place. They were discussing how they could get all the schools in London out on strike on Wednesday.[392]

The SAU had never disguised the fact that it received support from sympathetic adults, or that small numbers of adults assisted pupils to coordinate its activities. The SAU had affiliated to NADWR and it was as a result of this that Hunt had come to chair the SAU's national execu-tive, though at this stage the *Mail* was not aware of this. Nor had the SAU sought to conceal its broader revolutionary objectives, which were geared towards initiating fundamental change in the "adult" world as well as that of the school. It was inevitable that political links and alli-ances would be forged between the SAU leadership and other radical organisations on the left. In this sense the *Mail's* story was not "news-worthy" but its allegations of sinister, adult-inspired indoctrination were intended to undermine support for the pupils and to create a panic about the "manipulation" of pupils by mysterious revolutionaries.

Malcolm Stewart of the *Guardian* offered a more balanced perspec-tive on the eve of the Trafalgar Square demonstration, pointing to the moderate nature of the pupils' demands. "A large number of teachers, and not all of them young, hate enforcing petty school rules, particu-larly when they concern uniform, regard corporal punishment as an obscenity and are critical of headmaster-power". Teachers, he argued, "do not need to be revolutionaries to support these aims nor to be in favour of school councils and even regular consultation" with pupils. A *Times* editorial also offered a more nuanced approach to that taken by the tabloids. While not condoning "organised truancy, breaches of school discipline and possibly of the law", it noted that the "pillars of society would not tremble, even the school cloisters would not col-lapse, if all these demands were met in full".[393]

The Trafalgar Square demonstration went ahead as planned on 17 May, involving up to 2,500 children.[394] Like other tabloid reports of the day's proceedings, the *Daily Mail* sought to portray it as an unmitigated failure. "Pupil power", readers were informed, "ran out of puff yesterday after three hours legging it round and round Trafalgar Square".[395] The ILEA also dismissed the demonstration as "a failure as an attempt to get any widespread support from pupils for the strike", noting that the SAU had initially aimed to gather around 20,000 participants.[396]

The SAU *had* anticipated a higher turnout. However, it had succeeded, for the second consecutive week, in getting thousands of children to defy school and education authorities and take part in an organised strike. This was quite an achievement.

The forces of law and order in the capital (and, as we shall see, the prime minister) did not view the demonstration as insignificant. On the contrary, the police's planned and well-resourced efforts to disrupt and nullify the impact of the demonstration suggest quite the opposite. On their arrival at Trafalgar Square, the demonstrators found themselves surrounded by a large contingent of police officers, led by a Scotland Yard commander, who refused them access to the Square.

An orchestrated strategy of harassment ensued, involving the police harrying and hustling protesters, and deliberately targeting the SAU leadership for arrest. Initially, officers tried to arrest pupils for truancy, until it was patiently pointed out to them that if anyone was guilty of an offence when a child absented themself from school, it was the parent. This did not stop the police attempts to target and arrest the protest's "ringleaders". In all, 14 children and 10 young adults were taken into custody, including most of the SAU Executive. In another typically over-blown reaction, two female protesters whose parents had contacted the police in an attempt to prevent them from participating in the protest were picked up by officers and placed temporarily into local authority care.[397]

The arrests disrupted the organisation of the protest, but police attempts to disperse the demonstrators and force them away from Trafalgar Square were only moderately successful as pupils reacted with spontaneous acts of resistance. As the *Guardian* reported, efforts to drive the demonstrators across Westminster Bridge proved fruitless, as pupils "suddenly turned...and marched back towards Trafalgar Square—trotting across the lawns of the Ministry of Defence, jamming Craven Street and squatting on the steps of St-Martin-in-the-Fields".[398] More clashes between police and pupils ensued. "Arrests and scuffles with police as 2,500 children join school strike", was the headline in the *Times*, accompanied by a photograph of a head-locked pupil being forced into a police van by two Met officers.[399]

In the confusion, and in the absence of leadership that might otherwise have been provided by the arrested SAU national officers, the demonstrators were split into two groups.

Around 1,000 were led back to County Hall by a fiery 13 year old pupil identified by the *Guardian* as Eddie Ryan. He only narrowly escaped arrest when a banner he was carrying, demanding, "Ban Victimisation From Marylebone C of E School", was snatched by a Met officer who pounced from a kerb-crawling van. On arrival at County Hall the protesters were met by another police cordon, but several dozen pupils broke through into the courtyard whereupon scuffles with police took place. Several more arrests followed—in fact more arrests occurred here than at any other location. Eventually, following their confrontation with the police, the County Hall group headed to Hyde Park, where the second group of protesters had gathered to hear speeches from SAU activists who had managed to escape arrest. Steyne was one of the few members of the SAU's executive to avoid the Met's attentions, and he ended the demonstration with a clarion call for pupil activists to "Go back to your schools and organise".[400]

The seriousness with which the Met responded to the threat posed by the pupil activists belies contemporary claims that this was a protest of little significance. Richard Handyside, publisher of the *Little Red Schoolbook*, was one of a number of individuals who wrote to the press challenging this interpretation of events:

> Sir, In common with most other newspapers, your report (May 18) of the London schools strike and demonstrations talked of the children involved "playing truant". Apart from being typically condescending, this term is both inaccurate and misleading, as these children were clearly not "playing" at anything. They were taking seriously the rhetoric about "social responsibility" so often thrust at them and, despite more or less frenzied threats from headmasters and parents, demonstrating their intention to bring about badly needed changes in our schools... Neither over-reaction on the part of the police, as occurred yesterday, nor any amount of veiled mutterings and overt threats on the part of headmasters and education authorities is going to make these grievances disappear.[401]

The NCCL also entered the debate on the side of the SAU. Like Handyside, its general secretary Tony Smythe directed particular criticism at the media's entirely negative response to the children's demands.

The press, he argued, had sought to construct an "elaborate conspiracy theory" around the demonstrations without mentioning the merits of the reforms children were calling for:

Some of the aims of this particular demonstration correspond closely with the NCCL's call for the end to corporal punishment, the right of children to determine their personal appearance and for participation by pupils in the running of their schools. These aims seem modest enough in terms of a pronouncement by the General Secretary of the NUT to the effect that "when it comes to civil rights, children are the most underprivileged group in the whole community".

Children, the NCCL argued, had a "constructive contribution" to make in the debate over the future shape of education in Britain, and instead of "pouring scorn" on their attempts to air their grievances, commentators and policy makers should be "listening carefully to what the aggrieved party has to say".[402]

Nor should contemporary efforts to downplay the significance and impact of the demonstration be allowed to obscure the real sense of challenge that it represented. The *Guardian*'s Peter Wilby, who was covering the protest, was confronted by one stunned middle aged women who told him: "There's nothing left but to die or emigrate... That's the future of this country. They're a lot of bloody little Communists".

Wilby suggested that the march portrayal in the media suggested "that all order and authority was on the verge of collapse":

Television and newspaper pictures of a monstrous regiment of children marching across Westminster Bridge...to hand in a list of pupil power demands at the headquarters of the Inner London Education Authority...have been greeted by most parents and teachers with alarm and bewilderment.[403]

It was not only school authorities who had reacted to the protests with alarm. It seems their disquiet was shared by those occupying the highest reaches of the state apparatus.

Recently declassified secret documents show that two days prior to the Trafalgar Square demonstration Robert Armstrong, the principle private secretary to the prime minister, had written to the Home Office and the Department for Education and Science (DfES), informing them of Edward Heath's concern at the phenomenal rise of the pupil power movement. In this extract from the letter sent to Education Minister Margaret Thatcher, Heath demands not just information but also "special action" to combat the growing levels of pupil militancy:

> The Prime Minister has noted with some concern the emergence of militancy among London school children. When a similar development occurred in France in 1968, it caused a good many problems and proved very difficult to get under control. The Prime Minister would be grateful if the Secretary of State would let him know how she sees this development, and what steps can be taken to prevent its spreading. This may require special action at particular schools, to try and isolate the ringleaders of the militancy.[404]

Heath's sudden interest in the growing influence of the pupil power movement perhaps helps explain the police's response to the Trafalgar Square protests, which was far more aggressive than its reaction to the earlier 9 May demonstration. It also provides us with a fascinating insight into the establishment's views of the pupil power movement in the immediate aftermath of the strikes.

After receiving Armstrong's letter requesting that the prime minister be kept abreast of developments, the Home Office quickly sought to establish what intelligence the security services, special branch and the uniformed police had on the pupil power movement and their views on the potential threat it posed.

The Home Office received the security services analysis on 18 May. An MI5 briefing focused on the activities of the SAU, detailing its origins, operational structure, membership details and political influences. On the latter it went into some detail, documenting links with the Young Communist League, Trotskyists (the IMG), pro-Chinese communists and Maoists (in the form of the NADWR). Maxwell Hunt was identified as the chair of the SAU and the NADWR was said to have provided the "inspiration and organisation behind the recent demonstrations". The briefing described the Trafalgar Square demonstration as an "anti-climax" for the SAU, but ended ominously, noting that "the relative failure of the demonstration does not detract from its significance as a symptom of the subversive influence which is increasingly being brought to bear on schools".[405]

The Home Office's reply to the prime minister, dated 24 May, reiterated the ominous tone set by the MI5 briefing. The SAU, it noted, had "right from the start...attracted the interest of various extreme left wing factions...and although other groups have given support to the Union, the Maoists have maintained a hold on it" (though it noted that "not all branches are necessarily Maoist orientated"). Regarding the events of the 17 May, it was explained that "The police had to turn out in considerable strength on this occasion," and that the tactics adopted had enabled them to disrupt the protest "without too much difficulty". However, the prime minister was advised that the "relative failure" of the demonstration ought not to lead the government to underestimate the threat posed by the pupil power movement:

> Our impression is that there is a good deal of discontent [in schools] and that subversive elements, though not themselves responsible for the original discontent, are showing themselves ready to take advantage of it.

The acknowledgement here of a "good deal" of genuine, underlying "discontent" in Britain's schools is an admission that the stimulus for the pupil protests originated in the real conditions of schooling rather than being the inspiration of adult militants or "agent provocateurs" as the popular press suggested.

However, the remainder of the Home Office briefing to Heath was devoted to identifying the "subversive elements" said to be seeking to capitalise on this "discontent", outlining a strategy for containing their influence. Steyne and Finch were named as the "principal organisers" of the Trafalgar Square protest but younger adults, including Hunt, were also alleged to have been involved in its planning. A number of strategies for undermining the effectiveness of the SAU were under consideration, including a proposal to seek to destabilise and weaken support for the SAU via the media. However, it was felt that the already "favourable" tone of press reporting of the SAU dispensed with the need for any such intervention. "The Home Secretary", it was stated, "has considered whether anything useful might be achieved by further publicity about some of those involved. But the newspaper coverage has been pretty good". It had "already brought out the Maoist influence...given a good deal of publicity for example to Hunt...and to the fact that the General Secretary of the Young Communist League was one of those arrested on 17 May". Further intervention was, though, needed to monitor the activities of the pupil power movement more closely. Pupil activism, it concluded, was not a temporary phenomenon and the organisations responsible for promoting it would need to be carefully watched in future:

> Both the police and the Security Service think it likely that there will be a continuing problem here in the field of public order which is not to be lightly regarded. Steps are being taken to improve intelligence about the SAU, and the people behind it.

In recognition of the "gravity" of the potential threat, copies of the briefing were sent not only to Armstrong but also to Cabinet Secretary Sir Burke Trend and Sir Martin Furnival Jones, the newly appointed Director of MI5.[406]

The DfES's response to Heath's concerns bore a number of similarities to the Home Office's. It began by praising the Home Office for its handling of "the events of 17 May". "The police action seemed to us to be exactly right in all respects", it noted, and while there was a "need to be careful not to create martyrs", such public order offences needed to be dealt with firmly by the police and courts. However, the DfES admitted it found itself constrained in terms of the action that *it* could take against malcontents. The UK's decentralised system of education made direct intervention in disciplinary matters of schools difficult. This, together with the requirement that children of compulsory school age must receive a full-time education, "restricts the possibilities of action open to us". Teachers who were guilty of encouraging activism—Hunt was specifically named—could be charged with professional misconduct and dismissed. It was noted that Hunt had already been summoned to appear before an ILEA sub-committee as a result of earlier political activities that had resulted in a court conviction.[407] Regarding recalcitrant pupils, while acknowledging the limits of its powers the DfES would encourage schools to deter and punish the "ringleaders":

> Pupils may be suspended or expelled from the school, and it seems right in principle to take this line with older pupils whose persistent misconduct makes it clear that they are determined to reject the reasonable exercise of authority.

While sharing the authoritarian tenor of the Home Office's response, the DfES was more reflective, seeking to contextualise and explain the rise of pupil power. "The general outlook of the young has changed and is likely to go on changing", it stated. "Their attitudes towards authority and conventional rules are more challenging", and in "places, mainly, though not wholly, in metropolitan areas, there is a significant, but rather ill-defined and inarticulate discontent among secondary school pupils". While this sometimes expressed itself in "undisciplined or rebellious behaviour in school...some boys are already beginning to develop political attitudes" leading them to "engage more consciously in activities of protest". The DfES was careful not to give the SAU and its demands too much credence, but earlier drafts did come close to acknowledging the legitimacy of pupil concerns about the stultifying nature of the secondary school curriculum and the potential impact of this in prompting pupil protests. "We need to continue our efforts to make the curriculum more stimulating and relevant to various age groups", an earlier draft explained. "Some of the present discontents (and disciplinary problems) are rooted in the boredom of pupils with their work".

This was quite an admission and it caught the eye of Thatcher, whose handwritten scrawl in the draft's margins showed that she concurred with its sentiments. "How?" she demanded to know. "We are always saying this, but *we* do little about it [original emphasis]".[408] Thatcher's comments were spotted by W R Elliott, a senior DfES official, who quickly saw the potential risks of continuing with this line of analysis. He advocated a more cautionary approach:

> I note the Secretary of State's comment... We could, if necessary, fish up something in answer to her question, but do not let us put too much money on making the curriculum "stimulating and relevant". Much more important for these rebellious pupils is a satisfying relationship with those who teach them... and "good schoolmastering".[409]

The final draft sent to Armstrong reflected this more dismissive tone, and the offending paragraph was edited to convey a rather different message. "A great deal of work", it stated, "has been and is being done to make the curriculum more stimulating and relevant to the needs of different groups". This more guarded tenor permeated the final draft, which carefully avoided any hints at legitimacy of the pupils' claims. The DfES was also keen to emphasise that schools themselves were not responsible for growing levels of politicisation. There were, the DfES insisted, "more potent factors than education or its institutions in creating this new outlook"; "they seem either a reaction to, or an imitation of, the adult world they see around them," including "the example of militancy set by older students and by adults". "External factors, for example, the mass media, especially television, and parental attitudes themselves changing," were also influential. On the potential longevity of the pupil power movement, the DfES shared the Home Office's view that it was likely to become a permanent feature of the educational and political landscape:

> As for the future the present wave of militancy may well die down of its own accord; but it will probably be renewed when the time seems ripe.

Given that pupil activism was here to stay there was the thorny question of how it should be managed, and whether any recognition should be given to its representative organisations. On this the DfES was unequivocal. The SAU was untrustworthy, open to militant and adult influences and "bent on mischief". However, the newly formed NUSS "may have a different part to play" and officials "would not want to judge it too hastily". It was "in effect a junior wing of the NUS", and although communist and left wing elements were evident within the NUS, the DfES had found it "worthwhile" to give it some limited recognition. In addition the NUS was "in practice more moderate than the public speeches of its leaders might suggest". The inference was clear; if the pupil power movement proved a durable phenomenon, it might be possible to do business with the NUSS.[410]

While hardly a ringing endorsement, the mere fact that the DfES was contemplating recognising the legitimacy of organised pupil activism and engaging with one of its representative bodies is one of the major achievements of the May 1972 strikes. This would have been unlikely without the pupil protests. It was their shock and bewilderment at the mass demonstrations which forced senior figures within the state apparatus to take seriously the threat posed by pupil activists, jolting officials into earnest deliberation over which elements of the movement were more responsible and worthy of recognition. In a briefing written for ministers by an official in the DfES Schools Branch, the evaluation of the SAU could not have been more scathing:

> There can be no doubt from the style, vocabulary and content of the union's leaflets and the newspaper, of its left-extremist approach and it is perhaps reasonable to suppose that its adult manipulators regard its

present "demands"...as little more than a front and that their long-term aims are essentially disruptive of present, political, social and educational systems.

The NUSS was, by contrast, "markedly more moderate" and had sought to distance itself from the SAU's militancy. The DfES was not oblivious to the NUSS's YCL links (including those of its chair Mary Attenborough), but its judgement was that there was "no evidence of political affiliation", and at its inaugural conference "efforts were made...to stress the non-sectarian and non-political nature of the Union and its desire to cooperate with rather than to confront teachers". Again the inference was clear; if the state was to engage with pupil activism, it would be better to do so via the NUSS, not the SAU.

Within months DfES officials were seriously considering whether Thatcher, still the education minister, should receive a formal deputation from the NUSS to discuss, among other issues, the abolition of grammar schools, pupil representation on school governing bodies, the re-introduction of free school milk and greater levels of public spending on schools.[411] Had this deputation taken place, it would have been an unprecedented event in the history of pupil activism. As officials involved in the deliberations themselves acknowledged, it would have marked a formal acknowledgement of the legitimacy of pupil activism in shaping education policy. Ultimately Thatcher personally declined the NUSS's request to meet, but the seriousness with which its appeal was considered illustrated the shift in thinking within Whitehall in a short period of time.[412] In this sense the SAU-led protests of May 1972 had a very real impact on attitudes to pupil involvement in school policy at the highest levels of the educational establishment. This would prove one of the more lasting achievements of the strikes, although the SAU itself would not be the principal beneficiary.

How else can we gauge the success of the May 1972 pupil protests? The demand for an end to physical punishment was unsuccessful. Corporal punishment remained a feature of British schooling well into the 1980s, despite the fact that it had been abolished in Poland (in 1783), Holland, France, Finland (all in the 19th century) and later Belgium, Germany, Italy, Norway, Sweden and Denmark (all before 1970). In other respects the protests had some success. At the height of the disruption, some councils outside London conceded to some of the pupils' demands. Labour controlled Wolverhampton Council announced it would allow one pupil aged between 11 and 15 on each of the governing bodies of the town's 30 secondary schools. Brighton's Conservative controlled local authority proposed that two pupil representatives sit on the governing council of each of the town's 14 schools. In Manchester the Education Committee announced that it was minded to formally recognise the NUSS, stating that pupil activism could play a "very valuable part of children's education". Eventually even the Inner London Education Authority (ILEA) came to acknowledge the merits of the SAU's demands: "it was important to give careful consideration to the views of pupils and to give them opportunities to participate in decisions which affect them in schools through school councils or similar means".[413]

Just as importantly, the protest movement prompted a serious national debate outside the corridors of Whitehall about the merits of the demands being made by pupil activists. It soon became evident that not all were prepared to condemn the tactics adopted by the SAU or the reforms it was advocating. We have already seen that Handyside and the NCCL sprang to the defence of the striking pupils. They were not alone. The *Guardian*'s Peter Wilby, an otherwise outspoken critic of the SAU's tactics, acknowledged the legitimacy of many of its demands: "behind the sound and fury of the slogans, the pupil militants have raised fundamental questions about the role of democracy in education and the relationship of schools to society at large". The SAU activists, "in their muddled way, may have done education a small service".[414] The well-respected educationalist Christopher Price, who served as Anthony Crosland's parliamentary private secretary in Harold Wilson's 1964-1970 Labour government, was even more decisive in his defence of the demands made by the pupil power movement, condemning the "complacent hub of wishful thinking" that had typified the establishment's response to calls for greater school democracy:

> The predominant adult reaction to the past two weeks of pupil demonstrations has been bewildered irritation, a search for scapegoats and a refusal to take it very seriously; we have been told of sinister adults feeding wicked ideas into young, innocent heads. If only we deny them the publicity they seek, throw out a few troublemakers and let the rest go back to school, everything will be alright... It cannot,

however, be dismissed quite so easily... In the short run, the recent children's crusades may not have achieved very much. But they have aired some fundamental questions about the relationship between schools and society.[415]

Even the *Mail*'s Virginia Ironside showed support for the pupils' cause following the broadcasting of a BBC2 *Man Alive* documentary on pupil power. "When the shouting died down", she declared, "it was difficult not to come out on the side of the pupils".[416]

This greater willingness to assess rationally the manifesto of the pupil power movement provided as huge boost to the newly formed NUSS, which would soon succeed in positioning itself as the official organ of the pupil power movement in Britain. As a relatively well-financed adjunct of the NUS, now bestowed with tacit "official" recognition, it began to seem best placed to represent pupils' interests. As the *Times* noted, by June talks were planned between elements of the SAU and the NUSS with a view to uniting the two organisations, and thereafter the SAU's influence appeared to wane.[417]

As we show in the next chapter, the NUSS would prove to be no "establishment stooge" and there were certainly those within Whitehall, not least Thatcher herself, who viewed its activities and growing influence with apprehension. Thatcher's ideological predisposition was to be suspicious of the pupil power movement. Her suspicion intensified following an NUSS-related conversation in the Commons lobby with the Tory MP for Warwick and Leamington, Dudley Smith, in November 1972. Smith was a governor at the North London Collegiate School, which had seen a phenomenal rise in NUSS subscriptions among its pupils. He told Thatcher he and the school's head teacher viewed this with considerable alarm. They viewed the NUSS as a "subversive" organisation with "deplorable" aims, and their experience was that even "respectable and level-headed" pupils were having their heads turned by it.[418] At Thatcher's behest Smith wrote to her offering advice on countering the growth and influence of the NUSS. His view was that the organisation was using its NUS-linked fringe benefits (including cheap travel and free museum entry) "as a cunning way of gaining recruits, who may be influenced by many of its deplorable aims". He felt that "If there was a way of countering the "bribe" aspect of the Union's activities...far fewer girls (and boys for that matter) would join".[419] Thatcher was impressed but DfES officials sought to assuage her concerns. "I think", wrote one official, "that we can regard the NUSS as being one of the most moderate and constructive...of the various organisations of this kind that have emerged to date". Indeed, "much of what they are clamouring for has already been conceded, or there is an identifiable trend in the same direction". He recommended that the DfES continue with its strategy of tacit, constructive engagement with the NUSS:

> I do not feel that I am being bold in predicting that organisations of this kind are with us to stay and there seems to be no advantage in our pursuing any form of collision course with them.[420]

Thatcher was not convinced. She instructed officials to instigate a laborious, time-consuming audit of NUSS benefits to establish whether pupils would receive these without being members of the union. Like Smith she felt the appeal of NUSS membership would be weakened if it could be shown that the concessions it offered were largely worthless. Officials were clearly aware of the sensitivity of the task Thatcher had set them. One advised his colleagues to tread carefully and to avoid giving the impression that they were "gunning for the NUSS", which was precisely what they were being instructed to do.[421]

The outcome of this exhaustive review, which involved officials contacting all the major museums and attractions in London, travel services, London Transport and the Civil Aviation Authority, was communicated to Dudley Smith in January 1973. With some satisfaction Thatcher noted that few concessions directly accrued from NUSS membership and hoped that the information she provided would be useful in "countering any false claims that might be made". Doubtless Thatcher and Smith thought that they had uncovered a "smoking gun" they could use to undermine the NUSS. However, the whole exercise showed a spectacular misunderstanding of the NUSS's popular appeal among pupils, which in reality had little to do with the concessions that accrued from its membership. As Thatcher's own officials acknowledged, the pupil power movement—and support for its representative organisations—was based upon a set of grievances, and not a desire for cut-price admission to museums and galleries.

Heath's election defeat led to Thatcher's exit from the DfES and a thawing in the relationship between the Department and the NUSS.

Labour ministers and their officials seemed initially more amenable to its lobbying. In January 1974 new education minister Reg Prentice received a letter from Simon Keys, the new president of the NUSS, requesting a meeting to discuss broad aspects of NUSS policy.[422] Accompanying the letter was an NUSS policy statement, listing 30 aims adopted at its 1973 Annual Conference.[423] Again officials deliberated over whether the NUSS should be afforded a deputation. "The ministerial door should not be open to every caller" wrote one official, but "the NUSS has some claims to being responsible and a sizeable membership, so I would be hesitant about indicating that we judge them 'not worthy of an audience'. They seem to be the sort of people who might be received once in the lifetime of an administration".[424]

G F Cockerill, a senior DfES official, agreed; "the literature bears out my impression that this is a responsible body of young people, to be regarded quite differently from the Schools Action Union which was involved in school strikes and similar disruptive action". While some of their aims inevitably did not accord with government policy, they were "by no means disreputable".[425]

Another official went further, highlighting that a number of the NUSS's broader objectives were in accordance with the views of the current Labour administration, adding further support to the union's request for a deputation: "Some of the NUSS's views (eg on comprehensive education) would be acceptable to present Ministers and they will be sympathetic to others (eg the abolition of corporal punishment)".[426] The general consensus was that any deputation would have to be "carefully handled" because of the potential for adverse publicity, but in light of growing acknowledgement of the importance of listening to pupils' voices it was deemed that a meeting with a junior DfES minister would be an appropriate and "welcome gesture".[427]

The meeting did not ultimately take place. Just as officials were drafting a letter of invitation to the NUSS, Armstrong was approached by Stan Newens, a Labour MP generally considered to be on the left of the party, who urged him not to receive the union.[428] The precise nature of Newens' grievance with the NUSS is unclear, but it coincided with the publication of a *Morning Star* article on a jointly-organised NUSS/Black Students Action Collective demonstration in support of the "Brockwell Park 3", which was drawn to Armstrong's attention by the DfES's permanent secretary.

The "Brockwell Park 3" were three black youths controversially jailed for affray following a fracas with police officers in London's Brockwell Park in June 1973.[429] The convictions of all three were heavily contested by community activists, but that of 15 year old Robin Sterling was the subject of particular concern. Sterling's conviction would subsequently be quashed by the High Court and the NUSS's involvement in promoting his cause was commended. However, the *Morning Star* article detailing the NUSS's plans to leaflet and picket schools clearly troubled Armstrong. The NUSS was encouraging pupils to take strike action and participate in the demonstration to free the youngsters.[430] A *Daily Mail* account of the protest reporting that over 500 pupils "truanted" to take part was also brought to Armstrong's attention, adding to doubts about the wisdom of meeting the NUSS.[431] To make matters worse Armstrong was also shown a *Morning Star* article from April 1973 which hinted at the possibility of utilising the NUSS to establish YCL branches in schools.[432] The following day officials advised that the NUSS should be informed "that owing to the pressure of other engagements there is no possibility of a meeting".[433]

For the DfES the NUSS credentials had been tarnished, but this did little damage to the NUSS's credibility among school pupils themselves who continued to be attracted by its manifesto for change.

As we will see in the next chapter throughout the rest of the 1970s the NUSS would take on the mantle of leading the campaign for greater democracy in schools. It, and not the SAU, would now take forward the fight against corporal punishment and school discipline, defend the right of pupils to organise and protest, and, more generally, seek to influence education policy. Moreover, it would do so with a good degree of success. Like the SAU it would continue to sporadically attract controversy, but it would nonetheless develop a national profile of respectability that the pupil power movement previously lacked. Its affiliation to the NUS did help to achieve this. It afforded the NUSS a status and financial stability that the SAU never achieved, and in this sense the YCL's strategy of engagement with the NUS paid dividends. However, this should not serve to detract from the pivotal role played by the SAU in spearheading pupil activism between 1968 and 1972. Nor, as we have argued, should it lead us to underestimate the impact of the short but intensive burst of SAU-orchestrated pupil militancy of the summer of 1972. It is no exaggeration to suggest that the London school strikes of May 1972 rattled the foundations of the educational establishment and prompted a serious national debate about the merits of the demands being made by the pupil power movement. As we have shown, the NUSS would be the main beneficiaries of the more conducive political environment in the aftermath of the strikes, but the part played by SAU activists in contributing to this climate of change was crucial.

CHRIS FULLER (Norwich, 1974)
"We demanded real democracy in our school"

THE WORLD felt like a different place when I was growing up in Norwich. I was born in 1956 and one of my first memories was being taken by my dad to hear Harold Wilson speak at a rally in 1964. The hall was packed and I had to listen over a tannoy outside sat on dad's shoulders. After that I remember being at primary school and saying to my mates that I was on the "red team"!

It wasn't a very political household but mum and dad were Labour, dad was a trade unionist and it meant knowing which side you were on.

In 1972 I went to hear Arthur Scargill speak during the miners' strike. After the meeting I remember doing a collection for the miners at school. There weren't many miners who came to the Norwich meeting, but though there weren't many they then went and picketed—and shut down—the power station at Great Yarmouth.

All these things were great idea formers. The period I was growing up in helped shape me and my politics.

At the Arthur Scargill meeting I bought my first copy of *Socialist Worker*. I started to go to occasional meetings of International Socialism and joined Rebel, a youth organisation connected to IS.

The Rebel group had five members. Two of us were in IS, one was an anarchist and the other two were "non-aligned". We decided to join the National Union of School Students and tried to build the union. We regularly leafleted schools—but the school authorities made it difficult for us and tried to stop leaflets going into schools.

At my school we had a bit of success. We formed an NUSS branch and put regular leaflets in. There was already a school council which myself and some friends went to because we wanted a voice in the school. We were against school uniforms, we wanted more democracy in the school, we believed schools should respond to the wishes and demands of students. Some of our demands were less serious. I remember on one occasion we demanded greater choice of crisps in the school shop.

But it soon became clear the school council was a sham. It wasn't about giving us a real voice in shaping the school and its policies. We didn't even get the tomato crisps! So we tried other things.

In 1974 the miners were on strike again. It was very dramatic. There were power cuts and a three day week. It felt as if we were in the midst of a really important struggle and we felt we could win.

We did collections for the miners at our school. By now we had won the right to have an NUSS notice board, where we could put up information.

In April 1974 we decided we were going to have a rally for May Day. It didn't seem unusual. In 1974 it seemed normal to have May Day events. The school gave us permission to have a lunchtime meeting in the Assembly Hall.

But then the local press and TV found out about the meeting and turned up. The meeting was packed, much bigger than we expected— and far, far bigger than the school thought it would be.

I was speaking and then interviewed on the television, we were in the papers talking about the need for greater democracy in the school. We followed this up the following week with an NUSS recruitment and organising meeting in the school and about 100 students came along.

But now the school moved against us. They called my mum and dad in and gave me a warning. The head called my parents Communists!

We responded by posting an open newsletter on the NUSS notice board which called the head a dictator—an expression of our demand for real democracy in the school.

But he responded by first suspending me and then calling in my parents to another meeting. They were told in no uncertain terms to withdraw me from the school. It was, in effect, an expulsion. All done just before school broke up for half term.

It was devastating. It was hard for mum and dad, but they stood by me. It was hard for me, because I suddenly didn't know what I was going to do. It was a draconian punishment, an attempt to knock the rebel out of me. Even when I got in to a local college my application form had "Beware! Student rebel" written on the top!

We shouldn't underestimate the impact that victimisation has on people.

I didn't know at the time, but the day I was expelled the sixth form refused to go to classes and occupied their part of the school. It was a great show of solidarity, but the victimisation had an impact and broke the NUSS in the school at the time.

My NUSS activities shaped me in numerous ways. Actually in future years in the workplace I found bosses who tried to intimidate me and other union activists in a similar way to the head teacher. But the NUSS was a great apprenticeship. It helped form my views, it taught me how to organise and it helped shape me—a life long socialist, proud of my days as a student Rebel!

JIMMY ROSS (Teacher, Glasgow 1972-1973)

IN 1972 and 1973 I was a young English teacher at Cranhill Secondary in the east end of Glasgow. There were a number of school student strikes at the school and at the neighbouring St Gregory's. The two schools were separated by a park and the students at one of the schools would walk out, march across the park and bring the other school out.

The students had a number of demands:

- No school uniforms (and no ties)
- An end to corporal punishment
- An end to punishment for smoking and older students allowed to smoke at breaks

The strikes were organised and led by students some of whom were close to the Young Communist League (or whose parents were Communist Party members).

On one occasion I remember one of the science teachers I was friendly with at school (he was an anarchist) let his students occupy the science class! They were there for about 48 hours and had posters over the windows: "You are now entering Free Cranhill"! Amazingly, from the perspective of today, nothing happened to the teacher, he wasn't disciplined in any way.

I remember me and some of the younger teachers watching one strike unfold from the windows of the staff room. We were appalled at the response of the senior school management. The head teacher and others marched out with their leather belts over their shoulders to confront the strikers. Here were students striking and demanding to be heard and senior school staff responding with brutality!

At the time of the strike I was a union activist. The union sent out advice to teachers on what to do when faced with a student strike. Their advice was, essentially, "send for the police"!

Rank and File Teacher had just been set up and I stood and got elected to the EIS Glasgow local association management committee. There were three of us from Rank and File on the committee. When the strikes were being discussed we submitted an "objection to the minutes". This was a challenge to the union's advice. We argued we should not call the police, that students had legitimate grievances and should be listened to, that there should be no punishment of strikers, that school councils should be set up and that the National Union of School Students should be recognised. From the response we got you'd have thought the sky was falling in. We got one additional vote: four of us out of 45!

There was an interesting split among the teachers at our school at this time. Some of the older staff were very traditional and saw the belt as a key tool for controlling kids and classrooms. They were very traditional in their approach to education and quite aloof from the students. These teachers tended to live some distance away from the school and had little to do with the community.

But many of the new teachers came from the area where they taught. I had been brought up in Ruchazie, just next to Cranhill. We had grown up locally, we were among the first generation of people from the area to have gone to university and on to teacher training. It meant we had shared many of the experiences of the children we were teaching and were part of the local community.

We had been students during the late 1960s and early 1970s and had lived through the student activism of those years. Not all the teachers coming into schools at this time had been student activists, but the atmosphere at university was one that challenged authority and the dominant ideas.

Teaching was changing in two important ways. First the dominant ideas in teaching were starting to shift, moving away from rote teaching and "chalk and talk" towards more inclusive, progressive and comprehensive methods of education. And second, the expansion of schooling in the post war welfare state had started a process of proletarianising teaching. It was no longer an elite middle class profession, we were employees of the local state, joining the union and fighting for our rights as workers. As such we were much more open to the demands of students for greater democracy in the school.

7

The shifting politics of the NUSS: 1974-1981

We'll stop them in the schools!
We'll stop them in the streets!
We'll stop the Nazi bastards
Anywhere we meet!

So please don't listen to the NF scum
Set up SKAN ANL groups and have some fun
Organise Discos or Rock against Racism gigs,
Educate people to reject these racist pigs.[434]

THE CLASS conflict in Britain between 1974-1979 has been well documented. As Shepherd notes, this period is "often remembered for recurrent crises, poor economic performance and industrial unrest".[435] During 1978 alone 9.3 million working days were lost to strikes involving an estimated 979,000 workers. In 1979 this rose to 29 million days, with around 5 million workers taking part.[436] This was the "winter of discontent", a term still used to conjure up images of economic stagnation, apparently all-powerful trade union barons and political incompetence.[437]

But this was not a period marked only by economic and political failure. In the political arena, for example, it was, as Black et al note, a decade of an extraordinary ferment in ideas, which saw the growing confidence and influence of a range of new social movements campaigning around a wealth of issues: sexuality, disability, gender, race and ethnicity.[438] As we saw in the previous chapter, school pupils were also moved by the politics of liberation that characterised the 1970s, and in 1972 an embryonic National Union of School Students evolved out of the pupil power movement of 1968-1972. In this chapter we discuss the development of the NUSS in the 1970s. The NUSS sought to present itself as a mature body, with a legitimate right to engage in the corporatist form of policy making that characterised the period. We document the tensions that emerged within the pupil power movement, often linked to the strategy of incorporation advocated by the NUSS's Youth Communist League leadership.

In the previous chapter we saw that under the influence of the YCL, the NUSS leadership sought to present the union as a more moderate, responsible body than its predecessor the Schools Action Union. Stevenson argues that the YCL's view was that the SAU's "increasingly sectarian approach inevitably divorced it from the bulk of school students and led many activists into the blind alley of challenging authority *per se*, rather than building on genuine mass issues of concern". A more moderate form of engagement was required, it was argued, to build the union into a mass organised body that would command respect and legitimacy. The confrontational direct action favoured by the SAU was now seen as counterproductive to the NUSS's broader political aims. The YCL was convinced that "strikes should only be called if they are well organised and if other methods have failed to realise just demands", and this conviction would shape the NUSS's campaigning strategies between 1974-1978.[439]

Militant direct action was sidelined in favour of publicity campaigns, attempts to build alliances with potentially sympathetic organisations and cooperation with official inquiries into issues of concern to the union, such as student maintenance, corporal punishment and school democracy.

This did not rule out the passage of fiery resolutions at annual NUSS conferences, nor did it mean that the union did not support direct action involving pupil disobedience in schools. The NUSS backed the high profile campaign against school discipline waged by pupils at Islington's Highbury Grove comprehensive school. And in March 1976 the union initiated a national week of action against corporal punishment, encouraging pupils to refuse to be caned or strapped and for them to keep detailed records of beatings, which could be compared with official school punishment books.[440] A number of other such campaigns were sanctioned while the YCL retained control of the NUSS. However, the primary focus of the NUSS leadership during this period was directed towards enhancing the union's size and reputation through a policy of "constructive engagement".

This strategy was reflected in work conducted behind the scenes, aimed at transforming the union into an organised, effective campaigning body for pupils. The Department for Education and Science's (DfES's) file on the NUSS, appropriately titled "Information on the Union", was obviously originally intended as a repository of information on the NUSS's activities, including a raft of NUSS-produced literature. It also inadvertently helped to document the efforts the union's leadership were putting into establishing its reputation and status. Even its publicity material was given a "makeover", assisted by the injection of National Union of Students (NUS) funding. The low-cost, informal-style literature associated with the SAU was dispensed with in favour of more professional promotional material, branded with the distinctive NUSS clenched fist. An ideological de-toxifying process also occurred, reflecting the YCL's wider strategy of moderation. Gone were references to Marxism and socialism and the wider revolutionary aims that were a characteristic feature of earlier pupil power literature. Strenuous efforts were made to distance the union from its more radical, militant roots. "We are not a political body in any way", outgoing president Simon Keys told its 1974 annual conference.[441]

This approach showed signs of success in attracting potential allies to the NUSS's cause. The National Council for Civil Liberties (NCCL), an organisation that had previously supported some of the aims of the pupil power movement, began to provide more formal assistance to the union. It helped in the production of a range of documents, including complex legal guidance setting out, among other things, police powers to enforce attendance, school powers on discipline, expulsions and suspensions, and school students' rights to organise. A formal constitution was also drawn up with NCCL help, as were standing orders for national and local conferences. In short the NUSS was beginning to take on the appearance of a more formal, organised campaigning body.

The NUSS leadership's strategy was given a major boost in June 1974 when the House of Commons Select Committee on Expenditure invited it to give evidence on the question of grants for school students staying on in further education. It was one of only a small number of organisations asked to come before the Committee, enhancing the

NUSS's growing credibility and status.[442] The invitation was seen as a major coup for the union, seeming to justify its efforts to present itself as a responsible key player in the educational arena. The barrage of outrage the invitation generated among the NUSS's traditional foes seemed to provide further vindication of its strategy. The newly elected Tory MP Rhodes Boyson, a renowned self-publicist and the controversial former head of Highbury Grove comprehensive, lambasted the Committee's decision. The union, he argued, was an irresponsible "nonsense body", which "wanted schools run by committee with cleaner, cook, laboratory technician and the head teacher all having equal say". The Committee was wrong to give the NUSS the "kiss of recognition", Boyson insisted, and in the light of its decision it was "small wonders that good teachers were fleeing the classroom".[443]

The NUSS, however, seized the opportunity to contribute to the Committee's proceedings, well aware that it was the first pupil power organisation to be asked formally and officially to articulate its views on a key aspect of educational policy. As John Randall the union's then president acknowledged this was "the first time the NUSS has been recognised by an official policy-making body as being capable of speaking for school students".[444]

Together with the NUS, the NUSS submitted a joint memorandum to the Committee setting out among other demands a detailed and persuasive case for the introduction of educational maintenance allowances for FE students. A joint NUS/NUSS delegation also gave oral evidence before the Committee, with the NUSS represented by Simon Keys and Alan Walter (its vice-president). According to the Tory committee member Janet Fookes, Walter's appearance constituted the first ever occasion any person under the age of 18 had given evidence before a select committee—another apparent first for the NUSS.

The NUSS's influence on the evidence submitted to the Committee by the joint-delegation is clearly discernible, most notably in its demand that final year secondary school students, as well as further education students, be entitled to financial support. The impact of raising the school leaving age from 15 to 16 in 1972 had, the jointly written submission argued, placed an undue burden on poor parents.[445] Some level of maintenance was required, not just to compensate for the extra year of schooling but also to pay for books, extra-curricular activities and school uniforms.[446]

In their oral evidence Keys and Walter were not given the opportunity to defend the "school student allowance" proposal because the Committee's questioning focused entirely on the funding of FE students. However, they performed well on the day, dealing effectively with the combative questions of the Committee's chair Tory MP Neil Merten. For instance, in response to his inference that school students deemed "incapable" of benefiting from further education should be disqualified from post-16 educational maintenance support, they made an articulate, persuasive case for *all* young people to be entitled to assistance, irrespective of their academic qualifications. They also gave the Committee constructive advice on how to combat the widespread ignorance among secondary school pupils about the availability of existing discretionary grants for further education. Ultimately the Committee's recommendations made no mention of "school student allowances", but the NUSS suggestion that advice and guidance about FE maintenance allowances be more fully integrated into the earlier years of secondary schooling was accepted. Also accepted was the more substantive joint NUS/NUSS demand for an end to the inequitable discretionary variable grants system for FE students and for the introduction of a national educational maintenance allowance.

Significant though these recommendations were, of more importance to the NUSS was the boost that participation in the Committee's proceedings gave to its credibility and status. This was reflected in the comments made by Simon Keys in his presidential retirement speech to that year's NUSS conference. "The invitation to report to Parliament", he noted, "has been our major success in the past year. I think we are now getting a great deal of respect from all quarters".[447]

While the efforts the NUSS leadership were making to enhance the union's national standing were considerable, this did not prevent the union from supporting some high profile struggles waged by pupils at a local level. The NUSS had backed the Black Students Action Collective demonstration in support of the "Brockwell Park 3" (see chapter 5). On 4 April 1974 up to 500 pupils heeded the NUSS's call to strike and participate in a three mile march from Kennington Park to Brockwell Park.[448] Its support for this cause would soon be vindicated with the formal acquittal of Robin Sterling, one of the Brockwell 3. In truth, though, this was one of the now increasingly rare incidences of the NUSS providing overt support to a cause unrelated to its narrower, more sectional education-focused aims. Henceforth, the union's official backing tended to be restricted to action taken by pupils' campaigns for greater school democracy and against the authoritarian nature of state schooling, reflecting the NUSS leadership's inclination to avoid appearing overtly political.

The most notable NUSS support for a localised pupil-led campaign over school discipline occurred at Rhodes Boyson's former school Highbury Grove, where pupils were engaged in a concerted protest over its strict disciplinary regime. After the departure of Boyson the school's governing board made it clear they were searching for a replacement "capable of continuing Dr Boyson's standards of discipline and academic achievement". The acting head Barry Sharr launched a liberal usage of beatings with the cane and a series of suspensions and expulsions.[449] His efforts to impress the school's governors were not appreciated by pupils, and in early July 1974 a series of protests at the school began with a playground demonstration against "excessive authoritarianism". This was followed by a pupil strike and a march of around 70 students to the divisional education offices. The NUSS's intervention in the dispute was prompted by pupil claims that around 30 of these protesters had been caned and three expelled or suspended.[450] Plans for a further strike on the afternoon of 17 July were called off by pupils after they were faced with a barrage of hostile reporters and photographers at the school gates.[451] Incoming NUSS president Simon Emerson, a prominent YCL activist, had by now intervened directly on behalf of the pupils, putting their case forward to the media and seeking the assistance of the NCCL.[452] At an NUSS-organised press conference on 18 July, pupils claimed there had been a distinct hardening of discipline at the school since Boyson's departure. Given Boyson's reputation while at the school this was quite an allegation! They claimed that upwards of 30 teachers at Highbury Grove—roughly one quarter—supported their cause, and indeed that one teacher had put them in touch with the left-leaning Islington *Gutter Press*, which provided support in producing publicity material. As we noted earlier, in the 1970s many teachers had themselves come through the pupil power or student movements of the late 1960s and early 1970s and the growing divergence between "old school" and new teachers was an important division within the school.

The notoriety of Rhodes Boyson and Highbury Grove guaranteed that protests attracted national press coverage, most typically negative. True to form, features in the *Daily Telegraph* and the *Daily Mail* alleged that children were being "led astray" and that the disruption was instigated by hard-left adult infiltrators. Boyson's allegations that Communists and Maoists were "trying to wreck his old school" were widely publicised, as was his somewhat bizarre proposed solution: reducing the school leaving age to 14, thereby relieving the school of its disaffected malcontents.[453]

In truth the NUSS seemed to act as a moderating rather than militant influence on the proceedings at Highbury Grove, only becoming involved after the initial protests had taken place. Following its president's intervention, plans to hold a second walkout were suspended.

Many of the allegations made by Highbury Grove's pupils were justified. Boyson had bequeathed an extremely unpleasant environment for both teachers and pupils at the school. Many parents shared the pupils' view that it was a dysfunctional institution, run along dictatorial authoritarian lines. As the *Guardian*'s John Fairhall noted, many parents felt that it was an "elitist institution where the academically bright boys are pushed forward and the rest went under, and were kept under by a rigid unfeeling discipline and a liberal use of the cane". Nor were pupil claims about teacher support for their cause exaggerated. Less than a fortnight after the pupil protests some 20 Highbury Grove teachers tendered their resignations. Many, the *Guardian* noted, were "pleased to be getting away from the place", disillusioned at the institution's "elitist, repressive" regime.[454] Based upon estimates provided by Highbury Grove teachers the *Guardian* estimated the school staff turnover rate to be as high as 50 percent in 1974, providing further evidence of its dysfunctional nature.[455] Ultimately Sharr failed in his bid to obtain the headship at Highbury Grove, perhaps partly as a result of the NUSS success in drawing attention to the discontent his temporary stewardship had generated. However, this would be a hollow victory. Boyson was ultimately succeeded at Highbury Grove by the equally authoritarian Lawrence Norcross, a former Communist turned reactionary Tory, who would become notorious for his defence of corporal punishment well into the 1980s.[456]

The media's reporting of the Highbury Grove dispute served to illustrate the extent to which the NUSS continued to face hostile press coverage, despite the considerable efforts it was making to broaden its status and reputation. *Daily Telegraph* columnist Peter Simple's regular jibes at the NUSS were representative of this continuing negative commentary. His account of the NUSS 1974 annual conference was little more than a diatribe directed at NUSS activists and officials, who he described as "owlish, self-important or precociously politicised school children...unfailingly of the left".[457] In fact the carefully managed resolutions passed at this conference were hardly revolutionary. Predictably, this was insufficient to prevent other newspapers following Simple's overtly critical tone and producing equally scathing commentary on the conference proceedings:

> Ban the cane...no victimisation...solidarity with Chile...£10 a week for sixth formers...and free school milk! No we're not making it up. There really was a conference of the National Union of School Students in London yesterday. And pint-sized shop stewards solemnly spouted these demands in voices scarcely broken.[458]

Clearly the suggestion that children should not be arbitrarily beaten and victimised and that further education students should be provided with some much needed financial support offended the sensibilities of the *Mail*, which opposed even this relatively liberal NUSS agenda for schools. Like other significant sections of the press, and indeed the political establishment, the *Mail* could not bring itself to contemplate the possibility that pupils might have something legitimate to say about the way they were educated and treated in schools.

Despite the negative publicity that tended to surround the NUSS , many of the union's policy positions continued to reflect mainstream educational and political opinion. NUSS calls for the introduction of an educational maintenance allowance for FE students was supported by the all-party Expenditure Committee. The NUSS's demand that corporal punishment be abolished also commanded a good degree of political support and regular questions on the topic were submitted by MPs and peers to ministers in the Commons and Lords. The second reading of Baroness Wooton's Protection of Minors Bill in December 1973, which would have prohibited the practice, was only narrowly defeated by 67 votes to 51.[459] During the debate Wooton listed some of the countries that had already abolished corporal punishment: France, Belgium, Italy, Denmark, Luxemburg, Holland, Iceland, Norway, Finland and Sweden, and argued that it was "only a question of time before we are required to abandon a practice which has been discarded by so many of our partners—indeed the great majority of them—as archaic".[460]

The election of Harold Wilson's Labour administration in February 1974 increased the likelihood of action being taken against corporal punishment. The incoming government's assistant whip Margaret Jackson (known today as Margaret Beckett) was herself known to be opposed to corporal punishment, and she was not alone on the Labour benches. Outside parliament organisations such as the Society of Teachers Opposed to Physical Punishment (STOPP) and the NCCL lobbied continually for parliament to outlaw corporal punishment.[461] The NCCL had drafted Wooton's Bill, which it subsequently published in a pamphlet.[462] The issue continued to be the subject of considerable controversy throughout the 1970s, forcing the Department for Education and Science (DfES) to open two separate consultations on the issue in 1975 and 1976. The latter consultation was prompted in part by Jackson's promotion to undersecretary at the DfES, where she pressed for the introduction of legislation prohibiting corporal punishment. In short while the NUSS's critics may have railed against its calls for an end to the legalised beating of children in schools, the objective of its campaign commanded a good deal of mainstream support.

There was also political support for the NUSS case for greater pupil participation in school management. The cause was championed on the floor of the House of Commons in July 1974 in an adjournment debate on school democracy sponsored by Labour MP Bob Cryer. Cryer was a former teacher and lecturer and was sympathetic to the NUSS calls for pupil involvement. In the debate he argued that "students participate in a modest way in colleges of further education, and there is no reason why this participation should not extend to secondary education".[463] Significantly, the DfES minister responding to the debate, Labour's Ernest Armstrong, intimated his tacit approval of the sentiments underpinning Cryer's argument, again illustrating support for the NUSS calls for pupils to have a say in shaping their education. "Staff, parents and pupils have a vital part to play" in the running of schools, he acknowledged. "A few authorities have made provision for pupil membership of governing bodies" and his officials were "watching this development with interest".[464] By the end of 1975 around a dozen local authorities had followed a trend set by Sheffield and allowed pupils to be represented on school governing bodies. In April

1975 the Labour government appointed Tom Taylor, deputy pro-vice chancellor of Lancaster University, to undertake an inquiry into the governance and management of schools, the remit of which included assessing the possibility of appointing pupils as governors.[465]

The NUSS also had some success in securing invitations to participate in a number of key formal official inquiries on educational policy, including Shirley Williams' regional conferences on the "great education debate", the DfES consultations on corporal punishment (1975 and 1976) and Taylor's inquiry into the governance and management of schools. It was also asked to take part in a Commission for Racial Equality (CRE) working party investigation into National Front (NF) membership in schools. These invitations would also be interpreted by the NUSS leadership as vindication of their attempts to legitimise the union. They were at the table and had been given an opportunity to influence key aspects of educational policy.

Official recognition of the NUSS was a significant development, as illustrated by howls of disapproval the invitations prompted from the union's critics. For example, the Assistant Masters Association was furious at the invitation to the NUSS to participate in the Taylor inquiry. "We are absolutely against this", the AMA president told the *Daily Mail*. "It is absurd that we should be put in the position of even having to argue against the idea of children as governors".[466] Likewise, the National Union of Teachers took exception to the invitation the pupil's union received to take part in the "great education debate". Unlike many individual NUT members, the NUT leadership had never recognised the legitimacy of the NUSS. It contacted Shirley Williams, protesting at the DfES's decision to include the pupil union, demanding it be excluded from future official consultations. Apparently this demand was given a sympathetic hearing by Williams, highlighting the fragility of the NUSS's newly bestowed "official" status.[467] This fragility was confirmed months later when the NUSS's invitation to participate in the CRE's working party on NF influence in schools was withdrawn following an NUT threat to boycott the proceedings unless the NUSS were excluded[468] This decision prompted one NUT member to write to the *Guardian*, condemning the "intolerant attitudes shown by the National Union of Teachers towards the National Union of School Students, particularly in matters where the latter's representation of school students on official bodies is concerned".[469]

Despite this setback, many contemporary outside observers, including the NUSS's opponents, expressed reluctant admiration for the way the union appeared to have succeeded in promoting its interests. Towards the end of 1976 it was revealed that talks had been held between the Federation of Conservative Students (FCS) and the Conservative Party's National Executive on the possibility of organising a rival body to promote conservative values in schools. Mike Forsyth, the CFS's chair, acknowledged that the party was "alarmed" and that action needed to be taken to undermine the "firm bases" the NUSS had established in schools to promote its agenda, which included, among other apparently revolutionary aims, the abolition of the grammar school system, universal grants for FE students, free contraceptives and abortions.[470]

Significantly, the NUSS strategy of moderation and consolidation had also won it plaudits within the DfES. "Many of the objectives of the Union", one ministerial briefing noted, "were unexceptional and command wide support among adults". "As such" the document concluded, "the Department's earlier assessment that it is one of the more responsible bodies active in the field of pupil participation can be sustained". Officials did remain concerned about the political leanings of the union, especially the continued influence of the YCL. NUSS President Simon Emmerson, it was noted, had publicly acknowledged his Communist Party membership and there was "the obvious danger that the Union could, perhaps without too much difficulty, be persuaded to adopt less reasonable attitudes through its links with potentially disruptive adult influences". The Brockwell 3 and Highbury Grove campaigns were cited as "less reasonable" examples of NUSS activities. However, officials were of the view that the NUSS was, on the whole, a body with a series of rational, sensible educational aims which could be trusted to act responsibly. Its affiliation to the NUS, in particular, had provided a moderating influence and operated as "a restraining effect on the Union's activities".[471] This can be interpreted as something of a triumph for the NUSS leadership's attempts to achieve official recognition for the union.

However, the NUSS's success in presenting itself as a responsible voice of pupil activism masked a growing conflict over the direction the union was taking. The YCL's considerable influence was beginning to show signs of waning. Emmerson, as a senior YCL activist, submitted reports on the NUSS annual conferences to the YCL's Executive Committee. His report for 1974 lamented that only 12 of the 50 or so delegates in attendance were YCL members. Eight to ten were described as "dodgy or don't know"(a euphemism for membership of a Trotskyist group), and a further 26 were described as "more or less broad left" but without any clear political allegiances. Following the NUSS third annual conference in 1975 Emmerson's report to the YCL Executive was equally gloomy. He estimated that "for the first time delegates belonging to youth political groups were in a minority".[472] That said, the NUSS's expanding membership provided some cause for celebration; this was reported to have risen to around 15,000 by 1975, a reasonable achievement given the hostility many activists continued to face in schools. In addition the bulk of the 78 delegates in attendance supported the plea Emmerson made in his retirement speech to continue "to show themselves as a responsible organisation which wants to contribute positive ideas to education, and not cause disruption".[473] Emerson's request for "responsibility" reflected the YCL's continuing belief that constructive engagement with education authorities was the most effective mechanism of building wider popular support for the union and of achieving NUSS aims.

By 1977/1978 though, the YCL's grip over the union's leadership had been irretrievably undermined. Its own post-mortem into how this happened acknowledged that its focus on winning credibility and legitimising the NUSS had led it to underestimate the importance of grassroots activity with school students themselves. As the Official Report to the YCL's 1977 National Congress admitted, YCL work at a national level, including within the NUSS, was "not accompanied by effective campaigning and social, cultural and educational activity among the majority of young people". Any work that was undertaken was "confined...to a very small number of politically conscious young people", when its efforts should really have been directed at building "a bold and open approach to the mass of youth". This failure to engage with pupils and young people on the ground had, it was accepted, undermined the League's grip on the NUSS and indeed support for the union itself among school students. "Today", the report lamented, "some school students do not see the need to be members of the NUSS".[474] Worse still, the League's marginalisation from the NUSS threatened the very viability of the YCL itself:

This reduction of YCL work in the NUSS has meant that many potential YCLers have been lost to the League—an intolerable situation at a
time when League membership is falling and undoubtedly a contribu-
tory factor to that situation...it is of the utmost importance that the EC
re-emphasises that activity on the schools front is indispensable.[475]

The YCL's loss of control over the NUSS was reinforced at the
union's annual conference in 1978, when 16 year old Labour party
member John Mumford was elected president. Mumford had accused
the former leadership of being too "bureaucratic", of "sticking to proce-
dure" and "being extremely constitutional, rather than discussing what
needs to be done and getting on and doing it". "People have finally
begun to realise", he announced, "that we're not the Transport and
General Workers' Union".[476]

In particular the YCL and the NUSS were slow to relate to the
struggle within schools that was developing around opposition to the
far-right.

As the long post war boom came to a shuddering halt the Labour
government of 1974-79 implemented a series of drastic cuts to social
spending. Unemployment—especially youth unemployment—rock-
eted. By 1976 unemployment had reached 1.2 million.

In an atmosphere of crisis the nazi National Front started to grow.
From 1974 there were increasing clashes between skinhead Nazis and
anti-fascist activists and where the Nazis started to gain a foothold,
racist violence followed.

In the English district elections of 1976 the NF averaged 8.9 percent
of the vote in the 168 seats they stood in; in Blackburn eight National
Party candidates received over 40 percent of the vote. In the
Metropolitan and County elections of 1977 the NF took over 200,000
votes in the 413 seats that they contested—over 120,000 in London.[477]

Then in the so-called "hot summer" of 1976 issues of "race" and
racism were pushed to the fore in British politics. There was widespread
and inaccurate media coverage of two Asian families from Malawi being
housed in a hotel. William Whitelaw, Tory shadow home secretary,
attacked Asian arranged marriages. The old racist politician Enoch
Powell revealed the existence of the Hawley Report, a government report
that raised fears about the "uncontrollable" Bangladeshi entry to Britain.

And then in Southall a Sikh school boy, Gurdip Singh Chaggar, was murdered by a racist gang. In the aftermath BNP activist John Kingsley Read told a fascist gathering that Gurdip's death meant "one down, a million to go".

The language in the rest of Read's speech was incendiary, liberally dowsed with the most disgusting racist slurs—and resulted in him being charged with incitement. But at the trial in 1977 Judge Neil McKinnon directed the jury that the law did not cover "reasoned argument in favour of immigration controls or even repatriation". He added that it was difficult "to say what it is that this defendant is alleged to have done that amounts to a criminal offence". The jury found Read not guilty and he left the dock with McKinnon "wishing him well".[478]

In this atmosphere the NF attempted to organise and recruit among school students. Weyman Bennett recalls what life was like growing up in London at that time:

> I was brought up in the East End of London. It was a very political area. There were lots of gas workers and dockers in the area. The Communist Party had a presence and there were also a few families which included Holocaust survivors. My own family were Jehovah's Witnesses and a number of people in the local congregation were Holocaust survivors. And there were people who remembered and had been active in the Battle of Cable Street in 1936. So there was a "collective memory" about Nazism and what it meant.

But by the end of the 1970s the National Front were trying to move into the area:

> They started selling their youth paper *Bulldog* outside my school—and there were a group of us in school who were determined to stop them. We'd see these lads on the NF marches, or selling their paper in the town—but we knew they had to come back to school. So there'd be these nazi skinheads and then us—punks and soul boys—who were determined to get them out of the school. There would be fights in school and sometimes in lessons. I remember there was a pretty significant confrontation in a music class one day. And that then spilled out to the surrounding area. There were often running battles down Stratford High Street as we tried to clear them off the street. And it wasn't like now. There was no CCTV, the police response was often really slow so sometimes these battles would last for a couple of hours.

But eventually we physically removed the NF from the school and stopped them selling their rag.[479]

Through the Anti Nazi League, Rock Against Racism and School Kids Against the Nazis young people were drawn into a more activist politics that challenged the system, and demanded a different type of politics from the NUSS. The activities of SKAN and RAR were able to draw young people away from the Nazi organisations. John Newsinger remembers one case in particular:

> I was teaching in a school throughout the late '70s and '80s and well remember the impact the ANL and RAR had. The school went from being covered in NF graffiti to having a large contingent of kids go into Leicester to stop the NF marching. I remember seeing a kid who had started out sympathetic to the NF jumping up and down on the roof of a police car![480]

In terms of school student politics, by the late 1970s to many young left-leaning potential recruits the YCL had come to look politically and culturally moribund. Its "social, cultural and educational" activity, such as it was, palpably failed to tap into the emerging political movements in the later years of the 1970s, something that other parties of the left—most notably the Socialist Workers Party—proved remarkably adept at. As Smith notes, the SWP's youth oriented campaigns were particularly appealing to a new generation of young people, whose ideological instincts had been stimulated by the anarchic, more militant, confrontational political messages emanating from the emerging youth culture movements of reggae, ska and punk.[481] The anti-racist campaigns—Rock Against Racism, the Anti Nazi League and School Kids Against the Nazis—were especially successful in helping to politicise young people, and the SWP was central to the operation of all three groups.

While the pages of the YCLs youth journal *Cogito* discussed "Aspects of ideological struggle for the British road to socialism and the Young Communist League",[482] the first issue of SKAN wooed potential recruits with a collection of features on "Red Teachers", SKAN/ANL successes in fighting fascism, Brian Clough's opposition to the Nazis, and RAR (with Tom Robinson, Steel Pulse and the Sex Pistols namechecked).[483] Whereas the YCL advocated non-violent, peaceful opposition to the fascist National Front, SKAN accepted the need for physical confrontation where necessary, to the extent that it even helped to organise self-defence classes for school students in areas where fascists were active.[484] This message resonated with an increasingly alienated rebellious youth, who were inclined to favour direct confrontational political action. Rehad Desai, at the time a young SWP member and pupil activist, recalls the impact that the SKAN campaign had on school students who were attracted by its radical, combative style:

> A lot of youngsters had great success in their schools or their communi-
> ties organising around the ANL, School Kids Against the Nazis. There
> was pop culture, there was the Sex Pistols, you know, punk reggae and
> stuff. We were feeding into a subculture—Rock Against Racism, and
> we felt that, you know... It was generation revolt... We had a set of mili-
> tant politics. We were about actively fighting on the streets.[485]

The spectacular RAR gigs were the icing on the cake, exposing tens of thousands of young people to left politics in a way the YCL could not possibly hope to compete with, or replicate. The following account of the RAR Northern Carnival, held on 15 July 1978 and featuring Steel Pulse, the Buzzcocks and China Street, captures the sense of excitement that characterised RAR/ANL events:

> Starting at Strangeways, Manchester the enormous march wound
> through the city centre to Alexandra Park. Reggae, Punk and Steel
> bands on lorries, banners from Anti Nazi League branches, Trade
> Unions, anti rascist groups, political parties and SKAN (School Kids
> against the Nazis) and Anti Nazi League "lollypops" everywhere...
> Badge sellers were everywhere as well so all the spectating public
> seemed to be ANL supporters... At Alexandra Park the massive audi-
> ence enjoyed the fine weather and the bands. Numerous groups ran
> stalls and leaflets were given out galore. People of all ages from through-
> out the north of England had come to Manchester to have fun and
> stand up to be counted as one of the many to be firmly anti-racist.[486]

SKAN, RAR and the ANL were inspired primarily by a determina-
tion to destroy fascism, but their appeal inevitably expanded the SWP's powerbase among young activists generally, including those linked to the NUSS. And this occurred at a time when pupil activism had begun to take a distinctly more militant turn once more.

In March 1978, for instance, a series of school strikes swept across Britain, sparked initially by the cancelling of school meals due to industrial action by teachers. This shift within the pupil power movement took many contemporary commentators by surprise. The *Guardian*'s editorial on the protests expressed shock at the "wildcat walkouts" organised by activists within the "normally well-disciplined National Union of School Students".[487] The NUSS leadership itself was also taken aback at the rapid spread of militancy within its rank and file. In an interview with the *Guardian* in the immediate aftermath of the strikes the NUSS treasurer Martin Rosenbaum admitted that although "many… members had been involved in disturbances, no instructions had gone out nationally" and that he was "surprised at last week's trouble".[488]

"Rebellion", exclaimed the *Daily Mail*'s headline on 6 March in one of its articles on the March 1978 strikes. "Pupils took to the streets in their thousands" after "demonstrations of pupil power were held as far apart as Penrith and Portsmouth", it reported. As ever, it is difficult to ascertain the true extent of the protests, but the geographical spread of areas confirmed to have experienced school strikes—Penrith, Portsmouth, Birmingham, Stoke-on-Trent, Wolverhampton, Leicester, Telford, Hartlepool, Tamworth, Prestatyn, Barry, Middleborough, Bradford, Leeds, Canvey Island, Liverpool, Highgate—suggests large scale disruption.[489] Even pupils at Harold Wilson's former school, Huddersfield's Royds Hall Secondary, participated in the protests, barricading themselves in classrooms for most of the day.[490]

Attempts were made by sections of the media to convey the impression that the protests were overtly anti-teacher, doubtless with the intention of undermining support for the teachers' industrial action. The *Guardian*'s analysis was more circumspect, noting that the NUSS leadership had made it clear that, in most cases, the intention was to support, not oppose the teachers' work to rule, and to condemn the failure of local authorities to accede to the teachers' demands.[491] "We basically favour the teachers' pay claim", announced Martin Rosenbaum.[492] Rosenbaum was right. In many areas pupils were expressing solidarity with the teachers' cause. In Stoke-on-Trent, for instance, around 200 pupils marched to the education offices and presented a 600 signature petition demanding that the teacher's pay demands be accepted.[493] Pupils in a number of other towns and cities, including Bradford and Birmingham, pursued similar tactics, walking out of school and marching to local education departments to present their grievances. Council staff in Canvey Island had to be locked in their offices for their own protection when around 300 pupils tried to storm the building, "thumping on windows and shouting".[494] Pupils in Birmingham were said to have been the "most militant" and persistent in their protests, as "Hundreds of banner-waving and chanting pupils marched to the city's education office in relays all afternoon".[495]

The protests sparked a particularly authoritarian response from the police. Eighteen pupils from Willenhall comprehensive in Wolverhampton were arrested after their attempts to picket a nearby school led to a confrontation with police who tried to bar their path. A further 12 arrests were made in Hartlepool after windows were broken in schools. Heads across the country responded in an equally authoritarian manner, initiating a programme of mass canings of pupils suspected of being involved in organising the strikes. The *Times* reported on what it described as a "day of retribution", which included a series of suspensions, detentions and beatings. Up to 50 boys were caned at Poleworth School in Tamworth and a further 20 at Tudor Grange comprehensive in Solihull.[496] At Harold Wilson's former school in Huddersfield, 24 children were caned on their backsides for participating in the protests.[497]

In the aftermath of the strikes feelings were clearly running high. In Telford a decision was made by local police to close secondary schools until the Monday of the following week, disrupting the education of 2,600 of the towns' pupils.[498] Attention quickly turned to establishing the cause of the protests. Of course the possibility that the pupils were airing genuine grievances was barely considered. Rhodes Boyson wrote an extensive opinion piece in the *Mail* claiming that the strikes were mere "copycat" events, with children replicating the "irresponsible" behaviour of their peers:

> The pupils' action *does* prove that children learn from example. If the teacher is responsible and self-disciplined so will his pupils be. If he takes militant action and withdraws from pupil supervision, pupils will withdraw from pupil order and become irresponsible. In addition pupils see daily on television assorted groups of agitators and strikers chanting inanities and claiming rights at the expense of the community. Pupils have learnt to do the same.[499]

As we have maintained throughout this book, the incidence and scale of school student political action *has* invariably been shaped by the wider industrial and political context in which it has occurred. Pupil protests are more likely to develop during periods of protracted industrial and/or political conflict, and the school strikes of March 1978 certainly fell into this category. However, it is wrong to assume as Boyson did, that the protests were simply a "copycat" reaction, a case of children naively mimicking adult militant activity. Pupil activists will have taken inspiration from the growing militancy of their adult trade unionist counterparts (the growing rebellion of low paid workers against the Labour government's austerity measures) and this may have influenced the strategies they adopted to articulate their concerns. However, pupils themselves had genuine grievances. The cancelation of school dinners, for instance, constituted more than a minor inconvenience for the millions of pupils from disadvantaged backgrounds who were reliant upon free school meals for their daily sustenance. More generally the school environment continued to be an authoritarian, brutal experience for many pupils, as the UK remained one of the few European countries to continue to sanction legalised beatings of school students. Regarding the more militant tactics that were utilised—school strikes—pupils had every right to be disillusioned with the conservative collaborative approach that had hitherto shaped the NUSS political strategy. It had generated official recognition and status for the union but had ultimately failed to deliver on any of the pupil power movement's substantive aims, such as the abolition of corporal punishment and greater school democracy. A new more militant generation of pupil activists was emerging, one far more inclined to use confrontational political action to achieve its aims.

As had been the case with the pupil protests in the late 1960s and early 1970s, others located blame for the pupil disturbances with "Trotskyist agitators" polluting the minds of the nation's school children. Ron Cocking, treasurer of the National Association of Schoolmasters, a union notoriously hostile to the principle of school democracy, was among those who detected such an influence. "It is the extreme left wing idiots who are doing this", he said. "They really are abysmal when they try to make schools into a political playground."[500] Cocking's suspicions were seized on and reinforced by the media when it emerged that Labour Party Young Socialist activists in Birmingham, reportedly one of the more militant areas, had leafletted schools in the city during the strikes encouraging pupils to stand up for their rights and to join the NUSS. "Leaflets from the Young Socialists' national committee of the Labour Party encouraging school anarchy have been handed out in the Northfield area of Birmingham where there have been violent demonstrations during the past two days", stormed the *Mail*.[501]

Within days the offending LPYS leaflet, entitled *School Students Have Rights Too*, was the subject of parliamentary questions with Tory MPs and Lords alleging young militant Labour activists were responsible for provoking the burst of pupil protests. Fred Silvester, Tory MP for Manchester Withington raised the issue at prime minister's question time, equating the left's attempts to organise pupils with NF infiltration in schools.[502] Tories demanded the leaflet be withdrawn. The Labour government's initial reaction to the Tory demands, provided by Lord Donaldson, a DfES Minister, was relatively dismissive:

> Although the Government did not publish the leaflet, we support some of the policies contained in it, although not all. Obviously, the Government have no power to require the withdrawal of leaflets they did not produce; nor would they wish to have such powers.[503]

The commissioning of the leaflet had actually been approved by Labour's National Executive Committee (NEC) the previous July, which probably helps explain Donaldson's initially cautious response. However, the NEC had been unaware that respondents to the leaflet would be sent NUSS literature by the LPYS along with invitations to join the union.[504] Just two days after Donaldson's dismissive response to Tory allegations, the Labour leadership buckled. Prime Minister James Callaghan succumbed to the mounting pressure to act, announcing that Reg Underhill, Labour's national organiser, would conduct an investigation into the links between the LPYS and the NUSS.[505] As we saw previously, this was not the first time that a sitting prime minister would order an inquiry into pupil power activists. It was not just pressure from the Tory benches that forced Callaghan's hand. The NEC had also received complaints about the leaflet's contents from some of its own local constituency associations and MPs.[506]

Underhill's report was presented to the organising committee of Labour's NEC on 10 April. Particular attention was devoted to the five-page NUSS document that was sent out to the leaflet's respondents.

This was officially entitled *How to set up a branch of the NUSS at your school*, though Underhill gravely noted that sections of the press had referred to this as the "ABC to chaos in city schools". More controversially for the Labour leadership it also set out tactics for prosecuting campaigns over pupil grievances, including petitions, protests to the local education authority, press campaigns, occupations of premises, non-cooperation with school authorities, walkouts and disruptions.[507] Each of these tactics had been embraced by pupil activists in the recent spate of school strikes with a good deal of success, adding to the sense of alarm within Labour's Executive. Shirley Williams, the DfES's secretary of state, was said to be furious "that Labour Party funds should be used as a means of recruitment for a body that has no association with the party, and which is openly urging pupils to engage in demonstrations, occupations of school buildings and other actions to disrupt school life".[508] In response Andy Bevan, the LPYS's national officer, vigorously defended the leaflet. "There is a movement of anger growing in the schools", he insisted, before going on to defend the LPYS's efforts to politicise school students. "If you think you will keep politics out of our schools", he argued, "you are living in the past".[509] Needless to say, the LPYS's planned second reprint of *School Students Have Rights Too* was cancelled forthwith and after this the LPYS's work with school students was severely compromised.

By contrast the SWP began to play a much greater role in organising pupils. A 1978 pre-annual conference bulletin, written by Roger Green the party's Youth Organiser, highlighted the success of the SKAN, ANL and RAR campaigns, drawing attention to their potential for radicalising their young participants:

> A large number of school students and school leavers are rapidly becoming attracted to organisations and campaigns in which the SWP is active. We must discuss how they can be brought closer to us. Today's rebels in schools can become tomorrow's politically aware industrial militants and as party members they are a source of enthusiasm and new ideas... For example Rock Against Racism has encouraged the anti-racist element, and in terms of its size, has had a massive influence among rock fans.[510]

The militant turn that characterised pupil activism in 1978 had already provided young SWP activists with an opportunity to expand their influence within the NUSS, which had, according to Green, hitherto been little more than "a plaything of the YCL with a self-imposed 'no politics' rule". More though could be done. "It is clear", he stated, "that a youth movement must be built where youth are and that is essentially the schools. That is where we should direct our work". The enormous success of SKAN should, Green argued, be harnessed to build the party's support among school students:

> SKAN is based in the schools. This has a big advantage. It means that a few anti-nazi students can communicate their ideas to a large audience, the average size of a school today is well over a thousand. SKAN is probably more important than the Right to Work Campaign or RAR in terms of influencing and attracting large numbers of youth.

Young SWP activists finally gained control of the NUSS at its annual conference in 1979, when 16 year old Rehad Desai, who had "cut his teeth" in SKAN, was elected president. He remembers the day he and other SWP supporters succeeded in winning key national positions in the union:

> There were about ten or 15 of us...that went to the NUSS conference... in '79. I was 16 then. And we managed to work out the transferable voting system. The YCL was really dominant. They hadn't been doing anything. It had turned very much into a sort of lifestyle approach. You know, a lot about...sexual politics and stuff like that. We managed to win the day...together with some kids from the IMG, and I became the national chairperson of the NUSS [for two years].[511]

Erika Laredo, an NUSS activist from Leeds, also recalls that year's conference. She had arrived at the North London venue leading a sizeable collection of non-SWP delegates from Yorkshire, and remembers being struck by the dedication and organisational skills of the SWP activists she met there, who immediately identified her group as potential allies. Looking back, she remembers being impressed by her London-based SWP counterparts and their methodical, sophisticated approach to school student politics. "The SWP", she notes, "obviously had organisers there who understood student politics in a way that we didn't, or I thought that we didn't. But they obviously knew, because we had quite a big organised contingent, that maybe I was the person to talk to".[512] These talks led to a collaborative pact, which, in combination with other more militant delegates, culminated in her election as the NUSS's northern officer, and the election of Desai as president. Steve Marsh, another SWP activist, was elected as national officer.

Now under the influence of young SWP activists, the NUSS continued to move leftwards. This more militant swing was reflected in the political content of its campaigning magazine *Blot*. First published in 1978, *Blot* had initially been funded by a £1,600 grant from the Gulbenkian Foundation. It quickly generated considerable outraged commentary in the press.[513] *Blot*'s critics accused it of being an offensive subversive journal that threatened school authority. Of course, to an extent this was precisely what it was intended to be! Its seditious content led many schools to formally ban the magazine, and there were instances of pupils being disciplined and indeed suspended for distributing it. One NUSS activist, the 15 year old son of a prospective Labour parliamentary candidate, was transferred to another Luton school after being accused of merely *planning* to sell the magazine (not actually selling it!).[514]

As with the *Little Red Schoolbook* in the early 1970s, it was the *Blot* articles on subjects like "masturbation", "contraception" and "two-timing" that generated the most moral opprobrium and interest in the press. "Sex shock in school magazine" exclaimed the *Daily Mirror* on the day of the first edition's publication. "A shock magazine containing controversial sex articles will go on sale today at hundreds of schools", it announced.[515] However, from its inception *Blot* was a relatively sophisticated blend of personal, political and campaigning content, designed to appeal to *all* school students and not just those already interested in politics. The second edition, for instance, contained features on personal issues (puberty, abortion, being gay in school), on school-related matters (homework, school dinners, bullying, school uniforms, religious education) and politics (the Tory government's education cuts and the fight against racism and fascism). It also included sections devoted to the various campaigns waged by NUSS activists across the country, drawing attention to instances where pupils had successfully challenged authority.[516]

Although every edition of *Blot* had contained a political element, later editions became more overtly political, a tendency which accelerated as the SWP's influence within the NUSS increased. The election of the Tory government in 1979 coincided with this SWP "takeover" of the union, and thereafter *Blot* exhibited an explicit anti-Thatcherite stance. This was epitomised by the message *Blot* sent to the incoming Conservative administration:

> Well, Maggie, what are you and your Tory government going to do to make our lives better and give us more choices? You want to close down our schools, make us pay more for school dinners, throw teachers on the dole and cut down outside visits like going to swimming baths, sports centres and on school trips. And just to save money for you and your rich Tory friends.[517]

Another article in the same edition entitled "Cutting up our lives!" called for pupils to engage in organised political opposition to Thatcher's government:

> The Tories like calling all unions "wreckers" and "vandals" for nothing. The *real* wreckers and vandals are in the government—out to destroy our lives. FIGHT THE CUTS—JOIN THE RESISTANCE!! [original emphasis].

There was no sign here then of the collaborative, conciliatory strategy of the earlier NUSS leadership. The call for pupils to engage in direct political action was replicated in subsequent issues of *Blot*. In another 1979 edition of the magazine, plans to picket the inaugural meeting of the Youth Parliament on 25 October were announced. This was the International Year of the Child (IYC), and the incoming Tory administration had presented the Youth Parliament as an illustration of its commitment to children's rights. Controversially the proceedings were to be opened by Thatcher herself, a development that infuriated the new leadership to NUSS, who had inherited their predecessor's plans to send delegates to the conference. The NUSS had already been critical of the Thatcher government's commitment to extending children's rights throughout the IYC, particularly its refusal to ban corporal punishment or extend pupil democracy in schools.[518] The prospect of hearing Thatcher proclaim the virtues of children's rights at the Youth Parliament, particularly in the light of the education and welfare cuts that had recently been announced, was a step too far. Behind the scenes plans were made to disrupt Thatcher's address.

Erica Laredo recalls the considerable efforts herself, Rehad Desai and Steve Marsh put into organising the demonstration. Their view was that the NUSS's former leadership had uncritically collaborated with what was, in effect, little more than a stage-managed "pantomime" of a conference, and they were determined not to give credence to such an event:

> The [YCL] people before us were very, like, you know, would go along...with these people [the organisers of the conference], and they were quite bureaucratic about everything they did, and we were very "punk" about everything that we did. So we said, right, what we should do is have this disruptive event...because we knew it would get national coverage, because it was like an opening of the youth parliament... It would have been the very first one, and at the opening we got these very young people, our young people, to stand up and make protests... We... had people outside, but we had delegates, and as soon as it was all going to be opened, they got up and spoke... So that was a real high point. It took a lot of organising. [519]

On the day the conference opened the protest inside the hall was led by Rehad Desai. He defied the attendant Scout troops, who had been employed to keep order, and questioned the legitimacy of Thatcher's presence at the conference. "We deny you the right to speak", he interjected, "because you are breaking the UN declaration of the Rights of the Child. You are cutting our education left, right and centre". Desai was ejected for his barracking of Thatcher, but the disruption carried on when another group of NUSS activists continued to berate, slow hand clap and interrupt Thatcher before being removed themselves.[520] The plan had worked though, and the demonstration achieved national newspaper and television coverage. Much of this coverage was inevitably negative, but it did serve to expose the hypocrisy of the Tory administration's commitment to "children's rights". Erika Laredo views this as one of the high points of her period as the NUSS's national organiser.

A month later the publication of the NUSS leaflet *How to Disrupt your School in 6 Easy Lessons* confirmed the more militant tone of its leadership:

> First pick a campaign—any popular grievance like caning, uniform, petty rules, exams, "useless lessons" will do. Hold a meeting and organise a petition. When your petition is ignored (as usually happens), the school students will become angrier and be more prepared to take

direct action. Suggest a one day strike. Sometimes it's a good idea, if the head reacts by suspending people, to take some "shock action". How about an occupation?[521]

Before long many pupils across the country were heeding the call to demonstrate and strike. *Blot* documented many of these protests. Not all were entirely successful. The attempts of Birmingham NUSS activists to replicate the disruption caused by pupils in March 1978 were frustrated after strikers were harassed by police and threatened with arrest for breach of the peace. Chris, an NUSS activist who participated in the latest protest, was not disheartened by the experience—"we haven't been defeated", he wrote in *Blot*, "we have learnt our lessons and we're planning more strikes in the near future". Islington's NUSS activists were more successful in their protest against education cuts on 28 November 1979 and children from a number of schools heeded the union's strike call. Attempts by the police to disperse striking pupils failed and they made their way to a prearranged meeting point at Hyde Park. Barbara's account of the event, published in *Blot*, is worth quoting in some detail. As it explains, the pupils succeeded where their 1972 SAU predecessors failed, managing to break through security at County Hall to stage an occupation in the Inner London Education Authority's offices:

> By this time there were about 400 NUSS supporters along with masses of people from all over the country protesting about the cuts. Everyone marched to the Embankment where we were told to disperse and go home. For everyone else the demo was over but not for us—we decided to occupy County Hall, office of the Inner London Education Authority. We all sneaked into the building through different entrances. Once inside we barricaded ourselves in but the security guards were determined to get rid of us. They lashed out with chains that we were using to try and lock the doors. They threw chairs at us and even chucked one girl across the room. The police arrived and told us to leave—we agreed to. While we were leaving one girl was arrested for kicking a policeman (they said). We all crowded around the police car determined not to let it leave until we were told why she had been arrested. Again the police—like the security guards—used excessive violence and arrested another one of us. It just so happened that the two NUSS members arrested were black—could it be that the police are racist? The two of them were released and no charges made.[522]

Soon after, Red Rebel, the SWP's youth organisation hosted a well-attended conference of NUSS school pupil activists at the Polytechnic of Central London. The meeting, chaired by Daniel Ashton the NUSS's national secretary, listened to speeches on school democracy and activism from a range of speakers including Tony Cliff and Paul Foot.[523] Following the conference around 100 NUSS activists joined in a TUC mass demonstration against the Tory government, an act which infuriated the Tory MP John Carlisle, who called upon William Whitelaw, the Home Secretary, to ban the union:

> I am concerned that this union is inciting juveniles to break the law by playing truant from school. I would like to see it banned from all schools and strongly condemned by the TUC, the Labour Party and all education authorities.[524]

Thereafter Carlisle began something of a crusade against the NUSS, submitting numerous questions to ministers asking them to look into the union's activities, particularly in his Luton constituency. In April he asked the following question of Neil McFarlane, under-secretary at the DfES:

> Is my hon Friend aware of the activities of the National Union of School Students, which, with local Labour Party support in my constituency, is encouraging pupils to play truant as well as distributing obscene literature and disrupting classes? Will he consider recommending to local education authorities that that obnoxious organisation is banned from schools?[525]

"Such behaviour", McFarlane replied, "is to be totally deplored".

In reality the NUSS was already banned in many schools, the vast majority of which had never recognised the union. In the few schools where it was recognised it was invariably tolerated rather than embraced. Heads often rapidly moved to close the union down when demands made by activists moved beyond what they deemed acceptable. Chris Fuller's experiences in Norwich were fairly typical. The school head's initial lukewarm reception to the NUSS rapidly evaporated once its demands moved beyond a desire to have different flavoured crisps, culminating in a series of events that led to Chris's suspension from school:

> In my school, we did have quite a lot of [initial] success. So we organised NUSS meetings and people joined. I remember one meeting we

had in the lunchtime, and we had about 100 people there. And we managed to get things like an NUSS noticeboard... And then we organised a May Day mass rally in '74 in the main hall... It focused quite extensively on the extent to which the head had control of the school, and so as a result of that we were on the front page of the evening paper...and interviewed on *About Anglia*, which the head was obviously completely livid about... After the May Day mass rally my parents were called in to see the head. I think it was at that time that they accused us of being Communists (laughs) I think it was a warning really... So then it comes to a point where we use the school notice board to put up a sort of a flyer, a newsheet about what's happening, and it's in that newsheet that I'm pretty sure I call the headmaster a dictator, which, in effect, is the power that they have in the school. And following that my parents are called in...and told in no uncertain terms to withdraw me from school... I'd been suspended by that point.

On hearing of Chris's plight, his peers did hold an afternoon sit-in, refusing to attend classes, but ultimately the episode heralded the "effective crushing" of his school's NUSS branch. NUSS activists across the country faced similar levels of harassment, doubtlessly experiencing the same feelings of frustration and powerlessness that Chris still remembers to this day:

I remember that was really hard. I mean, you can imagine going through that...that was pretty tough. And you know that's probably something that people should remember, that when young people do this, it's not just that they're facing all the pressures that anyone else is facing when they're rebelling, but all the other stuff that they're dealing with as young people as well, and a feeling of powerlessness and so on. I feel quite strongly about that... It was hard for my parents as well, really hard for my parents, because it's quite public. [Interview with Chris Fuller, 19 March 2015]

NUSS activists had always faced victimisation and harassment from school authorities. While having severe consequences for many, including Chris, this did not necessarily threaten the viability of the union itself; it was a desire to resist and fight which inspired many thousands of pupil activists to join the NUSS in the first place.

However, by the late 1970s the union began to face another much more serious threat, this time from its ostensible senior partner, the

NUS. The NUS leadership, under the control of a "broad left" alliance of Communist Party and Labour Party members, had become concerned at the NUSS's growing militancy. It soon became evident that moves were afoot to separate the NUSS from the NUS and frustrate its work. In 1979 the NUS decreed that the NUSS should no longer be accommodated at its Endsleigh Street headquarters in London due to a "lack of space". This decision, which many saw as motivated by political rather than spatial issues, forced the NUSS to adopt a transient existence, basing itself in sympathetic London student union buildings. The NUS ratchetted the pressure up still further at its December 1979 conference, when delegates approved a national executive motion to reduce funding for NUSS from £7,000pa to £2,000.[526] A year later the NUS ceased funding for the NUSS altogether.[527] Steve Marsh, one of the SWP activists elected as a national officer of NUSS in 1979, recalls the difficulties they experienced as a consequence of this decision:

> The problem was, once the YCL had been kicked out, the NUS withdrew all its support and all its funding, and so we had no money and basically there were just people on the dole running the union out of different places around London... When I left [in late 1981], there was nothing more to do. They utterly destroyed it.[528]

The denial of much needed financial and political support made this a hugely difficult period for the NUSS's national officers. Some rank and file NUS members were sympathetic, but the NUSS was blocked from presenting its case for school student activism at key NUS conferences. Steve Marsh recalls the desperate measures they took to try and ensure their voices were heard. In one such instance, he and other NUSS officers armed with banners and placards, covertly sneaked backstage at a London NUS conference before bursting through the stage curtains to demand a hearing. Clearly unnerved by their dramatic entrance Trevor Phillips, the then NUS president, reluctantly allowed them make a short address to the 300 or so delegates. However, such opportunities became increasingly rare and the removal of NUS funding would ultimately seal the NUSS's fate.[529]

After 1980 the NUSS was kept alive through the voluntary efforts of its national officers. Funded by little more than weekly dole cheques and comradely assistance from supporters, Steve Marsh, Rehad Desai, Erika Laredo, Daniel Ashton and other activists sought to generate support for the union. Typically their tactics would involve unannounced visits to targeted schools where, armed with leaflets and a megaphone, they would seek to win over pupils to their cause. As Rehad Desai explains, the campaigning would entail:

> leafleting, meeting people, going to their school, impromptu meetings with a megaphone, seeing who turned up, seeing whether we could pull any action, and whether there was a willingness to take action. And that's how we set up, trying to set up branches where we could, and often we would be supported. We had quite an active student core around the SWP, and sometimes the follow-up work would be done by the students in the area.[530]

Their campaigns were not restricted to schools. Amusement arcades, shopping centres and other areas where pupils congregated would be targeted. Steve Marsh also recalls organising a week of action opposing army recruitment in his school, which culminated in an occupation of the local army recruitment office and the arrest of all those taking part![531] This direct approach to recruiting pupils to the NUSS was not appreciated by the authorities or the police. Sometimes the police would take them into custody, give them a stern warning, then release them without charge. On other occasions, as Rehad Desai recalls, they were bundled into police cars and driven into the countryside before being thrown out to fend for themselves:

> When I went…to organise students, I'd walk into the school and the police were called quickly and, you know, I'd be picked up a few times with the megaphone and dropped at the edge of town and told to "Fuck off back to London". You know, dropped in the middle of nowhere by police.[532]

As in the past, the press did not report pupil grievances objectively. Desai recalls a widely published image of him which was deliberately misconstrued to give the impression that he was a lawless, violent hooligan:

> It looks like I'm fronting a policeman… It looks like me, I'm telling a policeman, you know, "Come on…you want some?" And he's pointing his finger at me. But actually there's a fascist at the other side of the policeman, who's thrown a penny and told me "Go and have a wash,

you dirty nigger bastard", or something to that effect... It was quite an iconic image.[533]

There were some notable successes though, which galvanised the small band of NUSS national officers. Erika Laredo recalled her part in prompting a pupil protest in Leeds where, through leafleting and lobbying pupils, she contributed to a school strike in the city. Her efforts generated quite a stir locally. Edward Pollard, spokesperson for Leeds' Secondary Heads Association, took particular exception to Laredo's leafleting campaign. "It is not right that politics and political propaganda should be circulated in schools", he fumed. "Schools are there for purposes of education, and the children should not have political propaganda pushed down their throats". Local Tory MP Donald Kaberry was also affronted by one of Laredo's leaflets which he described as "obscene". He wrote to Attorney General Michael Havers asking if legal action could be taken against its authors. Apparently Havers agreed the article was "offensive" but did not think a prosecution would be successful. Laredo's efforts also outraged Labour's right-leaning Leeds MP Stan Cohen, who wrote to Home Secretary William Whitelaw and Education Minister Mark Carlisle, drawing attention to the "scurrilous literature distributed by the NUSS" in the city.[534]

Another noteworthy achievement, recalled by both Rehad Desai and Steve Marsh, was the demonstration they organised around the Right to Work campaign's 1980 March from Port Talbot to Brighton, where the Tory Party conference was being held. Youth unemployment had soared under the Tories. The number of under-19s without work had risen from 250,000 to 350,000 between January 1979-1980, and the Manpower Service Commission forecast that this would rise to 500,000 by April 1982.[535] The NUSS sought to drum up support for the Right to Work campaign via the pages of *Blot*:

> Since the Tories have got in, unemployment figures have shot up especially among school leavers. It will soon be getting to the stage where you're expected to be out of work when you leave school. That's why NUSS representatives all over the country voted at our last conference...to get down to Brighton on the day she speaks at the Tory conference on October 10 and give Thatcher a dose of her own medicine: A Short, Sharp Shock.[536]

In their attempts to induce pupils to support the march, Rehad Desai and Steve Marsh adopted the "megaphone" technique that they had used many times before, arriving unannounced at schools on the route, calling on pupils to back the demonstration. Their attempts in Port Talbot generated considerable alarm but little direct support, though pupils at a number of Brighton schools heeded their call to take action:

> I remember we organised strikes to coincide with the "Right to Work" march in the summer of 1980, which went from Port Talbot in South Wales to the Tory Party conference in Brighton... We tried to organise strikes in Port Talbot, not with a great deal of success, but we caused havoc at schools. Basically, Hardy [Rehad] and I walked into schools with megaphones and tried to get the kids to walk out, and we did the same in Brighton. In Brighton we had more success...a couple of schools came out. [Interview with Steve Marsh, 19 March 2015]

This would be one of the NUSS's final significant campaigns. The union was still partially active in October 1981, mainly due to the efforts of Steve Marsh, when a leaflet entitled "Make Blackpool Rock on 16 October" encouraged school students to demonstrate at that year's Tory conference. However, by then the NUSS had all but wound down.[537] While it was never formally dissolved, it effectively ceased to exist as a union as its exhausted national officials were no longer able to keep it afloat in the absence of any solid organisational structure or funding.

The demise of the NUSS was a blow for the pupil power movement but it did not herald the end of school student activism. Regular pupil strikes and protests over school-related matters continued in the early 1980s.[538] In addition the ANL continued to provide a platform for school student opposition to racism, and pupils were also attracted to the anti-apartheid campaign.[539] The Campaign for Nuclear Disarmament (CND) also attracted the support of large numbers of pupils. The campaigning body Schools Against the Bomb emerged to articulate the concerns and anxieties of school students about the issue, much to the dismay of conservative commentators and newspapers such as the *Mail*. True to form, they blamed pupil support for CND on left wing teachers and the proliferation of "peace studies" in schools.[540] As in the past they could not contemplate the possibility that school students were capable of articulating an informed, independent political standpoint.

This greater willingness among pupils to become involved in non-school related campaigns and protests is one of the key transformations during the period covered by this chapter. Pupils continued to express their dissatisfaction over issues related to their education. But from the late 1970s onwards the political battleground that pupils engaged with encompassed a much more diverse range of issues, many unrelated to their education. This is what fundamentally changed the ideological orientation and strategy of the union. It became a much more overtly *political* union for pupils, confronting the educational establishment and spearheading campaigns against, for instance, racism and unemployment. Other developments were also important in shaping the widening political horizons of pupils. More provocative forms of youth culture encouraged participants, including school pupils, to question and directly challenge all authority structures not just the school. Also significant was the election of a divisive Tory government, whose economic, social, defence and foreign policies alienated large sections of youth. The Thatcher government's support for South Africa's racist apartheid regime, and its role in generating a spiralling nuclear arms race, provided much of the impetus for pupil engagement with the anti-apartheid and CND campaigns. Nor were pupils and young people insulated from the educational and social security cuts imposed by the Thatcher administration, or the mass unemployment generated by their economic policies. These too would continue to prompt protest and opposition among school students throughout the early 1980s. In fact, as we show in the next chapter, it was concern over rapidly escalating youth unemployment rates that would influence the next major episode of pupil protest in 1985 when hundreds of thousands of pupils would march out of school in opposition to the Thatcher government's Youth Training Scheme.

STEVE MARSH (Sheffield, 1978-1980)
"There was an on-going war of attrition in the school"

I WAS brought up in Sheffield and in the 1970s the city was a very different place to what it is today. It was an industrial city, with strong labour movement traditions.

In 1978 I was 14 and I got involved with School Kids Against the Nazis (SKAN). A group of people who were a bit older than me leafleted our school about the Anti Nazi League. There was a contact address, so I wrote off and got heavily involved in SKAN and the ANL.

I very quickly became aware of power structures at school and I got in touch with others who were involved in SKAN across Sheffield. We wanted to set up a campaign about school kids' rights. And then, coincidently, we heard about the NUSS.

By this time I had joined the SWP and they put me in contact with other young people, especially in Leeds and then London. In the summer of 1978 I went to the NUSS annual conference. It was an incredible conference because the SWP and the IMG managed to kick the Young Communist League out of the national leadership of the Union.

I was very new to politics but I came back from the conference totally energised with a focus on building the NUSS in Sheffield.

At the time the NUSS had five basic demands.

- An end to school uniforms
- An end to corporal punishment
- An end to petty rules at school
- The right to organise as a union
- An end to education cuts

I went to a comprehensive in Sheffield. The city was one of the first to go comprehensive, but before that my school had been quite a prestigious grammar. So the staff were used to teaching mainly middle class students but now there were large numbers of kids from working class communities in the school.

The head teacher had been a former member of the Communist Party—but was an absolute authoritarian. Corporal punishment was used every day. It was a very brutal administration. And initially we were really quite respectful of authority, but that wore off!

My last two years of schooling were an almost constant battle with the authorities. We would leaflet the school regularly, sometimes national leaflets, sometimes written by us. This was the punk era and our leaflets reflected the punk aesthetic of the day.

We tried to spread out to other schools. We would turn up and leaflet a school and sometimes that would get new contacts. We also leafleted places where kids hung out in the town centre, amusement arcades and places like that. The leaflets would have stuff about racism, the Nazis, school, unemployment.

We organised lots of events. On one occasion we organised a public meeting and invited Rehad Desai to speak. The school authorities immediately tried to stop him speaking. Rehad produced a megaphone from somewhere and led the school out. The police were called. Everyone was really excited and it created an electric atmosphere in the school. It was a great day and remains one of the highlights of my life!

On another occasion we organised a week of action against army recruitment in the school and we ended up occupying the army recruitment office. We all got arrested.

There was an ongoing war of attrition in the school. And eventually they kicked me out. It was interesting—it took them two years to kick me out. In a sense that was because they were used to kicking people out for fighting or being violent. But in the NUSS we were clear that it was the schools and authorities that were violent. They used corporal punishment. We were non-violent and promoting greater democratisation of schooling and I think this gave them a problem as to how to deal with us.

Of course they tried to discipline us every day. They used the same tactics that the bosses were using against militants in the workplace: constant harassment and persecution. But actually kicking us out was difficult.

The year they kicked me out I stood for national office in the NUSS. I was elected as the national organiser—working with Rehad who had stayed on as president. I did the job for a year and then became the national Rebel organiser for about six months before I went back to college to do my A levels.

When I went to college the school informed them that I was a militant and should not be allowed to do my A levels! Luckily there was a network of comrades who taught me and helped me get through my exams.

My time in NUSS and my activity in school was a great period and it taught me an awful lot politically. I look back fondly on this time—they were heady days!

REHAD DESAI (London, 1977-1980)
"Stand up, speak out"

I WAS born in South Africa and brought up in exile in north London. The family had to leave South Africa because dad was heavily involved in the anti-apartheid struggle.

When I was 13 [in 1976] I remember watching the young people in Soweto and I was impressed by their bravery and their determination to tackle injustice. I decided I had to get involved. Dad directed me to some anti-apartheid meetings. I went along but these were full of people a lot older than me and the meetings weren't really appealing.

But by 1977 the women workers at Grunwick—the film processing plant in Willesden, North London—were on strike. They were tackling racism and fighting for their rights as trade unionists. It seemed much more vibrant, exciting and militant. I decided to go to the picket line. I remember getting up at 5am and joining the 7am picket. The day I went I remember Arthur Scargill and some miners being there.

In the aftermath I joined the SWP. I got heavily involved in School Kids Against the Nazis (SKAN). We wrote a fanzine which was about the Nazi threat, but it also covered a range of other political issues. In my school in Finchley it helped create quite a political atmosphere.

SKAN badges were banned in the school. So we used to wear them under our lapels. I went to the big anti-nazi demonstrations in Lewisham and then the Rock Against Racism carnival in Victoria Park in April 1978. My sister and I filled two coaches for the carnival just from our school. We had made our own school banner and we marched behind it into the park.

In our school the head was particularly unpopular. He ran the school with arcane rules, he liked to use corporal punishment. In later years he was revealed as a child molester.

But because he was so unpopular I got a lot of support—even from older students—when I raised political issues.

The end of 1978 was the Winter of Discontent. The caretakers at our school were out on strike. This meant there were problems with heating and the playgrounds were not salted even though it was icy. The school was very cold and dangerous. So we called a strike. Half the 1,000 students came out. We put pickets on and the dinner ladies refused to cross! We marched to other schools in the area and pulled three of them out.

I got an indefinite suspension. But dad was a lawyer and wrote to the school saying he would take legal action if I was not allowed back in. After a week I was back.

By this stage we had set up a Rebel group. There were a few SWP and Rebel students across the country and we went to the National Union of School Students annual conference. With the support of some members of the International Marxist Group we completely outflanked the Young Communist League and we were able to win key national positions. I became the national chair for two years from 1979.

We started to campaign against corporal punishment, school uniforms and for greater democracy in schools. In particular we had good groups in London and Sheffield. We led a lot of strikes, demonstrations and walkouts.

We produced 100,000 leaflets to distribute in schools. They were anti-authoritarian and got a good response. Militant working class kids were most concerned about corporal punishment and some were able to lead strikes against this. In some sixth form schools we managed to organise stunts against school uniforms. In a couple of schools the boys turned up in dresses and skirts and the girls in trousers.

In Brighton we managed to close quite a few schools down and marched with the Right to Work campaign to the Tory conference.

But once we were elected to leading positions in the NUSS the National Union of Students moved against us. At first we had free rooms in the NUS building and could use some of their facilities. But the Labour Party/Communist Party leadership of the NUS moved to try and shut us down.

The authorities moved against us as well. I would often turn up at a school somewhere in the country and be met by the cops. They would often shove me in their car, take me to the edge of town and chuck me out, telling me to fuck off.

By 1980 I was more or less running the NUSS on my own. We had very few resources. It was exhausting. For me, between the ages of 13 and 18 it had been full on. But by the end of 1981 I felt drained and dropped out for about nine months.

Though I returned to college and got involved again in the NUS.

I remain a committed revolutionary. My experiences in school student activism were very important. They taught me to stand up and speak out against authority. Schools are rule-bound, hierarchical places. It's not easy to speak out and challenge the authorities. But once you've done it, it becomes easier. It also taught me the importance if organisation. Of how to prepare, build support and organise to win.

ERIKA LAREDO (Leeds, 1978-1980)
"Strong campaigning can make a difference"

I WENT to Lawnswood High in Leeds. I was in the first year of a comprehensive intake, before that it had been a grammar school. There wasn't a great deal of politics at the school but I came from a political household. My dad was a political exile from South Africa. He'd spent time in Pretoria Central prison and so politics was part of family life.

I got directly involved in politics through the anti-Nazi struggle. The NF had a presence in Leeds and were pretty aggressive. I remember coming into the city one day and they were there making themselves felt. So I decided I had to get involved.

The ANL and Rock Against Racism were really strong in the city. Every Friday there were gigs. We were punks and the music, the cultural scene and the politics all merged together. The cultural stuff brought more kids towards us and created the milieu within which we could work politically.

I got involved organising coaches to ANL events. One demonstration in Leicester I remember as being particularly violent. The NF in Leeds used to target "red teachers" and "red students" and one day I got some razor blades sent through the post.

The anti-Nazi work fed into more general politics. Over the period we would get the same young people involved in CND activities, Right to Work marches, pro-choice events as part of the anti-Corrie Bill campaign. They all merged very much from what we were doing in the city centre.

We used to meet most Sunday afternoons in a pub. There would be

25-50 of us, all young, all wanting to do stuff. And interestingly the gender balance was excellent it was about 50:50 men and women.

We used to produce newsletters—in a fanzine style. The aesthetic was very punk. It was a time when we felt we could challenge and question all sorts of social norms. So we would have articles on all sorts of things. Unemployment, sexuality, racism, gender, music—they'd all be covered. I remember one time commissioning an article for a fanzine on masturbation.

In 1979 I went to the NUSS national conference in London. I wasn't a member of any organisation but it was a heated conference with a lot of debate over the direction school student politics should move in. I was 16 and got elected as the Northern organiser for a year. I left school and had a paid job to run NUSS activities in the north of England.

In was a contradictory job. In some ways it was quite lonely. You'd be in a basement writing and running off leaflets all day on a messy old Gestetner machine. But then it could also be very exciting if something happened or you managed to pull some activity. At Moorgrange Boys School in Leeds I leafleted over a period and eventually managed to get the school to come out over the issue of school uniforms. It felt good when you could deliver an outcome like this, when you'd worked hard to achieve it.

I spent a lot of time travelling from town to town. The reception was generally very good. I'd meet up with people, stay for a couple of days whilst sleeping on their floors and do some political work.

We would leaflet schools and try to organise some activity. Sometimes we were successful and could get a strike or a march, other times we were less successful and not much happened. I also got picked up by the police quite a lot. They rarely charged me, but I'd be picked up and kicked out of the town.

Organising in schools is difficult. There are short terms and just when you think you're getting somewhere there is a holiday, exams or something to disrupt the routine. The school authorities were also hostile and often they would try and involve the police. So there were often bursts of protest which were difficult to hold together. That's why, I think, we had greater success organising outside the school across the city.

I remember organising a demonstration at the very first Youth Parliament. We wanted proper recognition, representation and democratisation within the schools. This was one of the NUSS's key demands.

They set up the Youth Parliament. We felt this was a talking shop—an extension of the tokenistic school councils. It took a lot of work but as NUSS we organised a protest outside the meeting, but also had delegates inside. We got quite a lot of media coverage for our protest.

School student activism taught me a lot. It was an introduction to organised politics. It gave me confidence in myself and my politics. I remember talking at national demonstrations. I spoke in Trafalgar Square, I can't imagine myself doing that now!

It taught me that you could challenge authority and that strong campaigning can make a real difference. I'm convinced that our strong anti-Nazi campaigning made a real difference around Leeds.

Later I was a shop steward in NUPE and I used the same skills that I'd developed in NUSS work in the union as part of the rank and file network.

8

Striking for the right to work:
The Youth Training Swindle
and the strikes of 1985

THE NATIONWIDE children's strike against Youth Training Scheme conscription which took place in April 1985 occurred in the wake of the year-long miners' strike of 1984-1985 and was undoubtedly shaped by the heightened political atmosphere of the time. The miners' dispute evolved into a massive struggle between the employers, government and state on the one hand, and the miners and their supporters on the other. Like many others, school students were involved in support groups for miners and many were radicalised by their experiences of the dispute.

School students were involved early in the strike. Former pupil power activist Dave Gibson was working as a teacher in the Yorkshire coalfield during the strike. He recalls student strikes in March 1984. In three pit villages to the east of Barnsley students went on strike in solidarity with their mining relatives. The strike started at Thurnscoe and the striking students sent out flying pickets to the neighbouring villages of Goldthorpe and Darfield, where the school students joined them. The strike wave was stopped, not by repression or school discipline, but by the NUM. Head teachers asked the local NUM to come and talk to the students. Union officers thanked them for their solidarity but told them school strikes were not the way to win![541] As Dave says, though, what was interesting:

> was the instinctive solidarity of the kids who wanted to support their families and communities. They acted in ways—by sending out flying pickets, for example—that followed what was happening in the strike

and that their parents and brothers were doing at that point when they went to Nottingham to picket out miners there.[542]

The strike ended on 5 March 1985 when miners across the country marched back to work. But as the strike came to an end school students at a number of schools across the South Yorkshire coalfield re-joined the battle.

Dave worked in Honeywell School in Barnsley. The school was next to a working class estate where many mining families lived; many of the students in the school had dads or brothers on strike. By January 1985 there were a small number of miners in Barnsley who had gone back to work. Every dinner time there was a National Coal Board bus that would tour the estate and pick up those who had decided to go in. Dave remembers:

> A number of my fifth year students, today's year 11, were the children of striking miners. And their dinner time activity would be to go and join the protests—jeering at the scabs and throwing stones at the bus. By that time there was a feeling that the strike was going down to defeat and the students shared the feeling of frustration of their families. But I remember them discussing that they wanted to do more. And they decided to organise a strike in the school in solidarity with the strike, as an act of defiance. They brought the school to a standstill. The thing is, in the school, most of the teachers were sympathetic to what they were doing, even the head was sympathetic. But things spread from there. There was a one day strike at a number of schools in Barnsley and they held a march around the town.[543]

Just three days before the miners' strike finished students in the pit village of Armthorpe in Yorkshire struck, padlocked the school gates and formed a 150-strong picket line in front of the school. Bricks were thrown through the school windows, fences were torn down and strike-breaking pupils were harassed.[544]

Armthorpe had become accustomed to violent confrontations. The pit villages of Yorkshire had been under police siege for much of the previous year and the population had fiercely resisted persistent police harassment during the dispute. As the following comments made by a witness to a "police riot" that took place in the battle-hardened village illustrate, children were not insulated from the aggressive tactics adopted by the police:

The village was cordoned off for two days while the police tried to break the miners' picket line. Two children appeared on a television news programme to describe how they had seen police smash a local man's head against a lamp post.[545]

The head teacher at Armthorpe comprehensive suggested that the children who walked out of his school in March 1985 were simply copying scenes they had seen played out time and again by adults. Children, he said, "had dropped the game of cops and robbers in favour of police and pickets".

However, others within the school offered an alternative explanation. The head tutor for year three pupils said, "The strike was really about unemployment and, I suppose, if I really think about it, that the school perpetuates middle-class values in a working-class society". The school's deputy head supported this analysis: "It's becoming harder", he explained, "to make the pupils see the importance of school work. I just signed off three boys and said to them all 'just make sure you keep trying to find a job'...[but]...they almost all face disappointment—and unemployment benefits".[546]

School students in other pit villages embarked on similar protests. In February 1985 police were called to disrupt a demonstration at Edlington comprehensive near Doncaster after pupils marched out of school in solidarity with their striking parents. Six of the children who led the strike were suspended.[547] Like their counterparts in Armthorpe, these children had witnessed first hand the hardship, police harassment and violence that their parents had been forced to endure.[548]

In short the school strikes at Honeywell, Armthorpe and Edlington reflected the heightened political atmosphere in the coalfield in 1984/1985 and the realisation by students of the insecure future they faced on leaving school—a situation made worse by the threat hanging over the mining industry at the end of the strike.

The miners' strike had an impact beyond the coalfields as a number of student activists at the time make clear. Keir McKechnie from Glasgow told us:

> The activists of 1985 at St Augustine's school had had a year's experience of joining miners' support groups and had been radicalised by the strike.[549]

Hannah Sell lived not far from Cannock pit in the Midlands.

The miners' strike politicised us. I was in Wolverhampton, Cannock was not far up the road and everyone in the school was on one side or the other: you were either for or against the strike. I went collecting for the miners and the very idea of striking, in our young minds, had come from the miners. So there is no question that the miners' strike was key to what happened in 1985.[550]

Lois Austin from London was:

in a miners' support group and in my part of London we twinned with a mining village and I remember going up to take food and presents at Christmas. It had a big effect on us.[551]

Angela McCormick remembers:

[a]rguing about the miners' strike, defending the strike... In my Higher Modern Studies class there were some adult learners and I remember a mature student arguing with us about why we should support the strike. And I remember there were lots of students and former students from the school who you would see collecting on the streets for the miners and their families... The strike really dominated all our thinking in 1985![552]

In previous school strike waves the students had reflected the confidence of the general protest wave of the period, but the majority of the student demands were focussed primarily on the structure and organisation of education: school uniforms, corporal punishment, rote teaching methods, the demand for greater democracy in the school, etc. But the 1985 protests had at their heart much wider political concerns. The children involved in the mass school walkouts of 1985 were rebelling against what they perceived to be the failure of the government's economic and social policies, particularly in relation to youth unemployment.

School leavers were right to be concerned about their future prospects for work. At the time the national unemployment rate for 16 year olds was 23 percent. A further 45 percent were enrolled on the Conservative government's Youth Training Scheme (YTS), meaning that 68 percent of school leavers were without a proper job.[553] Even the government's Manpower Service Commission (MSC) could not fail to acknowledge the scale of the difficulties young people faced, referring in its annual report to a "bleak picture of worsening unemployment rates among the young and lengthening periods on the dole".[554]

The YTS was the principal mechanism Tory ministers used to manage youth unemployment in the early to mid-1980s. From its inception it was hated by young people forced onto the low paid schemes, and in March and April 1985 it was the spark that ignited the next wave of mass school strikes in Britain.

Introduced in 1983 to replace its predecessor the Youth Opportunities Programme (YOP), the YTS was ostensibly intended to provide young unemployed people with opportunities for training and work experience. Under the scheme employers were encouraged by the government to make 12 month "training" places available to out of work 16-18 year olds. The wages of the trainees in 1985 were £26 per week—about half the average for regular youth employment. These wages were paid entirely by the state along with an additional subsidy to employers to cover on-site costs. The wages themselves were the subject of considerable controversy and because of the low rates of pay, many young people came to see the scheme as little more than exploitative slave labour.[555]

The question of whether young people should be forced to participate on the YTS was another major area of disaffection and contention. When the YTS was initially conceived in a 1981 White Paper, the intention had been to include powers allowing the Department of Health and Social Security (DHSS) to deny access to supplementary benefit to young people who refused to participate. However, faced with opposition from trade unions and from within the MSC, the body tasked with responsibility for delivering the scheme, ministers grudgingly backed down.[556]

Theoretically then, participation on the YTS was voluntary and 16-18 year olds could remain on supplementary benefit if they chose to do so. But as Conservative ministers gradually tightened the social security system during the 1980s the pressure applied on young people to enroll on the YTS increased. For instance, as part of the DHSS's 1984 drive against "malingering", the Social Security Policy Inspectorate (SSPI) interviewed all young people declining to join the training scheme. The clear aim was to encourage participation through subtle, or not so subtle, coercion.[557] During 1984 the pressure on young people to engage with the scheme intensified. Careers officers were instructed to report to Unemployment Benefit Offices those who had refused or terminated a YTS placement, with a view to sanctioning their benefit for non-compliance.[558] In the Commons Ray Whitney, Tory parliamentary under-secretary at the DHSS, justified this shift with reference to an obscure clause in Labour's Social Security Act (1975).[559] Many careers officers felt that the moral and legal basis of this move was questionable and refused to comply with the instruction. Some did comply though, and between September 1984 and May 1985 309 16-17 year olds had their Supplementary Benefit reduced as punishment for not accepting a place on a YTS.[560]

The issues of low pay and compulsion were not the only aspects of the YTS to attract controversy. Contemporaries also raised questions about the quality of the placements offered under the YTS. They alleged that in most cases the training provided on the YTS was largely irrelevant to the needs of the trainee and that the opportunities on offer did little to open up avenues to permanent full-time work.[561] In fact the scheme did not contain any mechanisms at all for monitoring on the job training, making it impossible to assess the suitability or quality of placements even if there was political will to do so.[562]

Critics argued that the YTS was motivated principally by a desire to exert control over young unemployed people and to remove them from politically damaging unemployment statistics, while providing a cheap, disciplined pool of labour for employers.[563]

Analysis of internal unpublished and confidential SSPI surveys on the functioning of the YTS show that such concerns were justified. One such survey circulating around Whitehall at the beginning of 1985 provided a damning indictment of the scheme. Based on interviews with young people in different parts of the country, the research identified a number of reasons why school leavers were reluctant to enrol on the YTS. Many potential participants, the report found, took a "cynical view of it being cheap labour, achieving nothing, and leading nowhere". Two thirds of those interviewed "expressed hostility, or at best indifference" towards the YTS. The report also examined the reasons why participants frequently dropped out of the scheme. This was found to be due to poor quality placements rather than a lack of motivation or laziness. "They spoke of boredom, cheap labour, doing work they had not expected to do, not doing work they had expected to do, not being given any proper training, and so on." The author of the report, a senior SSPI official, expressed some sympathy for the plight of trainees who felt disillusioned after their YTS experiences. Many young people, he noted, "had embarked on YTS quite willingly, only to leave some time later, disappointed or even embittered". "One can understand", he went on, "the despair of a girl, embarking on a catering course with some degree of enthusiasm, being left to wash dishes for five weeks; or the lad whose placement in a garage involved a journey of 2 hrs each way".[564]

This was one of the first major in-house evaluations of the YTS, and it was not what senior DHSS and Department of Employment (DoE) officials had expected from one of their SSPI colleagues. Needless to say the findings were never made public. After reading the conclusions one senior DHSS civil servant expressed his alarm at the "rather jaundiced view of the YTS" presented by the research, adding that he "would not like to see the report published".[565] Another official concurred, noting that the "present instincts" of ministers "against publication of SSPI reports in general", and given the critical tone of the research findings, he could not see them disagreeing with recommendation "against the publication of this one".[566]

Clearly this kind of research had the potential to be politically explosive, given that it appeared to confirm much of what the trade unions and trainees were saying about the YTS.

The Labour Party did not oppose the principle of training schemes for young people but had raised misgivings about the YTS. When Norman Tebbit introduced it, Labour's employment spokesperson Harold Walker dismissed it as a "gangplank to the dole queue", which would do nothing to enhance the employment prospects of young people:

> Given the facts of the present situation—the abysmal prospects for young people, the wasted potential, the latent social backlash that we have already seen erupt in places such as Brixton and Toxteth—there can be no doubt that we have to create a new deal for the nation's youth. The Government's proposals…neither reflect the seriousness of the problems nor show much sign of understanding them.[567]

Labour's parliamentary campaign against the YTS contrasted the Tory programme with its own proposed £6 billion "Plan for Training", developed in collaboration with the Trades Union Congress (TUC). This was a voluntary two year youth training scheme which offered either a minimum inflation linked in-work wage of £34 per week or a £25 allowance for those wishing to continue with full-time study.[568]

Outside Parliament a range of campaigns developed to protest against youth unemployment. In the last chapter we looked at the interconnection between youth unemployment struggles and school student organisations with the NUSS's involvement in the Right to Work marches of the late 1970s and early 1980s. In the early 1980s Labour Party Young Socialists were involved in a number of campaigns against youth training schemes.

In November 1981 the Youth Trade Union Rights Campaign (YTURC) was launched to fight for improved pay and conditions and trade union representation on all government youth training schemes. The YTURC was made up mainly of LPYS activists, many former YTS trainees themselves. Although not constitutionally affiliated to the Labour Party, its close links to the LPYS allowed it access to Labour's Walworth Road as headquarters for campaigning. Up to 1985 it was generally seen as a legitimate voice of disenfranchised, unemployed youth within the Labour Party. Hence, at the 1984 Labour Party conference the YTURC was instrumental in securing the passage of a motion calling for a minimum YTS allowance of £55, the right for trainees to join trade unions, and for the right to a job at the end of the scheme.[569]

As youth unemployment soared and controversy over the Tory government's youth employment schemes increased, so did the profile of the YTURC. Although influenced by Militant supporters within the LPYS, it could call on a diverse range of support. Suggestions from Tory ministers that all young people not in work should in future be compelled to participate on the YTS widened YTURC's appeal still further. Its campaign against YTS conscription was formally launched at a press conference in the House of Commons on 24 January 1985 with musicians Paul Weller, then of the Style Council, and Brian Hibbitt of the Flying Picketts, and Labour MPs including Dave Nellist, Michael Meacher, Eric Heffer, Barry Sherman (Labour's front bench employment spokesperson), Chris Smith and Margaret Beckett.[570] Within weeks a veritable roll call of prominent musicians and celebrities signed YTURC's petition against making the YTS compulsory; they included Madness, Heaven 17, Bronski Beat, Big Country, Frankie Goes to Hollywood, Victoria Wood, Lennie Henry, French and Saunders, Robbie Coltrane, Tracy Ullman, Ruby Wax and Julie Walters.[571]

As the miners' strike came to an end a series of school strikes broke out across the country. In March 1985 an estimated 280 pupils walked out of Drummond Middle School in Bradford against the racist views of its head teacher, Ray Honeyford.[572] Honeyford's racist musings in the right wing *Salisbury Review* and the *Times Educational Supplement* were met with widespread opposition leading to his suspension and then forced retirement.

In other towns and cities including Newbury, Middlesbrough, Newcastle, Gosport, Havant, Portsmouth and Bradford, pupils engaged in protests about the disruption to their education caused by industrial action by teachers. These strikes could have been turned against the teachers but the intervention of activists made sure the strikes were anti-government rather than anti-teacher. In Havant and Portsmouth, for example, the LPYS produced a leaflet encouraging pupils to "Fight the Tories Not the Teachers". The leaflet also demanded an end to the "Youth Training Swindle", the abolition of corporal punishment and the establishment of school student unions.[573]

In Bradford a car was damaged and a shop window smashed as hundreds of pupils stormed the town hall in a demonstration over the cancelling of school dinners. A 13 year old boy's thumb had to be amputated after town hall security officers slammed a door shut on his hand in an attempt to hold back demonstrators.[574]

Galvanised by growing pupil activism across the UK, LPYS activists sought to harness and steer this into organised opposition to the Tories. Hannah Sell, a Wolverhampton school pupil in 1985, remembers how pupils like her took heart from the strikes occurring in all parts of the country:

> It was...the school student strikes in the coalfields which triggered the idea of a national demonstration... We thought that was a clear indication that young people could be mobilised to strike against youth unemployment and the YTS and that we could establish a mass school student movement".[575]

Nancy Taaffe concurs, arguing that there was a general feeling in the LYPS that "with Thatcher going after young people...there could be a movement, an opposition to youth training, to slave labour".[576]

In Glasgow YTURC activists began to organise a half-day strike for the 21 March against YTS conscription. The plan was to hold a rally at the City Halls where pupils would be treated to a gig by Scottish indie band the Bluebells, and speeches denouncing Thatcher's plans to make the YTS compulsory. An estimated 10,000 leaflets were printed and distributed encouraging those in years three (today's year 10) and above to participate in the demonstration. YTURC's secretary Tony Cox explained the rationale for the protest:

> All young people are under attack from this callous Tory government, and none more so than school students. Is it any wonder they get angry, when after eleven years of education the vast majority of them are offered a choice between the dole or cheap labour YTS. It is better for school students to get organised against the Tories rather than pointlessly lash out and riot.[577]

Despite attempts by teachers and education authorities to prevent the strike, the protest went ahead and pupils from schools all over the city descended on the centre of Glasgow. Support for the strike was overwhelming, taking the organisers by surprise. Pupils came from Motherwell, East Kilbride and Paisley, some hiring double decker buses to transport them to the protest. Jackie Galbraith, chair of the Scottish Young Socialists and one of the organisers of the strike, later described the day as "an unqualified success".[578] She described the jubilant scenes in City Halls:

> At the rally speakers and organisers were amazed when contingents of hundreds poured in, greeted with thunderous applause and roars of "here we go". Many waved homemade banners with slogans like "No slave labour" and "What about the future?"[579]

The biggest cheer of the day was reportedly for Denney Moohan, a sacked Musselburgh miner, who declared: "First it was the miners, then it was the teachers, now it's your turn. Don't let the Tories get you down. Stand up and fight".[580] The City Halls could not cope with the hordes of pupils seeking to gain entry, and the thousands unable to access the building descended on George Square for an impromptu mass protest. "Demo Chaos" was the headline of that day's *Evening Times*. Pupils, it reported, ran "wild through the city streets", chanting "We hate Maggie Thatcher" and "Down With the Youth Training Scheme".[581] James Doleman, a participant in the day's events, still remembers the electric atmosphere on the day:

George Square was mobbed. It was very excitable and a bit chaotic… It was a real carnival and the cops couldn't cope. I remember seeing some kids tapping coppers on their backs, they'd turn around and then someone else would knock their hat off![582]

Neither the education authorities nor the police had anticipated such high levels of support. Police in particular were taken aback by the scale of the protest. Angela McCormick, then a 16 year old pupil at St Augustine's Secondary, recalls a confrontation she and her friend Alison had with astonished police officers as they and other fifth year pupils led hundreds of children from her school on the 40 minute march to George Square:

We got to Saracen Cross…and we saw a police motor. We carried on walking and walking and two policemen stood in front of us on the pavement. We stopped, and they came up to us, and they go, " Where are you going, what are you doing?" I said "We're going to the city centre for the rally against the YTS… We're on strike"… And I'll never forget this…the policeman said, "School students don't go on strike". Me and Alison just looked at each other and said, "Well what do you call this then?" and we walked right round them. Brilliant…we just marched right passed them.[583]

The police had also underestimated the disruption once the march-ers reached the city centre. The *Glasgow Herald* reported, "At least 50 extra policemen were drafted in, some on horseback, to keep traffic moving and contain the youngsters." Special Branch and CID officers were also reported to have been hastily deployed, presumably to gather intelligence on the organisers of the demonstration. A police spokes-man described the events as "a very delicate situation".[584] Keir McKechnie recalls how the carnival atmosphere was soured by the more confrontational approach adopted by the police as the day progressed:

As the afternoon wore on the cops got really vicious. They raced horses into the packed Square—which was really dangerous. They were clearly trying to intimidate us. I remember being chased up one of the side streets by cops on horses. We just broke up and went off in different directions with the cops chasing us up and down streets. But as far as I can remem-ber there were no arrests. In the aftermath there was a witch hunt. The press accused pupils of destroying the flower beds in George Square![585]

Estimates of the number of pupils involved varied. The YTURC claimed up to 20,000 pupils participated, describing it as "the biggest strike of school students in Britain's history".[586] Official estimates were lower, probably in a deliberate attempt to downplay the significance of the demonstration. Strathclyde Regional Council's Divisional Education Officer Phillip Drake admitted (in a letter to Glasgow Springburn MP Michael Martin) that it was virtually impossible for him to identify precisely how many took part. He did point out that at least 32 out of 55 city schools were affected on the day and that a number of schools were hit by further protests the following day. There was little he or the school authorities could do to prevent the mass walkout. "At some schools", Drake gravely noted, "the pupils left in large groups and created disruption on the way to Glasgow".[587]

The Glasgow strike was an enormous success surpassing the expectations of the organisers. Labour figures in Scotland were less enamoured by the day's events. Jimmy Allison, Labour's Scottish organiser, immediately sought to disassociate the party from the strike. "The rally, unauthorised by us, was an act of irresponsibility by certain sections of the Young Socialists",[588] he insisted. Meanwhile, Michael Martin MP was outraged that the demonstration had occurred on his patch without his knowledge or approval. He wrote to Labour's General Secretary James Mortimer, expressing his irritation. The demonstration, he had been reliably informed, had "got out of hand, damage was done to public property, and also...children as young as 11 years of age were involved". He suspected the involvement of "subversive" elements on the left. "Knowing some of the personalities involved in this demonstration," he wrote, "I am convinced that the Militant Tendency are using the good name of the Labour Party Young Socialists for purposes which are clearly intended to bring the party into disrepute". He demanded that if any member of the party were found to have supported the strike, immediate "action should be taken to have them expelled".[589] On the same day Scottish organiser Allison wrote to David Hughes, Labour's national agent in London, informing him that the "very embarrassing half-day school strike" had been "organised by the LPYS without the permission of the Scottish Executive Committee". He questioned the legitimacy of the YTURC, demanding a copy of its constitution as well as information on its links with the party, its remit and its authority.[590]

Militant supporters within LPYS played a leading role in the Glasgow strike, but they were not alone. Keir McKechnie, then a young SWP activist, recalls the efforts made by all those on the Glasgow left to garner support for the day of action. "In the run up to the strike day we put loads of leaflets into the schools. There were LPYS leaflets, Militant leaflets, SWP leaflets and all were calling for strike action".[591]

It would also be wrong to suggest, as senior Scottish Labour officials did, that pupils were naively "seduced" into taking part in the protest. Firstly, this would underestimate the underlying insecurity and dismay many young people in Glasgow, as elsewhere, felt about their dismal employment prospects. As Keir recalls, "The anger at what was happening and what the Tories had done was almost touchable... The Tories had devastated the city. There were no apprenticeships, no jobs and our communities were being devastated by heroin, drugs, crime and desperate poverty". The strike, he insists, did not just "come out of the blue"; it was "an ideological strike, it was about students demanding resources, jobs and hope for a better future".[592]

Secondly, for many pupils their decision to participate was an informed, conscious choice. Angela, whose confrontation with police officers we describe above, was, she says, a model pupil; a prefect with an excellent attitude towards her schooling and an exemplary attendance record. Prior to the strike she was not particularly politically active. She is quite clear there were no Militant agent provocateurs lying behind her own carefully considered decision to take part. Indeed the lengths she and her friend went to to check the authenticity and legitimacy of the protest serves to reinforce our point that for many pupils this was a genuine, heartfelt demonstration against youth unemployment and Thatcher's YTS:

> I'd never had a day off school, never dogged school [ie played truant], I was a prefect... I was a good lassie! So my two best pals...said, "Are you coming out on strike? We're going out on strike!" And I said no, we cannae, we cannae dog school... So I said, "How do we know who's organising this... How do we know this is genuine?"... So what me, Audrey and Kathy did, was we went to Kathy's at lunchtime...and I said I'm not going until I find out that it's proper, that it's organised, so we looked up the Labour Party in the Yellow Pages and phoned them. I remember I said, "Hello, we're school students, and we hear that there's

a school strike, and we just want to know that it's bonafide". And the women on the phone was like... "Erm, I don't really know, I'll put you onto the Labour Party Young Socialists", and she put us through to, I think, Jackie Galbraith and she assured us that, "yes, this had been organised all over Glasgow, and yes, it wasnae just our school". And that was fine, so I said OK then, right OK, we'll go on strike.[593]

The Scottish Labour Party may have viewed the Glasgow strike with dismay but for others, particularly those taking part, it was a source of inspiration. As with previous school strikes discussed, for many participants it would be their first taste of political activism. It was an experience few would forget, and for many it had a lasting, formative impact encouraging them to engage with politics in a much more critical way. Angela's recollections of the awakening she felt are still vivid 30 years later. "As we marched into town", she recalls, "I remember my pal shouting at me: 'do you feel our power, Angela?' And I did! It was a great, exciting feeling".[594] She, like others we interviewed, is adamant that participation in the demonstration had a significant impact on her future political trajectory. Following the strike she and a number of her friends began to take a much closer interest in politics, attending rallies, reading political literature and joining in protest activities. Keir McKechnie also testifies to the strike's politically formative impact upon those taking part: "For a whole number of years afterwards many of the people involved in all manner of campaigns in Glasgow cut their teeth in the school strike. It was a great educator! It created a generation of Glasgow activists and militants".[595]

The Glasgow strike also acted as an inspiration for the pupil delegates attending the LPYS's Easter Conference at Blackpool a couple of weeks later. The March edition of *Socialist Youth*, the LPYS paper, described its conference, scheduled for 5-8 April, as "The Event of the Year".[596] In relation to its role in promoting the cause of pupil activism it certainly proved to be a formative moment. Hundreds of school pupils met separately from the main body of 1,500 delegates and, following speeches from Colin Baird and Jackie Galbraith, prominent participants in the Glasgow protest, they called for a half-day nationwide school strike of pupils over the age of 14 to take place on 25 April. Nancy Taaffe also spoke at the meeting, and she recalls how it quickly became evident that youth unemployment and the YTS were issues around which all young people on the left could coalesce and organise.[597] Lois Austin, a south east London pupil delegate to the conference, recalls the heady atmosphere that surrounded the event:

> There was loads of young miners there, Billy Bragg came and played at night and there was a massive fringe meeting—close to 500 young people at it—listening to arguments about why we needed school strikes against YTS. It was a great conference. I'd just turned 16 that month and, to be honest, I thought the revolution was coming![598]

Following the meeting, the pupil delegates formed a School Students Action Committee (SSAC) and set out a manifesto of demands that would be the focus of the demonstration:

- No to YTS conscription, real jobs for youth
- A Guaranteed job for all school leavers
- £30 grant for all 16-18 year olds who stayed on at school
- The building of a school students union
- Support for our teachers in their dispute[599]

At the close of the conference the SSAC and YTURC released a joint statement setting out a rationale for the day of action:

> The national school students' strike on 25 April will be the biggest ever show of pupil power in Britain. It is not anti-teacher or parents but anti-Tory and YTS, it will be a strike for the future of all school students. We...feel that by fighting against the government we can best guarantee a decent education system. We call on all school students in England, Wales and Northern Ireland to strike for their futures on 25 April. But we would advise those who have exams on this date to attend school.

The LPYS conference concluded on 8 April, leaving activists little time to organise the strike. In retrospect the short time-scale may have worked to the YTURC's advantage making it more difficult for the Labour leadership to move against the strike. In fact despite the SSAC/YTURC very public declaration of intent following the LPYS conference, Labour's hierarchy appeared to have been caught spectacularly unaware by the speed with which the planning for the protest developed. It was not until 16 April, at a meeting of the party's Youth Committee, that the matter was first raised as an issue of concern. Even then there was uncertainty about the timing of the day of action. Tom Sawyer, leader of the NUPE trade union and a loyal Neil Kinnock moderniser, chaired the meeting, informing those present of worrying reports "of an intended 'schools strike' to be held in some areas at the beginning of May". "It was unclear", he stated, "who the organisers of the intended strikes were but it was believed that the Young Socialists were involved through the organisation YTURC who had been producing leaflets from Walworth Road". The prospect of the strike clearly perturbed Sawyer, but the minutes of the meeting suggest his unease was not shared by all members of the Committee. While some "expressed concern about the school strikes and were anxious to obtain more information on all aspects of the matter", a motion that the issue be referred to the NEC for further consideration, and that LPYS "be instructed not to take any further action pending an investigation," was defeated by four votes to three.[600]

Sawyer, with the rest of the Labour leadership, were about to discover how immanent the protest was. On the same day that Sawyer chaired the Youth Committee David Alton, Liberal MP for Liverpool Mossley Hill, raised the issue at prime minister's question time. No sooner had Neil Kinnock sat down from the dispatch box than Alton rose to question Thatcher about Labour's irresponsibility in helping to organise an anti-YTS school strike:

> Despite the inadequacy of some of the youth training schemes, does the Prime Minister not agree that the calls made by some irresponsible members of the Labour Party for young people to come out on strike and leave their schools on 25 April is mischievous and irresponsible and is an attempt to use young people as cannon fodder.

Thatcher's response was entirely predictable:

> I understand that that is the action which the trade union rights group proposes to take on the 25 April. I deplore that politically inspired and counter-productive action. It is directly against the Youth Training Scheme, which is designed to help young people acquire more skills and better training in order for them to get jobs. The action is totally inspired by the extreme left wing of the trade union movement".[601]

Alton's question prompted a swift damage limitation exercise by Labour's leadership, which frantically sought to distance itself from the strike. Alton's intervention also alerted the press to the planned day of action. "Extremists have called on children to stage a class-room walk-out over the Government's Youth Training Scheme", railed the following day's *Daily Mail*.[602] As with the 1972 wave of school strikes, the *Mail* struck a tone of outraged indignation, alleging the influence of subversive Marxist skullduggery. Its coverage, mirrored in other tabloid newspapers, was a familiar blend of allegations of political manipulation and indoctrination supported by quotes from outraged Tory MPs, teachers' representatives and parents. "Militant squads call out children on school strike", was the headline a couple of days later.[603] Particular ire was directed towards the campaign's "inflammatory" leaflets being distributed at school gates by "left wing agitators", depicting a "disrespectful" image of Thatcher:

> The leaflets feature the slogan "Strike for your future. No to YTS conscription" and there is a caricature of Mrs Thatcher in SS uniform pointing Kitchener-style above the caption "We have ways of persuading YOU to go on YTS".

The *Mail* noted that at least 12 Labour MPs had signed an early day motion supporting the strike, including Militant supporters Dave Nellist and Terry Fields, citing this as evidence that the Labour Party had "blundered into an embarrassing split" on the issue.[604] This edition of the *Mail* also contained an "exclusive" opinion piece by Baroness Cox, a Tory peer and vociferous opponent of the "politicisation" of the school curriculum:

> Who would believe those recent stories of militant extremists succeeding in encouraging schoolchildren to walk out of class in protest against the Youth Training Scheme? Who would believe that Labour MPs could support a militant inspired school strike? Incredible... It is not surprising that some young people are growing up full of hatred for the police and other forms of authority.

Lest the message were not clear enough Cox's article was accompanied by a sketch depicting hundreds of school children standing outside a school forming the shape of a hammer and sickle.[605]

The *Mail* was, however, right to point to a division within Labour's ranks over the merits of the strike.

In the light of Labour's broader approach toward the principle of pupil participation in political life, there were good reasons why its leadership might have supported the strike's organisers. For example, in the week preceding the strike the party hierarchy published *Labour's Charter for Pupils and Parents*, which set out its strategy for encouraging the development of a more "caring", "compassionate", critically engaged young citizenry.[606] "In these last two years of secondary education", the *Charter* stated, "pupils should be prepared for adult life and to participate in a democratic society". "Young people", it insisted, "should be encouraged to use their critical and communication skills to develop their informed views".[607] The *Charter's* rhetoric held out the vision of an education system that would seek to cultivate informed, politically aware young people; the very sort of young people who were lending their support to the 25 April strike.

However, with the right wing press hard on Kinnock's heels political expediency took precedence over the principle of pupil participation.

Labour's Deputy Leader Roy Hattersley described the strike as "squalid" and "cynical", while privately admitting that he feared giving support to the protest "would rebound against Labour".[608] Echoing Tory ministers and the right wing press, Hattersley insisted that the Labour leadership "utterly condemn people who manipulate children for political ends".[609]

The day before the strike was due to take place, Labour's National Executive met. Tom Sawyer moved a resolution condemning the protest and calling for an inquiry into its organisers, in particular the YTURC. Michael Meacher, Tony Benn, Eric Heffer, Joan Maynard, Audrey Wise, Dennis Skinner, Jo Richardson and Frances Curran (the LPYS's NEC representative) voted against Sawyer's motion and moved counter-motions. Benn was reported to have told the NEC that "It's not enough just to get youth to listen to Billy Bragg songs. They've got to get organised".[610] The Labour leadership's determination to distance the party from the protest held sway and the following motion was passed by 17 votes to seven:

> That this NEC condemns this Tory Government's attacks on the rights and living standards of young people... As part of our campaign we recognise the importance of meetings, demonstrations, rallies and other events that bring together parents, pupils and trade unions. But we condemn the call for a school student strike... The National

Executive Committee requests the Organisation Committee to prepare a full report on the YTURC by clarifying its role and relationship to the Labour Party for the next meeting of the NEC.[611]

Immediately following the NEC meeting, Kinnock dismissed the strike's participants as a "bunch of dafties", accusing those responsible for organising it of being "more interested in their own delusions than the kids' realities".[612] Little support was forthcoming from national trade union leaders either. The TUC stated that the strike was "quite improper" arguing that it was wrong to seek to "exploit young people for political purposes". David Hunt, general secretary of the National Association of Head Teachers, argued that it was "a very sinister development, in which pupils are being misused and manipulated".[613]

Of course leading Conservatives condemned the action. John Biffen, at the time the Tory leader of the House of Commons, described it as a "most bizarre and deplorable episode".[614] Meanwhile, on the eve of the strike Margaret Thatcher felt sufficiently concerned to speak out in opposition to the protest for a second time, questioning whether this "was really the image...that should be projected to the industrialists of the world":

> I totally deplore and condemn this thoroughly mischievous attempt by left wing groups...to hide behind children in expressing concerns that they may have about the Youth Training Scheme. This is the worst possible example they could give to youngsters... The call to strike will be seen by all reasonably minded people as a clear political act of a totally negative nature.[615]

Despite media and political attempts to discredit the protest, the half-day demonstration went ahead as planned on 25 April, just three weeks after it was first muted at the LPYS Easter Conference. Lois Austin recalls the day vividly. For her it began with an appearance on BBC TV's *Breakfast Time* show, for an audience with Frank Bough, where she set out the case for the demonstration. This was not before she had been berated in the TV studio Green Room by Dame Vera Lynn, who was also being interviewed that morning. Lois recalls that "she was really having a go at us for being on strike". Lois's day concluded with her cutting short her protest in the centre of Woolwich to return to school and complete her Drama O Level practical.[616]

In parliament strike supporter Dave Nellist explained to MPs why those involved in the demonstration had felt compelled to undertake action of this kind:

> The 25 April strike was not anti-school, anti-teacher or anti-parent. It opposed YTS conscription and the Government who have destroyed the hopes of a generation of school leavers, 500,000 of whom have not worked since they left school under the Tory Government... In 1974, five per cent of 16 year olds not in full-time education were unemployed. That figure rose to 23 percent last year.[617]

Estimates of the number of children involved on the day vary. The *Times* claimed that backing was "minimal" in most towns and cities whereas the strike's supporters said 250,000 took part in the demonstration:

> A quarter of a million school children have given a crushing answer to the Tories, the press and the cynics in the labour movement. From Lands End to Newcastle, from Liverpool to Canterbury school students in their tens of thousands came out on strike.[618]

Upwards of 10,000 children participated in Liverpool alone, and a further 5,000 were reported to have attended a demonstration in London's Lincoln's Inn Fields, so it seems likely that support for the strike was considerably stronger than the *Times* report implies. Certainly critics of the strike were prepared to acknowledge the considerable disruption it caused on the day. Harry Greenway, Tory MP for Ealing North and a former London head teacher whose school had been affected by the 1972 strike, was incensed at its impact on schooling in the capital. "In some places", he told MPs in the Commons, "the strikes were organised to such a pitch that some pupils were observed following pre-arranged signals". He referred to an incident at Hampstead School, where teachers' car windows were broken and school windows smashed, as being symptomatic of the "anarchistic" chaos he alleged was a feature of the protests. He directed particular ire towards SWP activists who had leafletted the school encouraging pupils to strike:

> Those behind the recent strikes of schoolchildren were attempting to unleash something that they could not control, a process that could be damaging to the nation, the children and our whole way of

life—indeed, to our very democracy and our ability now to be debating the matter in the House. Such activity is outrageous and should be ended forthwith.[619]

Despite Greenway's apocalyptic language, the vast majority of the demonstrations passed without serious incident. Across the country the demonstrations invariably turned out to be well-organised, colourful and peaceful affairs. Typically the strikers marched to pre-arranged meeting points and listened to speeches from their peers denouncing the Conservative government's record on youth unemployment. Banners protesting against the government's record on unemployment were unfurled and placards accusing Thatcher's administration of betraying working class youth were waved by pupils. In instances where relatively serious disruption did occur this seemed to have been prompted by official provocation. In Liverpool a number of arrests were made prior to the day of the official demonstration. In their enthusiasm to back the protest pupils from four schools in Kirkby walked out of school on the Friday before the strike was scheduled. The *Times* claimed these pupils had "run amok in the town centre and outside school gates", leading to 14 arrests. This account contrasted sharply with that of school students' themselves, who spoke of police harassment and victimisation:

> We had a meeting of over 200 and the police arrived in vans and cars and drove at the meeting. Many of us were pushed down an embankment on to the railway lines. Some of those caught were hit with batons and kicked—and they have the cheek to say it was us rioting.[620]

Most accounts of the 1985 strikes place Liverpool at the epicentre of the events of 25 April. Certainly the protest here was one of the biggest, not least because the Militant-led city council had supported the strike announcing an amnesty for any pupils taking part. Accounts of the day in Liverpool can overshadow the sheer breadth of support for the strike across all parts of Britain. But in Liverpool backing for the strike surpassed the expectations of its organisers, one of whom recalls the "amazing sense of optimism" engendered by the overwhelming levels of support:

> There had been a leaflet campaign and a lot of word of mouth, but on the day we had no idea it was going to be as big as it was... It was

stewarded by Liverpool Labour councillors, but we lost control of it when that amount of people turned up... It was meant to be going from St George's Hall through the city centre to the Pier Head, but once the kids heard the words "Pier Head", they just went straight down Roe Street and Dale Street—they just ran... It was so fast, and the numbers were so big, that we couldn't stop them and redirect them.[621]

Once gathered at the Pier Head pupils listened to impassioned speeches from, among others, the Labour MP Terry Fields.[622]

The support offered to the strikers by Liverpool council and Terry Fields provoked outrage from their political opponents. "It is a serious matter", Tory MP Harry Greenway warned the Commons, "when Labour members of the Liverpool education committee vote unanimously to legalise truancy by guaranteeing children immunity from victimisation".[623] The reaction of Liverpool's non-Labour MPs was similar. On hearing of the day's events Liberal David Alton again raised the issue in the Commons expressing his outrage that children had been "led out of Liverpool this afternoon by a member of this House, causing chaos and anarchy in many of the schools in Merseyside". Alton called for an urgent debate on the issue.[624] The debate never took place, but Fields did not shy away from defending his support for the school strike in the Commons whenever the opportunity arose:

A myth has been created about it being wrong to politicise young people. From the cradle to the grave, the working classes' minds are poisoned by the ruling classes and the Tories... In my view, working-class youth should be politicised from the cradle, when they first start to speak and go on to read and talk about the nature of society. We must explain why there is no future for them under the present Tory Government and this capitalist system.[625]

Liverpool pupils themselves offered more nuanced justifications for why they participated in the protest than those offered by their critics. Debbie Riley, a school student at St Gregory's, challenged the media's claims that pupils were gullible victims of a left wing conspiracy. "We are not stupid", she insisted; "all we are saying is that if we're old enough to go on cheap labour YTS, then we are old enough to go on strike for our future".[626] Sean Boyle, a pupil at West Drayton comprehensive said, "We refuse to go to school when the YTS is the only result at the end of it. The education system offers us nothing".[627] Others, expressing a sense of desperation at the opportunities available to them on leaving school also commented on the inspiration they felt from striking. "We have got nothing to lose", explained 15 year old Paula Jones. "We have got nothing in Kirkby. YTS is the last straw, and this is more of an education than we could ever learn in school".[628] Selina Lambert, a pupil at Walton High, was more forthright also describing the threats of intimidation pupils had faced to deter them from taking part: "We were told we would get three days suspension, but we came out anyway. You sit in the exam room and think 'What the fuck are you doing this for?' It's not worth it".[629]

Apart from Scotland, where pupils had been encouraged by organisers to attend school and sit their exams, all areas of Britain were affected by the protest. In Birmingham around 400 pupils participated in the strike. Despite threats of expulsion and suspensions from head teachers, pupils here commented on the tacit support they received from teachers and condemned the Labour leadership's failure to back the protest:

> Many teachers, who could not admit it openly, made it known that they did support us... Kinnock describes the organisers of the strike as "dafties". But we are not dafties, we are young people with rights and we do not need crap from quislings like him.[630]

In Nottingham heavy handed police reaction to the protest led to three arrests, prompting a demonstration outside the police station and an occupation of the local radio station, where pupils got airtime to set out their case.[631] The pupils had earlier refused to talk to the Nottinghamshire *Evening Post* on the grounds that it was a non-union paper.[632] The *Evening Post* reacted with a patronising front page headline: "The Daft Wing", accompanied by a re-hashed report of Kinnock's "lashing" of the strikers as "dafties".[633]

In Manchester a series of rallies involved thousands of pupils. Here, the Labour controlled city council followed the lead of Liverpool by announcing no action would be taken against pupils taking part. The protest began with pupils laying siege to the city's education offices on Crown Square, where they were addressed by Labour councillor John Byrne, who reaffirmed the education authority's position. Interviewed afterwards, he stated, "We support their protest and if any youngster finds himself or herself in trouble over taking the half-day off, I have asked them to contact councillors or education officials". The pupils then marched to the Town Hall in Albert Square. "As the youngsters bawled soccer songs and shouted 'Maggie out' traffic jams built up", the *Manchester Evening News* reported. "Some children climbed scaffolding outside the Town Hall while others scaled the Albert Memorial".[634] Pupil protesters from one Manchester school wrote to the local paper condemning the YTS and denying claims that they had been passively brainwashed into supporting the strike. "We hope that your readers will realise we have analysed the situation carefully", they wrote, "and have not been indoctrinated by left wing extremists".[635]

Parts of Wales and Northern Ireland were also gripped by the protests. Well over 1,000 children joined the strike in Cardiff. In Pontypridd, 2,000 school pupils were joined by miners from several pits. The strike's organisers had called on the leader of the South Wales miners to lead them into town, which he duly did. In Newport the council attempted to disrupt a rally attended by over 1,000 school students by turning off the power to their PA system. Undeterred the school students marched to the courts to support a miner whose case was being heard before moving onto Newport Castle, where they raised the red flag. In Northern Ireland 2,000 were reported to have participated in Derry. In Belfast, in an impressive display of unity, over 3,000 Catholic and Protestant school students marched through the city centre behind a Labour and Trade Union Group banner. One trade unionist who witnessed the demonstration could not disguise his pride; "This is brilliant, just brilliant", he stated, "I haven't seen anything like this since 1969". Pupils participating in the Belfast strike also commentated on the unifying effect of coming together to collectively protest against a common cause:

> I think this strike has really shown that Protestants and Catholics can be united. We are going to see a lot of sectarianism in the run up to these local government elections, but this demonstration shows it can be beaten.[636]

Students in smaller towns across the UK also heeded the call to strike in impressive numbers. In Basildon 600 pupils marched through the town and occupied the jobcentre. One pupil was arrested but then released when demonstrators threatened to march on the police station. In Stevenage 500 were estimated to have heeded the call to strike, as did 600 pupils in Watford and 500 in Ipswich.[637] In the Midlands seven schools were said to be affected by the strike in Coventry, despite strenuous attempts by the school authorities to prevent pupils from taking part. Further north the estimated 2,000 pupils protesting in Bradford and Leeds were joined by around 400 in the smaller towns of Rotherham, Castleford, Barnsley and Grimsby.[638] In Preston, Lancashire over 300 children participated in the strike despite threats of suspension from the school authorities and a concerted campaign by the local newspaper. As in other parts of the country a number of those taking part were subsequently suspended. A contemporary account of the day by Phil Forrester, one of Preston's YTURC activists, recounts the political nature of the speeches made by school students:

> Speakers from schools explained how YTS was nothing but cheap labour, how it has allowed the Tories to doctor the real unemployment figures, and how it has been used to replace real jobs.

Forrester dismissed the notion that children in Preston had been mischievously enticed into taking strike action. "School students", he argued, "have become aware of the need to fight back not because of a few leaflets handed out by the Youth Trade Union Rights Campaign, but because of the way their own brothers and sisters have been treated by this government".[639]

In the aftermath of the strike the press continued to insist that pupils had been naively seduced into taking part. In an article head-lined, "Militants Help to Establish Pupils' Union", the *Times Educational Supplement* reported its growing concerns over "alleged political 'manipulation' of the school pupils by extreme left wingers, mainly supporters of the Marxist Militant Tendency".[640] Another article, headlined "Left Wing Groups Organise Pupils' Strikes", claimed that there were "strong links between militant school pupils and adult left wing activists who helped to organise the event, many of whom are Militant supporters".[641]

As evidence to support their claims critics of the strike pointed to adult involvement in the organisation of the demonstration. Many of those coordinating the 1985 protests, including within the YTURC, were no longer at school. However, although government spokespersons and the media claimed that the YTURC contribution to the children's strikes provided conclusive proof of a left wing conspiracy, its involvement stemmed from far less sinister considerations. As the *Times Educational Supplement* subsequently acknowledged, pupils themselves approached the YTURC asking it to assist in the setting up of regional strike committees. As one of the striking Liverpool school-children stated, "As far as we could see, the YTURC was the only organised campaign group that was trying to do something about YTS. What else could we do really?"[642]

Supporters of the strike sought to inject a sense of perspective in response to these criticisms. In parliament Dave Nellist responded directly to Tory accusations that he and others who backed the demonstration were guilty of political indoctrination. Such critics, he argued "should bear in mind that the first lesson [in politics] is given by the Tory government, who refuse to guarantee them a right to a job when they leave school". Commenting on the disruption to education, he reminded them of the disruption caused by the Tory government decision to close schools for the royal wedding a few years earlier. "What damage", he asked, "did that do to their education? Not one Tory member protested about every schoolchild having a day off when Charles and Diana got married in 1981". The half-day protest on 25 April was, he insisted, an "organised, disciplined and responsible political protest", and the children who heeded the call to protest should be congratulated for having the conviction to stand up for a cause they believed in. Nellist also condemned head teachers who disciplined participants in the strike. It was ironic, he said, that head teachers who complained about the half-day strike's impact on schooling were handing out "10 or 20 times that denial of education by suspending children from school as punishment".[643]

Support for the strike was not confined to the far left. Mainstream Labour and trade union activists in towns and cities across the UK were prepared to defy Labour's national leadership and give the strike their support. In Preston chair of the Labour controlled Education Committee Josie Farrington refused to condemn the town's pupils who walked out of school, noting that "the subject itself is one a lot of people feel very strongly about". "The major issue here", she argued, "is not the strike against the YTS but the very real social problem of youth unemployment. It is something that has got to be tackled".[644] Preston's Labour Party chair John Browne not only gave his support to the strike he actually attended the town centre demonstration. Asked whether the strike was irresponsible, he replied that, "With the present Government you cannot expect anything else but this reaction". Likewise in Harlow senior figures from the local Labour Party and the trades council backed the strike, addressing the demonstrators there.[645] In Newham South the local Labour party overwhelmingly backed a motion calling on the NEC to "applaud and support the work of the Youth Trade Union Rights Campaign".[646]

There was also considerable backing among parents, many affected by the high levels of unemployment across Britain. There were numerous examples of head teachers receiving notes from parents requesting leave of absence for their children to attend the demonstrations.[647] Letters to the local and national press across the country sought to counter negative coverage of the protest. "It is we, the parents, the educators, the politicians who are irresponsible, not the young people", argued one parent in a letter to the *Lancashire Evening Post*. "We do not listen to their unpretentious honesty, converse with them at any meaningful level (we talk at them rather than with them), we oppress their development as individuals by a variety of punitive means in an attempt to preserve the status quo".[648] Another parent whose daughter had participated in the strike wrote to the *Guardian*, defending the protesters:

> I feel school students should be able to absent themselves in support of their principles and their futures. Many local school students were actively prevented from attending the protest meeting, even to being locked in by their headmasters. Schools should be proud that their teaching has been such that their pupils feel able to form their own opinions on national issues.[649]

How should we judge the strike's overall impact?

The strike led to a re-think of government proposals for the YTS to become "compulsory". Plans to strip all 16-18 year olds of their right to social security benefits were delayed until 1988.[650] The strike's participants and supporters interpreted the government's backtracking as a major victory. At the time Terry Fields was unequivocal in his assessment of the protest's influence on this decision. "The demonstration and school strike this year", he told Parliament, had "brought about a climbdown by the government over the compulsory nature of the YTS".[651]

Participants in the 25 April demonstration are convinced of the crucial impact that the mass public display of opposition among school

students had on Tory plans. Hannah Sell says, "the strike was important. People forget but we actually defeated the Tories' plans to make
YTS compulsory".[652] Lois Austin is also adamant that the strike should
be seen as a significant victory: "Looking back it's sometimes easy to
forget that we won, and did do relatively quickly! Over the last 30 years
we have suffered a number of significant defeats and it sometimes
means we lose sight of the times we have won".[653]

The strike was also a success in that it showed a significant propor-
tion of working class children had not been swept along in the
Thatcherite tide, and that despite threats of disciplinary action and
suspension from school, they were prepared to vent their anger at what
they felt were profoundly unjust policies. For Lois Austin the school
strike was the culmination of a remarkable protest, the like of which
she has never experienced since:

> What I remember of it, was that it was a very quick and intense time,
> and I don't think I've been through a movement like that since. You
> know that any sort of strike or movement has a life of its own, has a
> build-up and a sort of apex... This movement, because it was so youth-
> ful...there was an element of chaos about it, uncontrollable chaos, and
> that's how I remember it. I remember it just going whoosh!

In the aftermath of the strike Nancy recalls there were "loads of
people looking for some sort of organisation".[654] The LPYS leadership
sought to capitalise on this and made immediate concerted attempts to
created a School Students Union (SSU). In the weeks and months following the strike the pages of *Socialist Youth* and *Militant* provided
coverage of attempts to build the new union. On 5 June 200 school
student delegates met in Manchester. After speeches from the LPYS
national chair John Hird and young Chilean and South African delegates a national committee, chair and secretary of the SSU were elected.

Dave Sirockin, the SSU's newly elected secretary, argued "School-
students...can now see that capitalism offers them no hope of a decent
future, and that the only way we can win our aims is to link up with
other workers in struggle".[655]

There were attempts to build SSU branches across the UK. The
inaugural meeting of Northern Ireland's SSU took place in June, at
Queens University Belfast, with pupils from Derry, Belfast, Ballymena,
Omagh, Coleraine and Enniskillen represented.[656] In Scotland a

Scottish SSU was formed following a conference in September with delegates from Dundee, Falkirk, Stirling and Glasgow present.[657] Considerable efforts were made to maintain this momentum and build the SSU into an effective representative body for pupils. Nancy Taaffe was one of those involved and she recalls the steps she and others made to promote the SSU in the aftermath of the strike:

> That summer I spent a lot of time trying to set up the union. We had stalls at Red Wedge festivals and we worked with the Youth Trade Union Rights Campaign. Out of that we managed to set up some branches—in London there was the LSSU and they brought out regular bulletins that we put into schools.[658]

As in the past the prospect of the creation of an organised union for school children horrified those on the political right. In Parliament an outraged Harry Greenway quoted, verbatim, an SWP leaflet distributed to Hampstead School, where 4,500 pupils had joined the 25th April strike:

> The school kids' strike was really one in the eye for Thatcher and her slave labour scheme. The panic it created among the headmistress and the school authorities shows our potential power... However, a one day strike will not defeat the Tories and all the crap they throw at us. To do this we need organisation in local schools to discuss how to build our own futures.[659]

"To attempt to subvert schoolchildren in that way", Greenway said, was "not only deplorable but dangerous, both to the children and to the future of our country", and he demanded assurances the SSU would be banned. "My right hon. Friend the Secretary of State for Education and Science should come to the House and assure us that the matter will be dealt with and that such organisations will be kept away from schools".[660]

Despite the widespread support for the strike, efforts to build SSU branches across the UK met with mixed success. By October the SSU leadership was able to point to the existence of branches in most major cities. In some of these the SSU had helped to coordinate demonstrations and strikes over localised grievances. In Wolverhampton, for example, Hannah Sell and other SSU activists helped turn an anti-teacher-strike demonstration at two schools into a ten-school strike against the Tories.

Pupils were persuaded to change their "Campaign Against Teachers Strike" ("CATS") banners to "Campaign Against Tories":[661]

> Me and others in the School Students Union said, "don't do that, don't do that, we're in favour of the teachers' strike!" And we convinced them to strike for the School Students Union, and then we marched around Wolverhampton and we got ten schools out. Dave Sirockin, the school student leader, came up to Wolverhampton...and we had ten schools out for a week, and we won the right to a School Students Union. We met in the council chamber on the Saturday afternoon![662]

The SSU acknowledged that there were "still whole areas of Britain where school-students have not been in contact with the SSU or the LPYS".[663] In truth despite the undoubted politicising effect of the 25 April school strike, activists found it difficult to mobilise pupils into an organised movement. As Nancy Taaffe, one of those involved in the SSU, said: "it was difficult to keep the network going, it was such a disparate group. The movement was like a great swell of water that engulfed us, but those that channeled it were scattered".[664]

Their efforts were also hindered by the Labour leadership's moves to neutralise the influence of the YTURC and, indeed, the LPYS.[665] The SSU did continue as a campaigning organisation—and in 1987 it helped to coordinate a series of pupil strikes in Manchester and London—but it never succeeded in fulfilling its early potential.

The 1985 strike could be seen as a more tangible and lasting success in other respects. Amassing such a broad constituency of support for their cause—among local labour activists, politicians and parents—was one the major achievements of the 25 April strike. It showed that children could not be ignored and that they could help inform and shape political debate. The fact that Tom Sawyer continued to be frustrated by the support shown for the YTURC in the broader labour movement as late as September 1986 testifies to the support for its anti-YTS campaign.[666]

On a national scale the strike also marked a development in children's political activism. Unlike the 1889, 1911 and 1972 children's strikes, which were much more narrowly focused on the organisation of schooling, the 25 April demonstration was motivated by wider political concerns. It was, in fact, one of a number of occasions (albeit an important and visible one) during the 1980s when children displayed a willingness to speak out and demand action on a range of national and international issues (such as nuclear disarmament and apartheid). These would not be the last generation of children to walk out of school in defence of passionately held political principles. In 2003, 18 years after the 25 April protests, children would again "strike" in protest against Britain's involvement in the war in Iraq.[667]

Angela McCormick (Glasgow, 1985)
"Feeling our power"

In 1985 I was a student at St Augustine's Secondary in Milton, Glasgow. It was a large Catholic school in a poor working class part of the city. I was in the fifth year [year 12] and there were very few of us who had stayed on—it was a school where the vast majority of students left at their first opportunity.

I wasn't very political at the time. But we had just lived through the miners' strike and I remember there were a lot of collections for the miners and arguments about the strike in our community and in our school.

Most people supported the miners. We all hated the Tories. We knew what they had done to our community. They regarded us with utter contempt and we all knew it. They had destroyed jobs across the Clyde and for many of us there wasn't much hope. We knew we would leave school and the best on offer was some crappy YTS—and now they were talking about making it compulsory.

On the day of the strike I came to school and there was a lot of discussion about the proposed walkout at the end of the lunch break. There were lots of arguments throughout the morning about what might be happening. I remember I was unsure. I wanted to know who was organising it!

At lunch time me and a couple of friends went to my house and we discussed what we were going to do. We decided to phone the Labour Party to see if this was a real march or what was going on. I think the woman on the phone nearly had a heart attack when we rang up! She blustered and then said she would put us onto the Labour Party Young Socialists (LPYS).

When we got through to the LPYS they told us that they weren't organising it, but the strike was happening across Glasgow. That was all we needed. We went back to school to join the strike.

When we got to the school gates there were teachers arguing with students to get in to class. But most of the fourth and fifth years were outside. As there were few fifth years we came to the front. We started to march around the school with the intention of then marching into the city centre where we had heard there was going to be a rally.

Just as we set off on the two and a half mile march an ex-student and local activist called Frank Doleman ran into the playground and shouted "everybody out". It was amazing: suddenly all the first, second and third year students rushed out the gates and joined us. Literally everyone in the school was on the march. We were all shouting and chanting. It was organised chaos, a real festival of the oppressed!

We tried to organise it so that the older students were at the front. The third year students were sent to be the marshals and make sure the younger kids didn't get knocked down! As we marched into town I remember my pal shouting at me: "do you feel our power, Angela?" And I did! It was a great, exciting feeling.

As we got closer to the town a cop car stopped in front of us. The cop came up to me and asked me what I thought we were doing. I told him we were going to the demonstration in town against the Tories and the YTS. "We're on strike" I told him. He just looked at me and said "school pupils don't go on strike". I remember just saying: "oh aye, then what do you call this?" And we pushed past him and went on our way!

When we arrived at George Square there were thousands of school students there. The estimate in the papers the next day was 10,000. The place was heaving. But it was also pretty chaotic. There were no speakers. The organisers had expected a couple of hundred and had booked a small room for a meeting, but this was something else.

There were anti-Tory chants and a lot of people having fun. Eventually the cops brought out the mounted police and tried to make us disperse.

We eventually all went home. There was some discussion about what would happen in the school the next day. Our school was pretty authoritarian. Lots of silly rules. You could get sent home for your hair being too high, your skirt too short, for wearing white socks if you were a boy. There were loads of rules about school behaviour as well— though the use of the belt had stopped when I was in first year. So people wondered what they would do about the strike.

But the amazing thing was they didn't do anything. At Colston Secondary [a neighbouring school] fewer students had come out and they were victimised. But at our school, where everyone came out, nothing. Let's face it they couldn't discipline us all. And that was a great lesson for me: if you stick together and act collectively it's much more difficult for them to victimise you.

JAMES DOLEMAN (Glasgow, 1985)
"The strike built a momentum of its own"

I REMEMBER the Glasgow school strikes of 1985 clearly. The strikes were about the YTS, about unemployment and about why we had to do something if we wanted any kind of future.

The strike happened just after the miners had gone back. For the previous year we had been watching what was going on in the mining communities. We had local support groups and the miners were something we had been discussing in school. That was the background to the school strike.

The main organisers of the strike were the Labour Party Young Socialists—and of course Militant were part of the LPYS at the time. They initially wanted a token event. They only wanted years 4, 5 and 6 to be involved because these were the students who would be leaving school. In some places they only wanted representatives of the school to come to George Square. I think they saw it as a bit of a stunt.

On the day Militant had booked a small room in the city chambers and they wanted that to be the rally. So they were expecting something very small.

But the strike built a momentum of its own.

In the run up to the strike we threw ourselves into trying to get the whole school out. We wanted first, second, third year students to join us. And, as it turned out, that was reproduced right across the city.

I spend the morning handing out leaflets and telling everyone to come and join the strike—and at St Augustine's everyone came out.

We marched into town. George Square was mobbed. It was very excitable and a bit chaotic. The organisers left and went to their meeting and that left school students everywhere: chanting, singing and running about.

It was a real carnival and the cops couldn't cope. I remember seeing some kids tapping coppers on their backs, they'd turn around and then someone else would knock their hat off!

But there were so many people there and no real organisation of the event so gradually people started to drift away and the cops came in a bit harder. In some senses it was an opportunity to do something, but lack of organisation on our side meant the atmosphere dissipated.

In the aftermath there was a witch-hunt in the press and from the

Labour Party. On the 25 April there were no strikes in Glasgow, though there were in other parts of Britain—an opportunity lost!

KEIR MCKECHNIE (Glasgow, 1985)
"The anger at the Tories was almost touchable"

I WAS 18 in 1985 and had been involved in politics in Glasgow for a few years. I first got involved with Youth CND, I was then involved in the local Miners' Support Group and I joined the SWP when I was 15.

I think you need to put the strike in its context and there were two elements to this.

First, there was the feeling of anger and frustration at what was happening in Glasgow. The Tories had devastated the city. There were no apprenticeships, no jobs and our communities were being devastated by heroin, drugs, crime and desperate poverty.

Many young people were even looking at the armed forces as a way out—their offer of an apprenticeship and a job was seen as the only option by some young people.

The anger at what was happening and at what the Tories had done was almost touchable.

This was all reflected in the campaigning work of the Labour Party, the trade unions and the SWP.

We had been petitioning and leafleting in the community and at our school against YTS for quite some time. In fact YTS was known as the Youth Training Swindle.

Second, many of us had been involved in political movements and campaigns. There was a very active Miners' Support Group. Many of us had been involved with YCND. The LPYS was really quite big and Militant were quite significant inside it.

At my school, in the north of the city, we had regularly petitioned and taken politics into the school. In the common room there was a space for older students to get involved in political debates and activity.

So for me the strikes didn't just happen. They didn't come out of the blue. Actually this was quite an ideological strike, it was about students demanding resources, jobs and hope for a better future.

In the run up to the strike day we put loads of leaflets into the school. There were LPYS leaflets, Militant leaflets, SWP leaflets and all were arguing for strike action.

We started discussions in the common room about what to do. In other parts of the city similar things were happening. In Pollock, in the south west of the city, the LPYS held community meetings arguing for a strike.

In some places only older students came out but we were clear, we wanted everyone out.

And to be honest, because myself and James were known as local activists a lot of the students came to us to ask us what we were doing about the strike.

On the day we marched into town. We soon realised there were similar feeder marches all over the city. On our way we stopped and called out other schools. Possil High, for example, was one school we pulled out on the route.

The local press said there were 10,000 students in George Square. There were possibly 20,000 students out across Clydeside. There were strikes in Greenock, Paisley, Dumbarton and in North Lanarkshire. The *Scottish Daily Record* said it was the biggest show of pupil power ever!

There were loads of homemade banners—and that just proves that it was planned and organised to some extent and not just a spontaneous event.

As the afternoon wore on the cops got really vicious. They raced horses into the packed Square—which was really dangerous. They were clearly trying to intimidate us.

I remember being chased up one of the side streets by cops on horses. But we just broke up and went off in different directions with the cops chasing us up and down streets. As far as I can remember there were no arrests.

In the aftermath there was a witch hunt. The press accused pupils of destroying the flower beds in George Square!

But the Labour Party distanced themselves from the events and used the strike to attack the left. They were starting their expulsions of Militant and this was used as part of their case.

The schools and the heads also tried to discipline students. There were threats of expulsions, cancellation of school trips and restrictions of activities at breaks.

Many of us were up for a second strike day in April. But actually nothing happened in Glasgow on 25 April. The leadership in the LPYS didn't follow through on the electrifying mood, under pressure from the Glasgow Labour Party, the media and the local state. I still think this was a mistake and a missed opportunity.

For a whole number of years afterwards many of the people involved in all manner of campaigns in Glasgow cut their teeth in the school strike. It was a great educator! It created a generation of Glasgow activists and militants.

HANNAH SELL (Wolverhampton, 1985)
"We defeated the Tories and stopped them making YTS compulsory"

I WAS a Militant supporter inside the Labour Party Young Socialists in 1985. LPYS was a mass youth movement with tens of thousands of members and supporters, and Militant, at the end of the miners' strike in 1985, was the most significant network operating within it.

During the miners' strike there had been a few strikes by school students in the Yorkshire coalfield. We thought that was a clear indication that young people could be mobilised to strike against youth unemployment and the YTS and that we could establish a mass school student movement—and that's what we set out to try and organise and create.

From a personal perspective, in 1985 I was at school in Wolverhampton. Cannock pit was just up the road and during the miners' strike the pupils were all on one side or the other—you couldn't be neutral. It was a very political time. I joined LPYS and got involved. We collected for the miners—and the very idea of striking, for us as school students, came from the miners and what we had seen over the previous year.

As the strike finished there had been a call for school student strike action in Glasgow. The response was massive. At the LPYS conference in April Militant supporters argued that Glasgow showed we could build a movement of school students. It was agreed to call for strikes in England and Wales on 25 April.

We leafletted as many schools as we could. It clearly was going to be very big. Breakfast television covered the strike on the morning of the strike and that undoubtedly helped make it bigger as lots of school students across the country realised what was happening. There were strikes in places where there were no Militant supporters, or where no leafleting had been done, so clearly the media coverage had an impact.

But in my school there was a lot of intimidation of students. We were told that anyone who came out would be suspended, and some teachers were actively identifying and naming activists. As a result in April 1985 the response in Wolverhampton was not as good as in other places—in my school only about 20 of us came out.

The following year we had a week-long strike in Wolverhampton. It started because some students at my school came out on strike against the teachers who were striking and working to rule. Their work to rule meant that school trips had been cancelled. So some students went on strike against the teachers! But we managed to convince them that the teachers were right, that they should support the strikes and that we should demand a school students union. We pulled 10 schools out for a week. At the end of the week we had a meeting in the council chamber and we won the right to representation!

But now the Labour Party started to move against the LPYS. They banned the Youth Trade Union Rights Campaign, the Labour Party NEC condemned the school strikes and eventually they moved to close LPYS down.

The strikes were important. People forget but we actually defeated the Tory's plans to make YTS compulsory—though they did bring that back in 1988.

One of the things worth pointing out is that, almost by definition, school students taking action don't bring the weight of previous defeats with them. They are young, angry and have a great belief that we can change the world. It's why, I think, young people are so often at the forefront of social protests and unrest.

LOIS AUSTIN (London, 1985)
"It was a very short, but intense movement"

I BECAME politically active during the miners' strike. I was still at school in south east London but we used to collect and raise support for the strikers. As the strike wore on I got more and more involved— and so did my friends and family. Our support group twinned with a mining community and I remember taking food, toys and money up at the Christmas of 1984.

The idea of the school strike started to form out of meetings at the LPYS conference in the April 1985. There were loads of young miners there, Billy Bragg came and played at night and there was a massive fringe meeting—close to 500 young people at it—listening to arguments about why we needed school strikes against YTS. It was a great conference. I'd just turned 16 that month and, to be honest, I thought the revolution was coming!

It was that meeting that put out the call for school strikes against Thatcher and her decision to make YTS compulsory. At the end of the meeting we had leaflets and posters and all left to go back to our schools and start to organise for the strike.

In the run up to the strike day some of the teachers in our school allowed us to hold meetings about the strike. The teachers were in dispute and had had several strike days. Many of them were very sympathetic—though I think they thought it was a bit gimmicky.

I remember the day of the strikes vividly. I started off the day being interviewed on Good Morning TV—by Frank Bough! Before I went on they put me in the Green Room and Dame Vera Lynn was there to talk about some anniversary. I remember she was giving us a hard time for going on strike! But during the interview I was able to put the case for the strike.

After the interview I had to get back to school and organise everyone onto buses to go down to Woolwich where I was meeting my sister and her class mates. It was wild!

We had organised a lunch time rally. We had brought some young miners down to speak. But it wasn't like most rallies. You would have a speech, then the students would suddenly run off somewhere. So we would go with them, there would be another speech, then they'd be off again. Normally in the trade unions there is a slower build up to any action and then a kind of controlled strike or march. But this wasn't like that. It was chaotic and very intense, but it was really exciting.

One of the things was that it was the day of my Drama O-level practical! So I had to leave at 3 pm and go back to school and take part in a play—because if we hadn't taken part everyone would have failed their exam.

Looking back it's sometimes easy to forget that we won, and did so relatively quickly! Over the last 30 years we have suffered a number of significant defeats and it sometimes means we lose sight of the times we have won.

But the strikes also changed me. I had been bullied at school, but the strike changed that. It gave me confidence and it got me involved in all manner of campaigns. And at school now the other students saw me changed. I remember a bit later I came into a class and some of the boys had written "Wapping Militant" on the board. It was a bit of fun—but I loved it!

NANCY TAAFFE (London, 1985)
"Our call chimed with people and produced the April strikes"

I CAME from a very political family, my dad was a leading member of Militant. But I didn't automatically become an activist. It was the miners' strike that brought things home to me. I started going to miners' support group meetings in Islington and collecting on the streets. I became active in LPYS during this time.

It was Militant supporters in something called FELS that started to argue for school strikes. FELS was Further Education Labour Students and because they were working with school and FE students they started to realise that youth unemployment and the imposition of YTS was becoming a big issue—something we could organise around. So in the summer of 1984 there was a meeting of Militant supporters who started to discuss organising through LPYS for school student action. We set up something called the School Students' Bureau and it was the mechanism we used to try and organise in the schools.

At the LPYS conference in April 1985 I spoke at a fringe meeting calling for strike action. I spoke with Jackie Galbraith, who had been central to organising the one day school strike in Glasgow. The key thing was identifying the issue around which we could mobilise. And in Militant we had debated this and identified the problem of youth unemployment and what they were going to try and do with YTS. So our call chimed with people and produced the response we saw in April.

If you think about school today, the design of the buildings makes it easier to contain students. Some of the academies are based on prison designs. But in the 1980s schools were much more open. There were no big fences, the schools were next to parks, or woods, or the main street. This meant it was easier for students to join the action and much more difficult for the authorities to contain the strikers.

After the strike we turned to organising the School Students Union. That summer I spent a lot of time trying to set up the union. We had stalls at Red Wedge festivals and we worked with the Youth Trade Union Rights Campaign. Out of that we managed to set up some branches—in London there was the LSSU and they brought out regular bulletins that we put into schools. We had a national conference in Manchester of close to 300 people and that was great.

But it was difficult to keep the network going, it was such a disparate group. The movement was like a great swell of water that engulfed us, but those that channelled it were scattered. Eventually the SSU merged with YTURC and FE and HE organisations.

MIKE MORRIS (Liverpool, 1985)
"I've never been on such a fast demo"

I'D JUST left school and was an apprentice joiner in Liverpool in 1984. I remember watching the miners' strike on TV and, in particular, the events at Orgreave. One of my mates in West Derby, Liverpool told me that the BBC had reversed the sequencing of their film (which we now know to be true). I was pretty stunned by that. It had a big impact on me and I joined the LPYS and became a Militant supporter.

By 1985 I was a Militant Young Socialist organiser and was heavily involved in the campaign against YTS and the organisation of the school strike in Liverpool in April that year.

The campaign kicked off for us after the Blackpool LPYS conference in April. We came back to Liverpool with leaflets and posters and started working to get people out.

We leafletted local schools. That was quite hard. Some teachers and some in the media were accusing us of trying to lead school students astray. But what I remember was how open young people were to the idea of a strike. In parts of Liverpool youth unemployment at the time was close to 80 percent. For many of those leaving school the choice was the dole or YTS—and now the Tories were trying to make the scheme compulsory. We likened it to slave labour; there was a real sense of grievance and anger at what was happening.

We leafletted and fly posted widely, but had little idea what was going to happen on the day. Some head teachers were threatening all sorts of punishments for any students who took part. Although this was mitigated, to some extent, by the decision of Liverpool City Council not to suspend or exclude any school striker.

I think it's fair to say the strike exceeded all our expectations. The scale of the strike was phenomenal. There were close to 10,000 school students at the start. Many had made their own banners, others had written all over their school shirts and uniforms. There were groups dancing and singing; others were chanting and jumping around. There was a real festival-like mood to the day. There were groups from schools that would traditionally have rivalries, but not that day, just a tremendous feeling of togetherness.

The other thing I remember was the speed of the demonstration. We had a planned route, but that was torn up as the school students just set off, at pace, for the Pier Head. I remember literally running to try and get towards the front!

At the Pier Head there were just school students everywhere. I remember when Terry Fields MP was speaking, I was near the front, just trying to hold people back—it was a bit chaotic, but there was a fantastic feeling of liberation!

And then it was over! The students left, but it was a tremendous, vibrant and exciting day and ultimately, they'd shown their power and won a victory against a government that was riding high on the back of defeating the miners, so it was some achievement to have done that.

9

Not in My Name: Student strikes against war in Iraq

IN THE aftermath of the horrendous attack on the twin towers in New York on 11 September 2001 the neo-cons at the heart of the US state administration launched what they termed a "war on terror"—a long-term struggle between "good and evil", in the words of George W Bush.[668]

The immense public sympathy generated by the attack was used to pursue a new global project dedicated to promoting US military and economic expansion. Condolezza Rice called "together the senior staff people of the National Security Council and asked them to think seriously about 'how do you capitalize on these opportunities' to fundamentally change American doctrine, and the shape of the world after 11 September".[669]

Washington based think-tank The Project for the New American Century, which had been in existence since 1997 and was staffed by leading members of the Bush regime, set out to offer a blue print for their vision of the world based around the interests and values of American free-market capitalism—a blueprint that was enshrined in the Bush administration's war manifesto, The National Security Strategy of the United States of America, published in September 2002.

The heart of the project was to utilise US military might to create and support a neo-liberal global regime structured to meet the needs of US multinationals. In the *New York Times* Thomas Friedman put it in brutally straight forward language:

> The hidden hand of the market will never work without a hidden fist. McDonald's cannot flourish without McDonnell-Douglas. And the hidden fist that keeps the world safe for Silicon Valley's technologies to flourish is called the US army, air force, navy and Marine Corps.[670]

Alex Callinicos[671] suggested that what we started to witness in the aftermath of the 9/11 attacks was the creation of a new "grand strategy" of the US Empire. The goals of this strategy being to protect and enhance US military and economic might, limiting the ability of regional powers (or future powers) to challenge US authority. The strategy involved (a) establishing US/Israeli control over the Middle East and its resources; (b) keeping the EU politically weak and internally divided by playing "new" Europe against "old"; (c) surrounding China with US bases and boosting the US military presence in the Asia-Pacific region; and (d) extending US military power into Eastern Europe and the former Soviet republics, thereby gaining access to regional resources and blocking any reintegration of "Soviet space".

The "Bush doctrine" offered an era of neo-liberal globalisation, welfare cuts, poverty for the many and vast riches for the already fabulously wealthy, and war. The end of Bush's time in the White House and his replacement by Barack Obama did not fundamentally alter the pattern of the US imperial mission.

Yet the priorities of the powerful did not go unchallenged. At the end of the last century a new mass movement came into being. It had many roots, but at the protests against the World Trade Organisation Third Ministerial in Seattle in 1999 the global social justice or anti-capitalist movement was born.[672] By the following summer it had spread beyond North America to Europe where it firmly took root at the protests against the G8 in Genoa in 2001. Youthful, vibrant and utterly opposed to neo-liberal globalisation, the movement was able to mobilise massive numbers onto the streets and—just as impressively—organise areas of open space for debate and argument about an alternative future at the World (and various sectoral) Social Forums.

Although the initial impact of the events of 9/11 was to throw the movement back (especially in the US), in Britain and Italy it quickly refocused energies into opposition to the Bush doctrine and the immediate threat of war against Afghanistan.

In Britain the Stop the War Coalition was formed at a large meeting in central London on 21 September 2001. It aimed to stop the endless war of the "war on terror" rather than any specific battle (in Afghanistan or Iraq, for example) within that war. It brought together new forces in a way that had not been seen for a generation. The anti-capitalist movement, peace activists (from the Campaign for Nuclear Disarmament and other organisations), trade unions and anti-war MPs including George Galloway, Alan Simpson and Jeremy Corbyn, far-left organisations, most significantly the Socialist Workers Party, and representatives from the Muslim community all joined together to form what was to become a truly mass movement on the streets of Britain.[673]

The movement started by campaigning against the attack on Afghanistan launched in October 2001. In January 2002 George W Bush used his state of the nation speech to denounce the supposed "axis of evil"—covering Iraq, Iran and North Korea—making it clear that regime change in Iraq was on the agenda. Throughout the rest of 2002 there was an immense ideological struggle waged between, on the one hand Bush, Blair and the US and UK states, and on the other the growing global anti-war movement.

In 2002 Stop the War grew in size and influence. By 28 September 2002 a massive march of close to 500,000 people, under the slogan "Don't attack Iraq", took to the streets of London.

In November a million people took part in the first European-wide demonstration in Florence at the end of the first meeting of the European Social Forum (ESF). At the ESF it was agreed that 15 February 2003 would be a day of coordinated European protest against the war. This date was soon to be taken up as a global day of protest.

The growth of the Stop the War movement was remarkable. Its size, global reach and diversity mark it out as one of the most remarkable social movements in British history. People engaged in a series of local, national and international demonstrations and actions against the threat of war.

In the weeks prior to 15 February the movement in Britain spread socially and geographically. Towns and cities across the country had meetings, local demonstrations and protests. On the day itself there were 600 known demonstrations across the globe and it has been estimated that 30 million people took part in the protests.[674] In Britain two million marched; in Rome approximately four million; a similar number marched in several locations across Spain; and in the US there was a massive demonstration in New York City.

Among those marching were hundreds of thousands of school students and the scale of the campaign led to the rebirth of the school student movement. Tens of thousands of US schoolchildren marched out of classes, calling for "books not bombs"; pupils in Switzerland walked out of school carrying rainbow flags for peace, followed by their classmates in Greece, Denmark, Sweden, Germany, Italy, Spain, Australia and Britain.[675]

In Britain Kate Connelly (16), soon to be one of the leaders of School Students Against the War, noted:

> The sense of power that everyone felt on that day [15 February] was immense... We felt in the majority and we felt very powerful. It made it so clear when you saw all those millions marching in the streets around the world.[676]

On the 15 February demonstration one of the Stop the War affiliates, the Socialist Party, used the opportunity to distribute thousands of leaflets calling for school student strikes. The call had met with some localised success but the campaign was given direction when the national Stop the War coalition facilitated a school student meeting in London on 22 February.[677]

Henna Malik (16) was one of the organisers of the meeting. She had been involved in anti-war campaigning since the September 2002 demonstration but after the 15 February demonstration she noticed a greater willingness among her friends and school colleagues to talk about the war and think about what could be done.

> It was after the February demonstration that people in school started talking about the war. There was a real politicisation going on and even very young kids were using words like "imperialism". Through the national Stop the War office I helped to organise the first meeting of School Students Against War (SSAW). We held a meeting in London and invited local groups to send representatives. About 200 school students turned up. We elected a national steering committee of 10 and I was elected the national coordinator. It was there that we set the date for the first national school strike on 5 March.[678]

Kate from Cambridge, adds:

> In the week after the 15 February demo we went up to London to a school student meeting. It started with reports from all these students around the country saying "we are organising a school strike" and when it came to our turn Ed (who was with me) said we were organising one as well—up to that point we hadn't been thinking about this,

but we felt we had to organise one because we had publically committed to it![679]

Kenny (16, Preston) also emphasised the link between the demonstration and the move to set up SSAW.

I went to the 15 February demo... There were 70 of us from our school
who went on the train organised by the local Stop the War Coalition.
On the way back, some of us got together and had a meeting. We decided
that on the Monday morning [17 February 2003], we would meet in the
city centre and march into school. We borrowed the coalition banner,
met at 8.45 and off we went. The following week, I organised a room and
we set up Preston School Students Against the War.[680]

In the weeks after 15 February school student "wild cat" strikes
started to break out across the country. In Glasgow:

Around 500 school, college and university students...struck and rallied
against war in the city centre on Friday of last week [28 February 2003]
[forcing] the closure of the army recruitment office.[681]

On the same day about 1,000 school students in Northern Ireland
and 400 more in Wales walked out of school.[682]

One of the youngest strikers who, because of her age, featured in an
article in the *Times Educational Supplement* was Olivia (10) from
Preston. She had been on the demonstration in February and attended
the Preston SSAW meeting. There she was part of a discussion about
how to organise a school strike. Following the discussion she took a
sign-up sheet to her primary school and got 28 pupils to agree to take
part in a strike against the war.

On 25 February, having signed up her classmates, she called the
strike. The young pupils were put under extreme pressure by the head
who kept them in the playground and refused to let them leave the
school premises. She threatened them with all manner of punishment. Some of the students started to falter. Three, including Olivia,
stood firm.[683]

Writing about the demonstrations Libby Brooks noted:

This spring...the country was witness to a new kind of protest. In the
most significant child-led campaign for a century, schoolchildren as
young as 10 walked out of their classrooms to attend what were, for

most, their first political demonstrations... These young people were organising and leading their own protests, leafletting at school gates, organising email networks and expertly working the media. Their determination to be heard was palpable. The results were awesome.[684]

Zoe Pilger, in the *Independent on Sunday*, argued:

Of all the carnage to come from a war in Iraq, one positive element has emerged. Young people of my generation are becoming more and more politicised. You can see it around you. It is now normal for me to over-hear 14 year olds discussing the pros and cons of military intervention, on the bus on the way home from school. Badges carrying anti-war slogans, such as "Not In My Name" are appearing on the lapels of school blazers and ties. It is common to turn on the television and see students under the age of 18 defying their teachers, waving banners and megaphones, and protesting in Parliament Square.[685]

As with previous waves of school strikes there is a tendency to view these as "spontaneous" outbursts. Indeed, Murray and German argue:

Of all the initiatives taken by the anti-war movement, the school walk-outs had the largest element of spontaneity.[686]

But we need to be careful not to over emphasise the "spontaneous" nature of the strike movement. Gramsci argued "pure spontaneity" does not exist. Rather, he argues, people talk of "spontaneous" rebellion because the "subaltern classes" and "indeed...their most marginal and peripheral elements...[leave] no reliable document...of the elements of 'conscious leadership'" shaping the events and their outcome.[687]

In other words the poor, the dispossessed and the marginal do not leave records of who argued what and who led the move from talk to action.[688] For the strikes to happen it needed local school students to step forward and make the case for action. The following words from Kenny (16, Preston) capture the elements of "self-conscious leadership" that some of the young people portrayed:

At our SSAW meeting we talked about getting organised and having a school strike. We made pledge sheets for people to sign. They signed them guaranteeing that they would strike. Some people signed them easily, some we had to convince, but this was a great way of committing people. On 5 and 6 March, we managed to get loads of students out on strike, we sat down on the road, demonstrated and really felt our voice was being heard. It was great.[689]

Some degree of coordination was offered by the fledgling SSAW network, but, as in 1985, there were many schools and school students who protested without any formal contact with the SSAW network. This can only really be explained by the rapidly changing context and the intense debate taking place about the threat of war in Iraq, and the confidence that many young school students gained by following what their peers were doing in the press, on television and via social network sites.

Lara and Amber from Mark Rutherford School in Bedford also provide an insight into the role of (their) leadership action within the general context of the time:

> We heard about the school strike the day before. We decided to get our school involved and began to spread the word. We expected 100 people to join in. We got 600. It was amazing.[690]

Across the country large numbers of young school students were stepping forward and courageously making the case for some form of action.

At the first SSAW meeting 5 March had been identified as the first national day of strike action. The date was chosen to coincide with proposed school strikes in the US on that day around the theme "Books not Bombs". Andrew Stone reports:

> An estimated 6,000 students took part, and many others were prevented from leaving school to join them. Hundreds of London students blocked the streets around Parliament and Downing Street.[691]

There were significant demonstrations in London, Birmingham, Leeds, Sheffield, Liverpool, Cambridge and Milton Keynes.[692]

Alys attended Alexandra Park School in North London. She was 14 at the time.

> This was the biggest political thing to have happened in my life...[on 5 March] there were initially just five of us taking the initial steps out of school... But the other kids had seen the handwritten leaflets in the corridors and toilets and when they saw us leaving other kids pretty much started running after us.
>
> I remember my form tutor running after me shouting "Alys, Alys we'll talk about this, just stay in school"—as if it was something

personal between her and me! But we just ignored her and headed towards Parliament Square.[693]

Kate tells the story of what happened in Cambridge:

When we marched out we started to head for town... In front of us was a really big policemen who told us to stop. I did—but everyone else just ignored him and walked on! The policemen told me that it was an illegal march and I said I couldn't control it and I wasn't in charge! I then got arrested and Ed, who had been organising with me, said "we are going to march to the police station"—so they arrested him! But what was important was that everyone else continued, they weren't cowed. They went to the police station and sat down outside. People felt very powerful—even though they were arresting people.[694]

Henna stood in front of her politics class in Coombe School, Kensington and said:

If you want a real politics lesson get your arses out and on to that demonstration...because there is nothing better than being involved in politics...don't read about it in a textbook...be part of it.[695]

Outside Parliament the BBC noted that some of the children "were as young as 13". Sam Beste from Fortismere School in North London told the BBC:

We just walked out of the school at break-time. There are now about 60 of us from our school. More would have come, but the teachers locked the gates after we left. We are against the war and this is the next step in our campaign to raise our voices against the war.[696]

Chris Smith (17) told the BBC there was no justification for a war and accused America of hypocrisy after its previous support for Iraq against Iran. Faced with the threat of war, he said:

[It's] no good sitting in front of your television if something like this is going on—you have to get up and do something.[697]

Sachin Sharma (16), a student at Prince Henry's Grammar School in Otley, near Leeds, argued that given students' lack of "democratic rights" they had no alternative but to take to the streets:

The majority of our school does not have democratic rights. They have no means to express themselves, and they don't have a voice in real terms. The only way we can, as minors, express ourselves is through demonstration.[698]

Over the next few days the strike wave spread. On 6 March there was a strike in Leicester with over 300 students congregating in the town centre. "The protest started at the Clock Tower in Leicester and was made up almost entirely of children from various schools around the city," according to the BBC.[699]

In Preston school students gathered in the central Flagmarket. The main organising centre was the large sixth form college in the city centre (Cardinal Newman College), whose students were 16-18 year olds. As the afternoon wore on small numbers of younger pupils joined the protest from a range of high schools across the city. Jess was just out of university and working for *Socialist Worker* at the time:

> We weren't sure what was going to happen. We had a SSAW meeting the week before and there were a lot of young people there. We knew most of them because they had been on our local demonstrations or had come down to London with us. The SSAW meeting had drawn up pledge sheets and people took them around their schools. But we were blown away by the response. We didn't expect so many pupils to come along and join us—suddenly we had a network of school students wanting to do stuff right across the city.[700]

The immediate reaction from the media and politicians was to label the strikes as "truancy" and to undermine the politics of those involved; something common to all school student strike waves.

In Birmingham the head teacher of Queensbridge School Christine Pitt wrote to parents warning them that the protest was not being sanctioned by the school. She wrote, "Students who stay off to be part of the protest will be marked with an unauthorised absence".[701]

In North London the Fortismere School deputy head teacher Martin Henson said he was "horrified" by the pupils' actions, claiming it was "irresponsible and dangerous". He blamed the older pupils who, he suggested, had "whipped up a frenzy" and would be "in a lot of trouble when they get back".[702]

The "trouble" he was threatening was, no doubt, similar to that in

Otley where the head teacher of Prince Henry's Grammar, John Steel, argued that the school "has a legal duty of care to its 1,360 students, and we must ensure the health and safety of our students during the school day. The school cannot advocate or legitimise actions that could put students at risk, and prevent us from exercising our responsibilities".[703] His fine sounding words about risk and protection were the pretext used to suspend two students for raising the question of a school strike.

Alys was also suspended for her role in organising the strike. She reflected on the irony of the move:

> I was excluded from lessons because I had missed lessons to protest against the war—where is the logic?[704]

In response to the claim that this was all just an excuse to skip school Henna argues:

> If people were just bunking off they wouldn't have gone on to protest, made their way into the town and city centres to take part in the campaign.[705]

Katrina (14), from Queensbridge School in Birmingham, said, "When we had our strike we were told we were truanting. We weren't. We were youth standing up for our political ideals in the world we're growing up in".[706]

The scale of the strikes on 5 and 6 March helped to spread the school student movement. More students were drawn into anti-war activity. This included involvement in the general Stop the War movement—participating in the regional marches that took place on 8 March—and organising debates in school:

> A London sixth form student reports, "Over 100 school students attended a debate between Lindsey German from the Stop the War Coalition and a representative from the US embassy at La Swap sixth form in Camden. By the end the US representative had to beat a retreat from questions he couldn't answer".[707]

On 12 March the first People's Assembly took place in Westminster Central Hall. Students from Pimlico School in central London walked out of school to attend the assembly. In front of the massive audience nine young children stepped forward, in turns, to give their reasons why they opposed the war:

(1) War is killing loads of people for no reason. (2) The US is only doing this for Iraq's oil, to protect its own financial interests. (3) The US wants to re-establish itself as the world's biggest superpower. (4) The US thinks it's the world's moral police, despite the corruption in its own country. (5) This war is immoral and no one wants it. (6) Blair is ignoring everyone. We should keep shouting so Blair can't ignore us. (7) War under any circumstances is always wrong. (8) This is breaking the rules of human rights and war by attacking Iraq when they haven't been attacked themselves. (9) We're children and it's our future Blair is destroying.[708]

The SSAW network now called for a second day of school strikes. The national network argued for a day of school strikes on 19 March and on "Day X", the day war starts. As it turned out this meant there were two days of school strikes on 19 and 20 March (Day X).

In preparation for the strike student activists organised banner painting sessions, signing up sessions to get class mates involved, meetings and a range of innovative activities to engage with those who were less convinced of their ability to act. For example, in Cambridge: "We organised banner painting...we put up posters and peace signs on the trees, and chalked around people on the floor to represent the Iraqi dead".[709]

Over the two days there was a massive wave of school student strikes. There were significant school closures in Belfast, Birmingham, Braintree, Bristol, Brighton, Cambridge, Cardiff, Carlisle, Dalston, Dundee, Dunmow, Edinburgh, Exeter, Glasgow, Glastonbury, Leeds, Leicester, Liverpool, London, Manchester, Milton Keynes, Newcastle, Newry, Nottingham, Plymouth, Preston, Scarborough, Sheffield, St Just, Stirling, Studley, Swansea, Torquay, Wolverhampton and Wrexham.

On 19 March some of the demonstrations were very large indeed. In Birmingham 5,000 students surrounded the main council building and 3,000 pupils blocked Manchester city centre. In Edinburgh 2,000 took part:

At 1300 GMT, as the traditional gun blast sounded from Edinburgh Castle, the youngsters lay down in the middle of the road in what they described as a "die-in".[710]

The movement swelled further after the bombs began falling that night. The 20 March was now Day X. About 5,000 protested in

Glasgow, 2,500 blockaded Sheffield's major roundabout, 2,000 protested in Brighton and 1,000 more in Leeds.

> School students dominated the 3,000-strong demonstration that wound through east London to Whitehall, where they joined thousands more from throughout London in shutting down Parliament Square.[711]

In central London the atmosphere around Parliament was described as "festive" as thousands of school students left school to join the protest. Here is Libby Brooks in the *Guardian*:

> Packed lunches were shared out. Cigarettes were smoked, slyly, cupped in hands held behind backs. "No War, Blair Out" stickers were plastered across taut, bare tummies and on tracksuited bottoms. Boys checked out girls, checking out boys, chanting, "Who let the bombs off? Bush! Bush and Blair!"[712]

Suzanne was at school in Hackney, London:

> In 2003 I was a student at Haggerston School in Hackney. After weeks of planning for Day X...when it came hundreds of students and some teachers walked out. We marched to Hackney town hall, where we joined with students from schools across Hackney and collectively marched to Parliament Square to join thousands of young anti-war protesters.[713]

Adam was in Stratford, East London:

> At lunchtime the streets [of Stratford] were filled with hundreds of schoolchildren who had come to show their opposition to the war. The mainly Bangladeshi and Pakistani school pupils poured onto the roads blocking traffic on Stratford Broadway... The school children were mainly between the ages of 11 and 15.[714]

On 5 and 6 March some schools had locked their doors, buildings and fences to try and stop students joining the protests. In response a number of students turned to picketing, stopping the students before they got into the school and before they could be locked in. As the BBC reported on 20 March:

> School children picketed many schools across London this morning to gather protest supporters, because they said they thought their teachers would stop them leaving if they went inside.[715]

The breadth and scale of the pupil protests took many by surprise.

In London police were forced to close off the main entrance to the House of Commons as schoolchildren marched on Parliament Square. Police on horseback were subsequently used to clear a sit-down protest and to prevent an attempt to climb over the gates to Downing Street. In Manchester the police used pepper spray against protesting pupils.

Bob Carstairs, assistant general secretary of the Secondary Heads Association (SHA), expressed his dismay at the speed with which the protests spread:

> It seems to have escalated each day… Children are getting blanket text messages telling them to join in. In other cases one child will get a message which refers them to an e-mail site. That's how it's spreading. This is the biggest event I can remember in 30-odd years in teaching.[716]

The reaction of the police was often brutal. Kate describes their behaviour in Cambridge when the school students sat down in the road.

> The police moved in with batons and started dragging people off, it really was very unpleasant…nose rings were pulled out, eyebrow rings pulled out. You could see people being whacked against the pavement.[717]

Henna remembers:

> We were involved in a road block and then the police came and pushed us up against a wall—they kettled us, though I don't think we called it that then! Then they started lifting people, throwing them around, hitting them… Up until that point I thought the police were there to protect me and individual citizens…but obviously not. That's not what they are there for. They were there to protect the state and the interests of the state.[718]

The scale of the demonstrations was not the only interesting feature of the protests. For those who argue that young people are apathetic, the justifications pupils gave for their actions were considered, reasoned and articulate.

Daniel (16, Liverpool) put it this way:

> This is not a war against dictatorship—there are many dictatorships around the world that Bush and Blair support. This war will not make the world safer, but more unstable, especially the Middle East. This war

will not only target Saddam's elite troops, but ordinary Iraqis, men, women and children—those who already suffer from UN-imposed sanctions and Hussein's brutal regime. No, this war is about oil and US interests. It's imperialism.[719]

Zuned (15, Preston) said, "What about Israel? They have nuclear weapons and biological weapons. Every day they kill young Palestinian children, yet nothing is ever said. Why? It's because America supports them".[720]

Olivia (10, Preston) focused on the children of Iraq: "Bush and Blair will kill thousands of Iraqi children, just like me and my friends. My teachers told me I was too young to protest, but if I'm too young to protest, they're too young to be killed".[721]

Journalists interviewing school strikers also reported equally clear and thoughtful responses from young people justifying their decision to walk out. Most expressed a profound scepticism over the rationale for military intervention. Clare (16, Newcastle) explained that she and 200 others walked out of school and demonstrated at the city's war memorial because they wanted to send a strong message to the prime minister:

> We all feel strongly that war is wrong. There is no valid reason for war on Iraq, dropping bombs will solve nothing and innocent lives will be lost. Young people have a voice and Tony Blair needs to listen to us.[722]

Jaswinder (13, Birmingham) explained that he and 350 children walked out because they believed that "innocent people shouldn't die so George Bush and Tony Blair get their oil".[723]

Amanda (15, Belfast) told a rally that "Bush is not giving the real reason. It's not to get rid of a dictator, it's all about oil. We want Bush and Blair to know that the youth are not behind them".[724]

As shown in earlier chapters, in previous waves of pupil protests in Britain the state responded brutally. Children had in the past faced intimidation, discipline (in many cases physical), suspension from school and arrest when challenging and questioning the legitimacy of the school authorities and the local and national state. In 2003 the reaction of the educational establishment to the protests mirrored this. The reaction of Chris Woodhead, former chief inspector of schools for England, was fairly typical:

Firstly, I am concerned about truancy, whatever the motivation for truancy, because I see a slippery path towards anarchy and kids being in school at all. And secondly, I suppose the older I get, the more complicated life becomes. There aren't any simple issues, and I suppose I worry a bit about encouraging young people to articulate judgements and feelings, however strongly they are held, when they haven't got the evidence, they haven't got the experience to really understand the full ramifications of what they are talking about.[725]

In light of Woodhead's conservative reputation in education, his response to the pupil protests is not surprising. However, teacher associations adopted a similarly recalcitrant line, interpreting pupil protests as a disciplinary problem. David Hart, leader of the National Association of Head Teachers, argued that head teachers had to either stop children "running amok in the country's high streets" during school strikes he described as "deplorable" and "irresponsible", or face discipline problems in the future.

Heads should ban all protests during school. They should take disciplinary action against any members of staff who encourage the demonstrations and against any pupils who are absent when they should be in school.[726]

Most local education authorities (LEAs) took Hart's advice, and many children who participated in protests faced disciplinary proceedings and suspensions. Elena Grice, a 15 year old pupil at Helena Romanes School in Dunmow, Essex was excluded from school for 30 days for helping to organise a 200-strong anti-war rally.[727] Five pupils at Abbey Grammar School in Newry, Ireland were suspended for eight weeks for attending a mass walkout on 5 March,[728] while 20 pupils at Cape Cornwall School in St Just near Penzance were suspended after joining a demonstration on 19 March.[729]

Most LEAs issued guidelines stating that protests during the school day, off premises, should be seen as unauthorised absences and treated as acts of "common truancy".

Intimidation and threats of exclusion and suspension did little to deter pupils, most of whom participated in anti-war protests in the full knowledge that their actions could result in them being disciplined.

Fiona Bagworth (14), who walked out of Beecham College in

Oadby, Leicestershire said, "When you believe in something so strongly, you just have to do it. We were warned about suspension and being put on report but it doesn't matter".[730]

Mirren Kelly (15), of Heaton Manor School, Newcastle said, "Lots of pupils in our school have been told they will get into trouble but we think it is more important to make a stand. People my age feel very strongly that bombing Iraq would be wrong".[731]

The pupils' protests were shaped by a high level of political understanding—reflective of the general movement against war in 2003. But like the previous school student strike waves the initial burst of activity faded; though there were sporadic school strikes around anti-war themes when first George Bush and then Condoleezza Rice made formal visits to Britain in 2003 and 2006. SSAW remained an important campaigning organisation of school students within the anti-war movement and it produced off-shoot organisations such as Force Watch, which campaigned against army recruitment in schools.

But as in the past, a more permanent political network of school students was difficult to hold together once the initial strike wave receded. Nevertheless, the school student strikes of 2003 stand as the largest example of school student collective action in British history and, in this sense, the high water mark of the school student movement.

Henna Malik (London, 2003)
"It was my education"

In 2002/03 the campaign against war in Afghanistan and Iraq and for freedom in Palestine was massive. I got involved after reading on teletext that there was a demonstration in support of Palestine in Hyde Park. I said to my mum "we should go" and that was my first involvement with the Stop the War movement. I was 16 at the time.

Things moved very quickly. Over the next few months I became very involved. I started going to demonstrations, both national and local ones. I got involved with the local Stop the War Coalition and went, with mum, to the European Social Forum meeting in Florence. The Florence meeting announced there would be a European day of action against war on 15 February 2003.

In the run up to that demonstration there were loads of things to do. I was involved in meetings, leafletting, fly-posting—it was just a blur of activity. And on the day it was unbelievable, the number of people marching in London was just tremendous and to be part of that was indescribable.

In the week after the demonstration we held the first meeting of School Students Against War at Friends Meeting House in London. There were about 200 school students there. We elected a national organising committee of ten—and I was elected national coordinator.

I remember at the meeting there were various people outside from a range of organisations, but we were very strict in the meeting: we only let school students in. Of the ten elected to the steering committee only two were members of political organisations (I had just joined the SWP) but eight of the committee were "independent".

The committee now met regularly at the StW offices and we started to plan for the school strike. We wanted to have a massive school strike on the day they started their war. We wrote leaflets and got them distributed to all the school students who had said they were interested. We were on the phone all the time. The 200 who came to the London meeting were phoned to make sure that they had leaflets and posters, that they were organising stalls and that they were taking "pledge sheets" around their school.

The pledge sheet was important. It was a way of talking to students, getting them to agree to come out and a way to build our network.

From the pledges we had new names of people who wanted to get involved: it was like a rolling snow ball, we were gathering new names, new people, new activists almost daily.

On the day the war started there were strikes across the country. All our hard work, all those phone calls resulted in somewhere in the region of 20,000 school students walking out and protesting. Across the country school students marched, demonstrated, sat down in the road and caused a huge amount of disruption. This was something we were proud of, and it's something I remain proud of today. Blair was launching a war that would result in the deaths of hundreds of thousands of Iraqis. School students struck and made it clear he was not doing this in our name.

In London the students made their way to Parliament Square. I got there about 12ish. It was crazy. It was very noisy and very vibrant. You could hear the noise as soon as you left the tube station.

The square was absolutely rammed. We had speeches, there was singing and chanting and I must have had a thousand conversations with people about what we should do next.

Some of the students then sat down in the roads—causing huge disruption. The sit downs weren't planned, they were spontaneous events that happened after a few kids took the initiative.

As the day progressed the police tried to block us in. Today we would call this "kettling". I remember seeing one really quite young boy stuck in the kettle. Across the road was his even younger sister. She was crying and the boy went to a copper and asked if he could go to her. The cop just punched him in the face. It was really shocking for me to see that, to see how aggressive and violent the police were that day.

I stayed in the square till quite late. I was interviewed by Jonathen Dimbleby late that evening in a live link from the square.

My involvement in those few months had a big impact on me. I often tell people it was my education. In those months I found out more about inequality, war, imperialism, the state, the role of the police and the power of collective action than I'd ever learnt at school. An education which continues to shape my thinking today.

10

Conclusion: That was then, this is now!

In 2015 journalist Adi Bloom asked, What happened to the rebelliousness of youth?

She suggests that the days of youth rebellion may be over:

> Rebelling against the rules of one's elders used to be a teenage rite of passage. It was the defining point of teenage existence... Today's teenagers, however, seem increasingly happy to follow the rules, whether in school or out.[732]

Bloom's argument draws on data showing a decline in school exclusions, teenage pregnancies and suggesting declining use of cigarettes, drugs and alcohol, to argue young people are being drawn into the mainstream.

The pressure on young people to pass exams and get to university has focussed minds. Moves by a range of institutions to include young people in their decision making processes and give them a voice have incorporated the young and dissipated their general rebelliousness, Bloom says.

She contends that part of this process includes a rejection of politics. Joining political parties, voting, protesting and demonstrating are passé. Today if young people want to express their views, they will do so via Twitter, Facebook or other social media—but politics and protest? No thanks!

Bloom echoes a more general dismissal of young people's political engagement. But things are not so straightforward. As we noted in our introduction, young people remain engaged in a range of political movements—though attachment to the mainstream political parties is more tenuous than in the past. The last few years have been marked by regular school student protests and strikes over a range of issues (though these often remain hidden as schools and local authorities try to conceal them).

But in the aftermath of the May 2015 British election it was hard to ignore the influx of young people joining anti-government protests. The election saw the Conservative party returned to power with a small majority on a minority vote. The result was met with a mixture of disbelief and despair in many activist circles—but soon despair turned to anger. On 9 May there were demonstrations across the country, including significant clashes between protestors and the police in central London. One noticeable feature was the youthfulness of the demonstrators.

The largest of the protests was organised by seven school students in Bristol. Four thousand joined the demonstration they called at three days' notice. Huw Williams, writing in *Socialist Worker*, reported that the "Bristol Against Austerity march was overwhelmingly young and included swathes of school students..."[733]

One of the organisers, Hannah Patterson, told the crowd, "We are young, but our voices will not be silenced. We will not sit around while the rich get richer and the poor poorer".[734]

Another organiser Megan Foster Flaherty argued:

Like many others we felt lost and hopeless after the election, but seeing the London protest [the action in Downing Street] inspired us to take action, peaceful action, to get our voices heard... It's about helping the most vulnerable to survive austerity in the bleak years to come. We felt, "If not us, who? If not now, when?"[735]

Katie Forster, writing in the *Observer*, noted the apparent paradox that "Young people are the least likely to vote—only 43 percent of those aged 18-24 did so in May [2015]—yet grassroots initiatives can have a far-reaching effect on disillusioned youth".[736]

If nothing else, the return of young school students to the streets and their engagement with the anti-austerity protests should question Bloom's thesis that the young are no longer rebellious. By the summer of 2015 the movement for change around the Jeremy Corbyn Labour leadership campaign drew a significant number of young people into debates about the future of British politics and alternatives to austerity. It would seem premature to suggest young people are no longer interested in politics or engaging in collective action.

We have argued the highest form of student protest is the school strike. It challenges the authority of head teachers, schools and educational authorities and, more recently, has been an expression of young people's broader political engagement with national and international issues. But the strikes are often recorded in ways that hide their true intent. In a world of school league tables and comparison between competing schools, school strikes are not "on message".

What is also noticeable is the complete lack of imagination those in authority have when school students strike From 1889 onwards school and education authorities have blamed students for copying adults, being "easily led" by outside activists, really being truants who are unable to understand complex political ideas and putting themselves at risk by leaving the school to take part in the protests. Young people have been met with derision, suspension, expulsion, beatings and other punishments, and investigations by schools and educational authorities. Their demands are given little real legitimacy but, remarkably, in almost all cases time has shown their perspectives to be more accurate than that of their so-called betters in positions of power.

Because of the pressures placed on young people by those in authority, student strikes are not easy to organise. There are a range of risks facing leaders. As many of the vignettes from activists have emphasised, schools and educational authorities can be vicious and vindictive in their treatment of school student activists. Educational authorities discipline, suspend and expel students who question the ways schools are governed, organised and run. Organising school action potentially brings young people into conflict with the police and even, as in the late 1960s and early 1970s, makes them the subject of state surveillance.

Despite this, the remarkable thing is that school student strikes are far more common than is usually assumed. Indeed we were pleasantly surprised by the number and range of strikes we discovered in the 12 months prior to submitting our manuscript for publication. The school strikes take two forms: the sporadic strike, usually about a school-specific grievance, and the more generalised strike wave where groups of school students across the country join to protest school conditions or broader political conditions (such as youth unemployment, school funding arrangements or war).

It is often difficult to organise school students into unions and lasting formal networks. Activists leave and move on. The excitement of the strike and protest is in contrast to the more mundane, routinised work of school student unionisation. There are few resources—financial and human—making the task of keeping a union together very difficult. But the remarkable thing is the recurrent attempts by school students to organise themselves and to engage in collective political activity.

School student strikes are vibrant, energetic and, generally, short lived political eruptions. They challenge the status quo and open up new ways of seeing for those at the heart of the disputes. We may not know when or where, but history tells us that we are likely to see another explosion in our schools at some point, when young people engage in collective action as part of campaigns to establish a better world.

Notes

1   Jamie Ross, "What 7,000 teenagers talked about during The Big, Big Debate". BBC News 11 September 2014 http://www.bbc.com/news/uk-scotland-scotland-politics-29157668.

2   James Sloam, "Bringing out the youth vote? Young people and the 2015 General Election", http://www.election analysis.uk/uk-election-analysis-2015/section-2-voters/bringing-out-the-youth-vote-young-people-and-the-2015-general-election/.

3   M Lavalette (ed), *A Thing of the Past? Child Labour in Britain in the Nineteenth and Twentieth Centuries* (Liverpool, 1999), pp123-128.

4   G Rude, *The Crowd in History 1730-1848* (London, 1981), chapter 14.

5   M Armstrong, *The Liberty Tree: The Story of Thomas Muir and Scotland's First Fight for Democracy* (Edinburgh, 2014), p4.

6   Ibid p7.

7   L Raw, *Striking a Light: The Bryant and May Matchwomen and their Place in History* (London, 2011).

8   J Charlton, *It Just Went Like Tinder: The Mass Movement and New Unionism in Britain 1889* (London, 1999), p10.

9   Raw, 2011, pp202-210.

10 Ibid, p212.

11 P Ryan, "Apprentice strikes, pay strikes and training in twentieth century UK metal working industry" in C Brown, B Eichengreen and M Reich (eds), *Labour in the Era of Globalisation* (Cambridge, 2009), pp317-353.

12 Dave Lyddon, "Postscript: The Labour Unrest in Great Britain and Ireland,

1910-1914: Still Unchartered Territory?" *Historical Studies in Industrial Relations*, no 33, 2012, pp241-265.

13 Ibid, p247.

14 Ibid, pp251, 252.

15 D J K Peukert, *Inside Nazi Germany: Conformity, Opposition and Racism in Everyday Life* (trans R Deveson), (New Haven, 1982/1987).

16 Ibid, p159.

17 Ibid, p166.

18 Ed Vulliamy "Brave Old World", *Observer*, 4 July 2004. http://www.theguardian.com/theobserver/2004/jul/04/features.magazine17. On Antek see http://themichmashcenter.blogspot.com/2011/07/little-insurgent-of-warsaw-maego.html.

19 Taylor Branch, *Parting the Waters: America in the King Years 1954-63* (New York, 1988), p757.

20 Ibid.

21 David J Farrow, *Bearing the Cross: Martin Luther King and the Southern Christian Leadership Conference* (New York, 1986), p250.

22 Branch, (1988), p770.

23 E P Thompson, *The Making of the English Working Class* (Harmondsworth, 1963), pp338, 366-370.

24 Daniel Defoe, *A Tour Thro' the Whole Island of Great Britain Divided into Circuits or Journeys Giving a Particular and Entertaining Account of Whatever is Curious and Worth Observation* (four volumes), (London, 1748).

25 A Davin, "When is a child not a child?" In H Corr and L Jameson (eds), *Politics of Everyday Life* (Basingstoke, 1990), pp37, 38.

26 Huggermugger—in this sense Davin means socially hidden or concealed ie not recognised as children with distinct needs.

27 Davin (1990), pp38, 39.

28 There is considerable debate on the social causes of child labour exploitation in the early phase of capitalist development. Ivy Pinchbeck, *Women Workers and the Industrial Revolution* (London, 1930/1981), and others argue that in the cottage industries children worked long hours doing repetitive and mundane tasks. These continued, during the early phase of industrial production, with the exploitation more open and visible. As a result it motivated philanthropists and politicians to enact legislation to control the worst forms of child labour exploitation. In contrast E P Thompson (1963) argues the exploitation of child labour during industrialisation was one of the most brutal episodes of the industrial revolution. These debates are explored in M Lavalette, *Child Employment in the Capitalist Labour Market* (Aldershot, 1994), where it is argued that the debate misses the key turning point, the intensification of child labour exploitation which came about with the growing hold of the market from the 17th century onwards.

29 A Davin, "Child labour, the working class family and domestic ideology in nineteenth century Britain", *Development and Change*, 1982, 13, 4, p634.

30 M Lavalette (1999).

31 Davin (1982), p636.

32 M Lavalette, "Child labour: Historical, Legislative and Policy Context" in B Pettit (ed), *Children and Work in the UK* (London, 1998).

33 M Lavalette (1994).

34 A Davin, *Growing up Poor: Home, school and Street in London 1870-1914* (London, 1996).

35 E Hobsbawm, *The Age of Empire* (new ed), (London, 1988).

36 M Langan and B Schwartz (eds), *Crises in the British State* (London, 1985).

37 G Steadman Jones, *Outcast London: A Study in the Relationship Between Classes in Victorian Society*, revised edition, (London, 2013).

38 See F D Hyndman, *Record of an Adventurous Life* (London, 1911/2013), pp330-332.

39 Ibid, p331.

40 "Less eligibility" was a concept established in the New Poor Law (1834), the notion that the "idle poor" are always looking at ways of getting "something for nothing", making it essential to stop benefits becoming attractive to the idle poor—or more attractive than work—so they must always be paid at a rate lower than the lowest paying job on the labour market.

41 P Thane, *The Foundations of the Welfare State* (London, 1982).

42 J M Winter, "Military fitness and civilian health in Britain during the First World War" *Journal of Contemporary History* 15; 2 Apr 1980 pp211-244; T E Jordan, *The Degeneracy Crisis and Victorian Youth* (New York, 1993), p165.

43 B Harris, *The Origins of the British Welfare State* (Basingstoke, 2004).

44 D Dwork, *War is Good for Babies and Other Young Children: A History of the Infant and Child Welfare Movement in England 1898-1918* (London, 1987).

45 H Hendricks "Children and social policies" in H Hendricks (ed), *Child Welfare and Social Policy* (Bristol, 2005), p34.

46 S Steinbach, *Women in England 1760-1914* (London, 2013), chapter 7.

47 H Hendrick, *Child Welfare: Historical Dimensions, Contemporary Debate* (Bristol, 2003), p19.

48 E Frow and R Frow, *The Half Time System in Education* (London, 1970).

49 S Humphries, *Hooligans or Rebels? An Oral History of Working Class Childhood and Youth 1889-1939* (Oxford, 1995).

50 *Educational News*, editorial, 5 October 1889, pp685-686.

51 Of course this is not the only role performed by the school system, as we discuss in chapter 2. But on this aspect, see for example, P Willis, *Learning to*

Labour (London, 1977).

52   R Adams, *Protests by Pupils: Empowerment, Schooling and the State* (Bristol, 1991), p2.

53   *Socialist Worker* (2010), "Rolling coverage of student protests on Day X3" http://socialistworker.co.uk/art/22937/Rolling+coverage+of+student+protests +on+Day+X3,+Thursday+9+December.

54   D Sewell "A Generation in Revolt" *Socialist Review*, January 2011, http://socialistreview.org.uk/354/generation-revolt.

55   A Gabbatt and D Batty, "Second day of student protests: how the demonstrations happened", *Guardian,* 24 November 2014, http://www.theguardian.com/education/ 2010/nov/24/student-school-pupils-protests-walkout; "Day X: Young People Show How To Fight Back", *Socialist Worker*, 24 November 2010, http://socialistworker.co.uk/art/22781/Day+X percent3A+young+people++show+how+to+fight+back. M Taylor, P Lewis and B Van der Zee, "School pupils plan national walkout over tuition fees" *Guardian*, 19 November 2010, http://www.theguardian.com/education/2010/nov/19/students-school-pupils-protest.

56   S Coughlan, "Students stage day of protests over tuition fees rises", BBC News, 24 November 2010, http://www.bbc.co.uk/news/education- 11829102.

57   A Gabbatt and D Batty, "Second day of student protests: how the demonstrations happened", *Guardian*, 24 November 2014, http://www.theguardian.com/education/2010/nov/24/student-school-pupils-protests-walkout.

58   D Casciani "eyewitness: London students protest over fees", BBC News, 24 November 2010. http://www.bbc.co.uk/news/education-11834784.

59   S Ruddick, "Students: The birth of a movement", *Socialist Worker*, 30 November 2010, http://socialist worker.co.uk/art/22814/Students perce nt3A+The+birth+of+a+movement.

60   S Coughlan "Student tuition fee protest ends with 153 arrests" BBC News, 1 December 2010, http://www.bbc.co.uk/news/education-11877034.

61   Joe, Charlie and Sophie interview in "Rolling coverage of Student protests on Day X2", *Socialist Worker,* 30 November 2010http://socialist worker.co.uk/art/22800/Rolling+coverage+of+student+protests+on+Day+X2.

62   Ibid.

63   P Walker and J Paige, "Student protests—as they happen", *Guardian*, 9 December 2010, http://www.theguardian.com/education/blog/2010/dec/09/student-protests-live-coverage.

64   "Royal car attacked in protest after MPs fees vote", BBC News, 10 December 2010, http://www.bbc.co.uk/news/education-11954333.

65   Ben Turner, "Hundreds of Merseyside secondary school students set to walk out of class for tuition fees protest", *Liverpool Echo*, 22 November 2010, http://www.liverpoolecho.co.uk/news/liverpool-news/hundreds-merseyside-secondary-school-students-3391134.

66   Ibid.

67   *The Star* (Sheffield), "Student protests: City students vent their fury at Clegg" 25 November 2010, http://www.thestar.co.uk/what-s-on/out-about/student-protests-city-students-vent-their-fury-on-clegg-pictures-1-2969945.

68   *Socialist Worker*, "Sheffield school students on the march", 7 December 2010, http://socialistworker.co.uk/art/22930/Sheffield+school+students+on+the+march.

69   S Robinson, "Camden sixth form students begin their sit-in", *Socialist Worker*, 8 December 2010, http://socialistworker.co.uk/art/22934/Camden+sixth+form+students+begin+their +sit-in.

70   M Taylor, "School walkouts planned to coincide with public sector strikes", *Guardian*, 20 June 2011, http://www.theguardian.com/world/2011/jun/20/student-walkouts-public-sector-strikes.

71   C Harman, *The Fire Last Time: 1968 and After* (London, 1988).

72 S Tarrow, *Power in Movement: Social Movements, Collective Action and Politics* (New York, 1994), p155.

73 T Booth and D Coulby (eds), *Producing and Reducing Disaffection: Curricula for All* (Milton Keynes, 1987).

74 See also S Humphries, *Hooligans or Rebels: Oral History of Working Class Childhood and Youth 1889-1939* (second revised ed), (Oxford, 1995).

75 S Humphries "Who has the power? Memories of school strikes", in Booth and Coulby (1987), p248.

76 R J Rubel, *The Unruly School: Disorders, Disruptions and Crimes* (Lexington, 1977), p83

77 South Africa History online, "Youth and the national liberation struggle", www.sahistory.org.za/topic/June-16-Soweto-youth-uprising?page=3

78 Ibid.

79 See the excellent resources at South Africa: Overcoming Apartheid Building Democracy website www.overcomingapartheid.msu.edu.

80 B Hirson, *Year of Fire, Year of Ash: The Soweto Revolts, Roots of a Revolution?* (London, 1979).

81 "Soweto student uprising", South Africa: Overcoming Apartheid, Building Democracy, www.overcomingapartheid.msu.edu/sidebar.php?id=65-258-3.

82 J H Stokes, *Students on Strike: Jim Crow, Civil Rights, Brown and Me* (Scholastic Press, 2008).

83 Ibid, p65.

84 National Association for the Advancement of Coloured People.

85 Ibid.

86 A Goodman and J Gonzalez (2006), *Walkout: The True Story of the Historic 1968 Chicano Student Walkout in East LA*, http://www.democracynow.org/2006/3/29/walkout_the_true_story_of_the

87 See the excellent clip from the documentary *Or Forever Hold Your Peace* (1970), also.gov.au/titles/documentaries/or-forever-hold-your-peace/clip2/.

88 K Kinyanjui "Secondary School Strikes: The Art of Blaming the Victim", Institute for Development Studies, Kenya Discussion Paper no 243 (University of Nairobi, 1976), available at opendocs.ids.ac.uk/opendocs/bitstream/handle/123456789/658/dp243-316869.pdf?sequence=1.

89 C Rose, "Student Power" (British Council 2011), http://learnenglish.britishcouncil.org/sites/podcasts/files/LearnEnglish_MagazineArticle_Student_Power.pdf.

90 M Reichetseder, Germany: 100,000 on the streets in a massive student strike Friday, 14 November 2008, http://www.marxist.com/germany-massive-student-strike.htm.

91 L Rafetseder, "60,000 school students strike on 24 April", 30 April 2009, http://www.socialistworld.net/doc/3555.

92 B Wharton, "Students Strike at Montclair High School", 27 April 2010, http://www.examiner.com/article/students-strike-at-montclair-high-school.

93 J Coca, "School students go on strike" 2012, http://www.demotix.com/news/1527858/school-students-go-strike#media-1527831.

94 N Lennard, "High Schoolers on Strike" Salon 24 April 2012, http://www.salon.com/2012/04/24/high_schoolers_on_strike/.

95 C Snook and K Doll, "Mass school students' strike in Hamburg against deportations" 22 December 2013, http://www.socialistworld.net/doc/6597.

96 Rebellion "thousands of students strike in Austria", http://www.marxist.com/austria-thousands-of-school-students-on-strike.htm.

97 "Arab state school students join Christian schools' strike", *Times of Israel*, 7 September 2015, http://www.timesofisrael.com/arab-state-school-students-join-christian-schools-strike/.

98 I Lazareva, "Christian Schools Accuse Israel of Discrimination as Students Strike", *Time*, 16 September 2015, http://time.com/4036257/christian-

schools-israel-discrimination/.

99 S Humphries "Who has the power? Memories of school strikes", in Booth and Coulby (1987), p249.

100 BBC News, "Southall pupils strike over teacher sacking", 8 February 2011, http://www.bbc.co.uk/news/uk-england-london-12390962.

101 M Fricker, "Pupils go on strike after school bans charity bracelets in honour of classmate suffering from leukaemia" *Daily Mirror*, 19 March 2014, http://www.mirror.co.uk/news/uk-news/joel-smith-leukaemia-charity-bracelets-3262135.

102 Ben James, "More than 100 Brighton and Hove pupils given detention for going on strike", *The Argus*, 29 March 2014, http://www.theargus.co.uk/news/11111826._/.

103 Emily Pearce, "Students strike at Cowes school", County Press Online, 4 April 2014, http://www.iwcp.co.uk/news/news/students-strike-at-cowes-school-55184.aspx.

104 Jennifer Smith, "Pupils plan strike action on 3 June to stop London school being turned into an academy", *London Evening Standard*, 30 May 2014, http://Www.standard.co.uk/news/education/pupils-plan-strike-to-stop-london-school-being-turned-into-an-academy-9459608.html.

105 K Jacobs "School students strike against academy plan at Crown Woods College in Eltham", *Socialist Worker*, 3 June 2014, http://www.socialistworker.co.uk/art/38292/School+students+strike+against+academy+plan+at+Crown+Woods+College+in+Eltham.

106 All three quotations from K Gould, "Pupils go on strike" *South London Press*, 11 March 2015, http://www.southlondonpress.co.uk/news.cfm?id=27257&headline="PUPILSpercent20GOpercent20ON percent20STRIKE".

107 K Gould, "Students strike at academy proposal", *South London Press*, 6 March 2015.

108 T G Higdon, *The Burston Rebellion* (1923, reprinted by The Trustees of the Burston Strike School, Diss, 1984).

109 "Stepney Words, Poetry And A Schoolkids' Strike", Stand Up and Spit, https://standupandspit.wordpress.com/2016/01/14/stepney-words-poetry-and-a-schoolkids-strike/.

110 Ibid.

111 J Charlton, *It Just Went Like Tinder: The Mass Movement and New Unionism in Britain 1889* (London, 1999).

112 M Haynes, "The British Working Class in Revolt", *International Socialism* 2:22 Winter 1985; J Newsinger, *Them and Us: Fighting the class war 1910-1939* (London, 2015).

113 D Marson, "Children's Strikes in 1911," History Workshop Pamphlet, no 9 1973.

114 BBC Radio 4, *The Long View*, http://www.bbc.co.uk/radio4/history/longview/longview_20030408.shtml 08/04/2003.

115 T Evans, "The Great Unrest and a Welsh Town", *International Socialism* 131 2011, http://www.isj.org.uk/index.php4?id=744&issue=131.

116 D Marson (1973).

117 C Harman (1988).

118 A Callinicos and M Simons, *The Great Strike: The Miners' Strike of 1984-5 and its Lessons* (London, 1985).

119 A Murray and L German, *Stop the War: The Story of Britain's Biggest Mass Movement* (London, 2005).

120 R Luxemburg, *The Mass Strike* (London, 1906/1986), pp46, 50

121 C Harman (1988), pp39,40

122 Chant sung by striking children from Burmondsey Board School, demanding an end to school fees. "School children's strikes", *Daily News*, 11 October, 1889, issue 13577.

123 John Charlton (1999).

124 T Taylor, "As the old cocks grow, the young ones learn: The school strikes of 1889 and the New Union movement", *History of Education*, vol 24, no 1, 1994, pp89-106.

125 *Times*, "Scotland", 30 September 1889.

126 *Times* (1889).

127 *North-Eastern Daily Gazette*, "School children in revolt: Strike against long hours and home lessons", 1 October 1889.

128 *Manchester Guardian*, "Summary of news", 2 October 1889.

129 *Times*, "The schoolboys' strike in Scotland", 4 October 1889.

130 *North-Eastern Daily Gazette*, "Shorter hours and no home tasks", 5 October 1889.

131 *Manchester Guardian*, "The schoolboy strike", 5 October 1889.

132 *Pall Mall Gazette*, "The schoolboy strike's extending", 5 October 1889, issue 7660.

133 "Parsing" was the term contemporaries used to describe the rote learning of grammar.

134 *Pall Mall Gazette*, 1889.

135 *Lloyds Weekly*, "School children on strike", October 6 1889, issue 2446.

136 *The Graphic*, "The strike of school children", 19 October 1889.

137 Ibid.

138 *Dundee Courier and Argos*, "The strike of school children", 9 October 1889, issue 11312.

139 S Humphries (1981), *Hooligans or rebels? Oral History of Working Class Childhood and Youth, 1889-1937* (Oxford, 1981).

140 *Leeds Mercury*, "The school children's strike", 1 October 1889.

141 *Pall Mall Gazette*, "The schoolboy strike in Barnet", 7 October 1889, issue 7661.

142 *North-Eastern Daily Gazette*, "School boy insubordination", 10 October 1889b.

143 *Lloyds Weekly*, "Spoiled infant candidates for the birch", 13 October 1889a.

144 *Dundee Advertiser*, cited in C Bloom, *Violent London: 2000 Years of Violence, Rebellion and Revolts* (Basingstoke, 2010).

145 *Manchester Guardian*, "Judge Hughes on the schoolboys' strikes", 22 October 1889e.

146 C Bloom, (2010).

147 T Taylor, "As the old cocks grow, the young ones learn: The school strikes of 1889 and the New Union movement", *History of Education*, vol 24, no 1, (1994), pp89-106.

148 D A Wells, *Recent Economic Changes and Their Effect on the Production and Distribution of Wealth and Well-Being of Society* (New York, 1891), pp1-2.

149 E Hobsbawm (London, 1987).

150 B Simon, *Education and the Labour Movement 1870-1920* (London, 1965).

151 G Pearson, *Hooligan: A History of Respectable Fears* (Basingstoke, 1983).

152 G Steadman Jones, *Outcast London: A Study in the Relationship Between Classes in Victorian Society* (second edition), (London, 2013).

153 B Simon (1965).

154 TUC, 1885, cited in S Cameron, "Earning Learning and Income: An Historical Analysis of Barriers to Accessing the Educational Ladder", PhD Thesis (unpublished) (UCLAN, 2014), p47.

155 *Observer*, "The schoolboys' strike", 13 October 1889.

156 *Times*, "Free education in Scotland", 10 September 1889.

157 *Manchester Guardian*, "Summary of news", 1 October 1889.

158 *London Standard*, "The Provinces", 5 October 1889, p3

159 *Leeds Mercury*, "Extension of the school students' strike", 9 October 1889.

160 *North-Eastern Daily Gazette*, "School children in revolt: Strike against long hours and home lessons", 1 October 1889.

161 *Northern Echo*, "The schoolboys' strike", 10 October 1889, issue 6124.

162 *Pall Mall Gazette*, "A Schoolmaster on the schoolboy strike", 11 October 1889a, issue 7665.

163 *London Standard*, "The schoolboys' strike", 11 October 1889.

164 *Observer* (1889).

165 Education Commission, "Final Report of the Commissioners Appointed to Inquire into the Elementary Acts, England and Wales" (London,1888) C5485.

166 E P Thompson, *The Making of the English Working Class* (Harmondsworth, 1975), pp 32-3.

167 *Women's Penny Paper*, "Miss Edith Lupton on the school children's strike", 19 October 1889.

168 *Times*, "Schoolboy strikes", 10 October 1889.

169 *Lancashire Evening Post*, "The schoolboy strike", 11 October 1889.

170 Ibid, 15 October 1889.

171 B Simon (1965).

172 Education Commission Final Report of the Commissioners Appointed to Inquire into the Elementary Acts, England and Wales (London, 1888), C5485 p180.

173 B Simon (1965), p119.

174 Ibid p118.

175 Cited in T Taylor (1994), p99.

176 *Pall Mall Gazette* (1889a).

177 *Manchester Guardian*, "Letter from J M Yates, school master", 18 October 1889.

178 *North-Eastern Daily Gazette*, "The schoolboys' strike", 9 October 1889.

179 *North-Eastern Daily Gazette*, "School boy insubordination", 10 October 1889.

180 *Dundee Courier and Argos*, "The strike of school children", 9 October 1889.

181 *Preston Guardian*, "The school strikes", 19 October 1889; *Times*, "The schoolboys' strikes", 9 October 1889.

182 *Glasgow Herald*, "The schoolboys' strike", 10 October 1889, issue 243.

183 *North-Eastern Daily Gazette*, "The schoolboys' strike", 9 October 1889.

184 *The Star* (St Peter Port), "Strike of Schoolboys", 12 October 1889.

185 *Northern Echo* (1889).

186 *Western Mail*, "Strike of Cardiff school children", issue 6364, 9 October 1889.

187 *Daily News*, "School children's strikes", issue 13577, 11 October, 1889.

188 *Glasgow Herald*, "The school boys' Strike", issue 242, 9 October, 1889.

189 Ibid.

190 *Preston Guardian* (1889).

191 *Times*, "Schoolboys' strikes", 14 October 1889.

192 *Lloyds Weekly*, "Schoolboys playing at strikes", 13 October 1889.

193 *Times*, "The schoolboys' strikes", 11 October 1889.

194 Ibid

195 *Lancaster Gazette*, "A magistrate on the strike of schoolboys", 16 October 1889.

196 *Times*, "The school strikes", 9 October 1889.

197 *Manchester Guardian*, "The schoolboy strike", 5 October 1889.

198 *Lloyds Weekly* (1889b).

199 *Lancashire Evening Post*, "The school strike", 10 October 1889.

200 *Times*, "The Schoolboys' strikes", 12 October 1889.

201 *Glasgow Herald*, "The schoolboys' strike", issue 243, 10 October 1889.

202 *Exeter Flying Post*, "The schoolboy strikes", issue 6984, 12 October 1889.

203 T Taylor (1994), p96.

204 *Manchester Guardian*, "The 'strike' of schoolboys", 10 October 1889.

205 *Lancaster Gazette* (1889).

206 *Preston Guardian Editorial*, 12 October 1889.

207 *Daily Mail*, "Children's rights", 13 September 1911f.

208 C Williams, *The Fifty Year March: The Rise of the Labour Party* (London, 1949).

209 P Foot, *The Vote: How it was Won and How it was Undermined* (London, 2005), p214.

210 J Newsinger, *Them and Us: Fighting the Class War 1910-1939* (London, 2015), pp19-20.

211 E Halevy, *History of the English People in the 19th Century* (London, 1924).

212 G Dangerfield, *The strange Death of Liberal England* (New York, 1961).

213 Ibid.

214 Cited in T Cliff and D Gluckstein, *The Labour Party: A Marxist History* (London, 1996), p47.

215 T Evans (2011).

216 G Dangerfield (1961).

217 BBC Radio 4, *The Long View*, 08/04/2003, http://www.bbc.co.uk/radio4/history/longview/longview_20030408.shtml.

218 R Grigg, "The origins and significance of the school strikes in south Wales, 1911", *The Local Historian*, vol 33, no 3, (August 2003).

219 *Times*, "A 'strike' of Liverpool school children", 9 September 1911.

220 Ibid.

221 *Daily Mail*, "Schoolboy strike", 13 September 1911c.

222 Cited in D Marson, "The children's strikes in 1911", *History Workshop Pamphlets* (9) (1973), p5.

223 *Manchester Guardian*, "Schoolboys 'strikes'" 13 September 1911.

224 Cited in S Humphries, *Hooligans or rebels? Oral History of Working Class Childhood and Youth, 1889-1937* (Oxford, 1981), p97.

225 *Manchester Guardian*, "Mr Clynes on the school-boys 'strike'", 21 September 1911.

226 S G Tarrow, *Power in Movement: Social Movements and Contentious Politics* (Cambridge, 2011).

227 Home Office, Colliery strike disturbances in South Wales: Correspondence and report, November 1910, Cmd 5568 HMSO (London, 1911), p34.

228 *Daily Mail*, "Loss of life at Llanelly", 21 August 1911.

229 Ibid.

230 *Guardian*, "Last night's rioting: Half-a-dozen bayonet charges: List of injured", 20 August 1911.

231 *Daily Mail*, "Official reports", 16 August 1911a.

232 *Guardian*, "Men shot down: Prison vans mobbed in Liverpool", 16 August 1911a.

233 *Guardian*, "The Liverpool strike: Inquest on the men shot", 1 September 1911b.

234 Cited in *Daily Mail*, "Shoot 'em down", 25 August 1911b.

235 *Times* (1911).

236 Ibid.

237 *Times*, "The schoolboys' 'strike': Charges of theft at West Hartlepool", 15 September 1911b.

238 D Marson, (1973), p16.

239 *Times* (1911).

240 *Daily Mail*, "Down with the cane: Thousands of children on strike", 12 September 1911c.

241 *Manchester Guardian*, "Schoolboys' 'strikes'", 13 September 1911d.

242 D Marson (1973), p21.

243 *Manchester Guardian*, "Schoolboy 'strikes'", 12 September 1911c.

244 *Manchester Guardian* (1911d).

245 *Daily Mail* (1911c).

246 *Times* (1911b).

247 D Marson (1973), p16.

248 S Humphries (1981).

249 D Marson (1973), p7.

250 P W Musgrave, "'Corporal punishment in some English elementary schools, 1900-1939", *Research in Education*, no 17, May 1973; E P Thompson, *The Making of the English Working Class* (Harmondsworth, 1975), pp32/3; S Humphries, (1981).

251 Commons, *Hansard*, 2 March 1908, c343-4.

252 *Manchester Guardian*, "Damages against a Manchester teacher", 13 October 1908, p10

253 Commons, *Hansard*, 5 October 1909, vol 11, c1838-1841.

254 Commons, *Hansard*, 20 July, 1914, vol 65, c 24-26.

255 M Lavalette, *Child Labour in the Capitalist Labour Market* (Aldershot, 1994); S Cunningham, Child labour in Britain, 1900-1973, PhD Thesis (unpublished) (UCLAN, 2000).

256 *Manchester Guardian* (1911d).

257 *Times*, "The 'strike' of schoolchildren: Demonstrations in Sheffield and Hull", 13 September 1889a.

258 *Times*, "The schoolboys' 'strike': Street processions in the provinces", 14 September 1889b.

259 Cited in D Marson (1973), p16.

260 *Times*, "A 'strike' of Liverpool school children", 9 September 1911.

261 D Marson (1973), p16.

262 *Daily Mail*, "Schoolboy strikers", Correspondence from W P Waston-Thomas, 15 September 1911e.

263 *Lancashire Daily Post*, "The schoolboy strikes", 14 September 1911.

264 *Times*, "The great rebellion", editorial, 16 September 1911c.

265 *Times*, "Schoolboy 'strikers' punished", 16 September 1889.

266 *Times* (1911).

267 *Manchester Guardian* (1911d).

268 *Manchester Guardian*, "Corporal punishment in schools", 13 February 1912.

269 *Daily Mail*, "The elementary cane", 15 April 1914.

270 P W Musgrave (1977).

271 S Humphries (1981), p120.

272 Young Communist League (1969),

Manifesto for Secondary Schools (Working Class Movement Library (WCML), Young Communist League box 1, 36015097.

273 Britain was not the only country to experience a pupil power movement. Perhaps the most renowned was France's Comites d'Action Lyceens, though similar organisations emerged in other countries. In Sweden the Sveriges Elevers Central Organisation (SECO) represented some 320,000 13-19 year old members in over 600 schools and colleges, even receiving a government subsidy to do so: C L Taylor, "The shape of pupils to come?" *Guardian*, 14 February 1970. In Germany the national school student movement was AUSS, and corresponding organisations emerged in Holland, Belgium and Switzerland: Schools Action Union (1969), *Vanguard: Magazine of the Schools Action Union*, no 7.

274 P Barberis, J McHugh and M Tyldesley, *Encyclopaedia of British and Irish Political Organisations* (London, 2005), p172.

275 G Stevenson (1982), *Anatomy of Decline: The Young Communist League 1967-1986*, available at www.grahamstevenson.me.uk/index.php?option=com_content&view=article&id=692:anatomy-of-decline-the-young-communist-league-1967-86&catid=29:miscellany&site mid=53.

276 Ibid.

277 Ibid.

278 F Boyd, "Young Liberals bring out strike guide for school children", *Guardian*, 30 January 1968.

279 Anthony Chenevix-Trench, Eton's headmaster, was concerned about developments, though his feeling was that the threat posed by the pupil power movement had been somewhat exaggerated. Ultimately delegates at the Headmasters' Conference concluded that a "mass takeover of schools by pupils seems unlikely": R Bourne, "Heads happy to let pupils participate", *Guardian*, 11 June 1968. A similar debate occurred at that year's conference of assistant grammar school masters, where delegates were warned that "'student power' may be followed by 'pupil power'—the revolt of the 16 year olds against outdated institutions and traditions": *Times*, "Pupil power the sequel to student revolt", 30 September 1968.

280 Dave Gibson, interview with authors 30 June 2015.

281 Leeds Schools Socialist Federation (LSSF), "We Stand For" "not to die but to be reborn", *Handful of Dust*, no 1, 1968 (Autumn/Winter), p3.

282 Ibid.

283 The magazines had different styles of titles and subheadings, settling for a standard title and style with number three. The first two issues sold for 3d, by number four this was up to 4d and for issues five, six and seven it was 6d. Issue one announces itself as a "free press" to which any young person can contribute and which will "act as a means of communication of news and information" (p1); the second issue, LSSF (1969) *HOD* 2 "Mag of young Leeds", *Handful of Dust* (February), starts with a long and very critical letter from a reader who complained about the spelling, punctuation and grammar of the first issue! The letter writer dismissed the publication as "juvenile" communism, claimed the poetry was not worthy of the name and the writing full of clichés about the evils of capitalism and alienation! After the letter there is a long piece on R D Laing, followed by a round-up of the Leeds scene; LSSF (1969) *HOD*, *Handful of Dust*, no 3 (March), looks at the attempts to ban *HOD* in some Leeds schools. *HOD* had been denounced as "obscene" and "communist propaganda". It then covers the attempt by the National Union of Students to organise school students— and comes down on the side of militant school students in the Schools Action Union (for more on this see chapter 5).

284 Stevenson (1982).

285 *Guardian*, "Teacher urges pupils to form

school councils", 6 December 1968.

286 P Newell, "Should pupils have a voice?" *Illustrated London News*, 1 November 1969, issue 6796.

287 *Daily Mail*, "Pupil power: Students new target is the schools", 1 February 1969.

288 P Newell (1969).

289 She was particularly impressed by the fact that the girls had managed to maintain close contact with the French Lycee rebels of 1968: S Rowbotham *Promise of a Dream* (New York, 2001).

290 Dave Gibson, interview with authors 30 June 2015.

291 Leading to the famous slogan: "Thatcher, Thatcher, milk snatcher!"

292 *Times*, "Pupils try to stir 'red Wednesday' revolt", 15 May 1972.

293 *Guardian*, "Protest march by children", 3 March 1969; *Times* "250 children march in protest", 3 March 1969; P Newell, (1969).

294 Dave Gibson, interview with authors 30 June 2015.

295 D Gray, "School power: Sixth sense", *Guardian*, 22 March 1969.

296 C Foster "When school students fought they system", *Solidarity*, no 99, September 2006.

297 *Times*, "Maoist threat?" 24 July 1969.

298 P Newell (1969).

299 S Wilkins, "Harrow boys sign up for pupil power", *Daily Mail*, 4 July 1969.

300 *Times*, "Eton targets for militants", 12 July 1969.

301 B Turner, "Pupils who demand the right to strike", *Observer*, 20 January 1970.

302 Schools Action Union, *Vanguard: Magazine of the Schools Action Union*, no 7, 1969.

303 Schools Action Union (1969).

304 M Dean, "Push off Mr Chips: Malcolm Dean on the Schools Action Union", *Guardian*, 26 February 1970a.

305 M Dean (1970a).

306 P Newell, (1969).

307 D Gray, "School power: Sixth sense", *Guardian*, 22 March 1969.

308 The response of the Incorporated Association of Headmasters in its defence of Baxter was unapologetic. Its members, it insisted, "must be free to include any relevant factual information" they saw fit when writing references for students: *Daily Mail*, "Student invaders demand to see files", 25 February 1970; R Nash, "Join our fight, pupils ask teachers", *Daily Mail*, 23 February 1970.

309 M Dean, "School for martyrs: Next week comes the crunch for striking pupils at Dulwich", *Guardian*, 22 January 1970.

310 M Dean (1970).

311 L C Taylor, "The shape of pupils to come?" *Guardian*, 14 February 1970.

312 J Stead, "Next, mini-militants", *Guardian*, 26 November 1969. In fact, the "spectre" of what this journalist referred to as a new generation of "mini-militants" had already arrived to haunt the political classes. MPs had been given a taste of what *Guardian* described as "toddler power", "when a group of under-fives ran round the lobbies of Westminster with a petition for better nursery facilities throughout the country": *Guardian* editorial, "Victory for toddler power", 22 January 1969.

313 L Lee-Potter, "Listen to Eve, in front of the classroom strikers", *Daily Mail*, 4 November 1969.

314 M Dean (1970a).

315 Commons, *Hansard*, 17 July 1969, vol 787, c856-7.

316 For a suggestion of early special branch surveillance see: B Turner, "Pupils who demand the right to strike", *Observer*, 25 January 1970, p3.

317 P Newell, "Midget with a mighty kick", *Times Educational Supplement*, 2 April 1971, p6. Apart from Handyside, the identity of the editors remained a closely guarded secret, and this article only cites their first names; Alan (a teacher), Elizabeth, Hilary, Roger (a sixth former) and Ruth.

318 S Hansen and J Jensen, *Little Red Schoolbook* (London, 1971), stage 1.

319 The book had also been published in Sweden, Norway, Finland, Holland, Germany and Switzerland, but had been banned in France: O Pritchett, "A little red rite", *Guardian*, 3 April 1971.

One estimate suggested that 500,000 copies of it had been sold across Europe by April 1971: M Stuart, "Police seize 'school book'" *Guardian*, April 1 1971, p1.

320 *Sunday Telegraph*, "Children are told drugs are fun", 28 March 1971.

321 J Stevenson, "Not exactly kids stuff", *Daily Sketch*, 29 March 1971.

322 P Newell (1971).

323 S Hansen and J Jensen (1971).

324 G Nabarro, correspondence with Reginald Maudling, 29 March 1971, National Archives, ED 207/168.

325 Handwritten note to Miss Cartwright, March, 1971, National Archives, ED 207/168.

326 J Banks, Note on the *Little Red Schoolbook*, 30 March 1971, National Archives, ED 207/168.

327 G E Dudman, Note on the *Little Red Schoolbook*, 30 March 1971, National Archives, ED 207/168.

328 S R Chapple, Note to the Private Secretary to the Solicitor General on the *Little Red Schoolbook*, 30 March 1971, National Archives, ED 207/168.

329 C Turvey, Report on the seizure of the *Little Red Schoolbook*, 6 April 1971, National Archives, DPP 2/4976/2.

330 M Thatcher, Correspondence with Miss Vera Finlay, 7 March 1973, National Archives, ED 207/168.

331 J A Hudson, Note to Mr Clark on potential witnesses for the DPP's case against *The Little Red Schoolbook*, 30 March 1971, National Archives, ED 207/168. Hudson was responding to a request from the DPP for the Board of Education to identify "suitable" witnesses for its case against the book's publishers.

332 M C Whitehouse, Statement of witness, 3 May 1971, National Archives, DPP 2/4976/2.

333 L Berg, in *Where: Information on Education*, no 58, June 1971, p164. The April issue of *Where* had called for the introduction of a children's "charter" which would include the abolition of corporal punishment, greater pupil participation in school management and the right to impartial advice about sex, contraception, drugs and alcohol: S Jewel, "Call for charter to protect children from adults", *Times*, 8 April 1971. See also: *Guardian*, "ACE says suppression of 'Red Book' is wrong", 3 September 1971, p7.

334 C Walker, "Leading publishers form group for defence of *Little Red Schoolbook*", *Times*, 8 May 1971, p2.

335 P Harvey, "Fight to save 'Red Book'", *Guardian*, 2 July 1971, p1.

336 T Morris, letter to *Times*, 7 August 1971, p11.

337 Cited in R Handyside, "*Little Red Schoolbook*", *Times*, 7 July 1971, p15.

338 P Harvey (1971).

339 R Handyside, Statement following conviction, reprinted in *Tolpuddle*, 1971, vol. 1. Working Class Movement Library (WCML), Young Communist League Periodicals, A-Z.

340 Inner London Quarter Sessions, The Appeal of Richard Handyside: Judgement of Judge Hines, 29 October 1972. National Archives, DPP 2/4976/2.

341 *Daily Telegraph*, "Young Liberal plan for 'Red Book' extracts", 6 August 1971.

342 *Times*, "Red Book out again", 15 November 1971, p2.

343 *Sun*, "A child's guide to love, sex and the pill", 4 November 1971, p9. For confirmation on the DPP's decision not to instigate proceedings against the edited edition, see *Daily Mail*, "'Red Book' cleared", 7 December 1971, p11.

344 In London, flanked by police outriders, SAU activists marched to the Greater London Council's headquarters where they delivered a letter demanding full democratic rights for school students: *Guardian*, "Militant pupils on the march", 13 July 1970. In Leeds police were called in to investigate SAU activists at Leeds Grammar School after they had distributed leaflets alleging inappropriate discipline and "interrogation" techniques: D Brown, "Police inquiry on school leaflet", *Guardian*, 15 April 1971. In Manchester the city's Education Department was

forced to publicly clarify its position on caning and racism in schools following SAU allegations of racism and inappropriate beatings: *Guardian*, "Pupils want to ban cane", 18 May 1971. In Dagenham police were called to deal with a strike involving 300 children at Mayesbrook Comprehensive school, which had been sparked by the headmaster's decision to repeatedly send a child home for being inappropriately dressed despite his parents' inability to afford a uniform: *Daily Mail*, "No uniform, say demo girls", 18 September 1971.

345 B MacArthur, "Sixth-form power campaign", *Times*, 19 March 1969, p3.

346 Schools Action Union, *Vanguard: magazine of the Schools Action Union*, 1969, no 7.

347 The NUS's "open letter" called for sixth form bursaries, student representation on school governing bodies, and also pointed to the need to address the "problem of school uniform": B MacArthur, "Sixth-form power campaign", *Times*, 19 March 1969, p3. "It is clear", argued the SAU, "that their 'proposals' have been pirated and diluted from programmes previously put forward by independent schools action groups, who saw them as levers to mobilise school students, and not, as the NUS sees them; the limits of our struggle": Schools Action Union (1969).

348 LSSF, *HOD: Handful of Dust*, no 3, March 1969, p7.

349 Schools Action Union, *Vanguard: Official journal of the Schools Action Union*, 1970, no 10, p3.

350 N Mitchell, "What is to be done?" *Tolpuddle*, vol 1, 1971, Working Class Movement Library (WCML), Young Communist League Periodicals, A-Z.

351 *Tolpuddle*, vol 2, Working Class Movement Library (WCML), Young Communist League Periodicals, A-Z.

352 J Ezard, "Kid stakes", *Guardian*, 22 November 1971.

353 G Stevenson (1982).

354 A Disney, "The day of the militant kids is approaching", *Daily Mail*,

22 November 1971.

355 R Darlington and Lyddon, *Glorious Summer: Class Struggle in Britain, 1972* (London, 2001).

356 T Cliff and D Gluckstein, *The Labour Party: A Marxist History*, second edition (London, 1996), p309.

357 A Disney, "The day of the militant kids is approaching", *Daily Mail*, 22 November 1971. See also, *Guardian*, "Pupils in half-fare protest", 1 November 1971, p7.

358 *Times*, "Full fare for bus ride back to school", 5 January 1972, p3.

359 R Tyler, "Mrs Thatcher meets pupil protest", *Daily Mail*, 2 December 1971, p9.

360 P Healy, "Children's ombudsman call by civil liberties group", *Times*, 28 September 1972.

361 J Ezard, "Pupil power", *Guardian*, 7 March 1972, p17.

362 Labour MP Joan Lester was among those supportive of the SAU's other key demand—the establishment of pupil unions within schools: T Rocca, "Kids' Lib seeks £16.50", *Daily Mail*, 13 March 1972, p3.

363 J Ezard (1972).

364 P Lillay, "More school strikes threat", *Guardian*, 7 May 1972, p2.

365 *Guardian*, "Boys in school protest", 4 May 1972, p10.

366 R Poter, "A day's work for schoolboy wrecker", *Daily Mail*, 5 May 1972, pp12-13.

367 R Tyler, "Trendy, these rebellious antics", *Daily Mail*, 5 May 1972, p12.

368 D Hughes, "Now prefects launch a counter revolution", *Daily Mail*, 6 May 1972, p7.

369 *Times*, "Pupils stone police van in walkout", 5 May 1972.

370 P Wilay, "More school strikes threat", *Guardian*, 7 May 1972, p2. See also J Ezard, "Pupil power backed by student union", *Guardian*, 13 April 1972, p6.

371 The founding conference of the NUSS was held on 20 May 1972 and attended by 100 delegates from the 30 area conferences. A 12-strong national executive was elected, half members of

the Young Communist League:
G Stevenson (1982).

372 *Daily Mail*, "'Pupil power' leader
arrested in strike demo", 9 May 1972,
p16-17. See also R Bourne, "Pupils and
police in clashes", *Guardian*, 9 May
1972, p5.

373 *Guardian*, "£15 fine for pupil leader",
8 June 1972, p8.

374 *Daily Mail* (1972).

375 *Times*, "Marching pupils are truants",
10 May 1972.

376 Ibid.

377 Ibid.

378 D H Griffiths, Organisations concerned
with promoting "pupil participation",
1972, National Archives, ED 269/100.

379 R Shears, "March of 5000 truants",
Daily Mail, 10 May 1972.

380 *Times*, "Marching pupils are truants",
10 May 1972.

381 *Daily Mail*, "Children's union calls a
strike", 11 May 1972, p9.

382 J Nicholson, "Head locks out the demo
girls", *Daily Mail*, 12th May 1972, p9.

383 R Bourne, "Heads get moral boost in
pupil strike threat", *Guardian*, 17 May
1972, p8.

384 J Webb, "Please don't sack teacher",
Daily Mail, 13 May 1972, p13.

385 *Times*, 10 May 1972.

386 G Wansell, "Headmasters advised to
take a liberal view of student 'general
strike'", *Times*, 17 May 1972; see also
R Bourne, "Heads get moral boost in
pupil strike threat", *Guardian*, 17 May
1972, p8.

387 G Wansell (*Times*, 1972).

388 R Tyler, "Go easy on classroom rebels,
education chief tells heads", *Daily Mail*,
17 May 1972, p2.

389 *Daily Mail*, "Down with slogans",
11 May 1972, p6.

390 L Watkins, "These childish little rebels
without a cause", *Daily Mail*, 12 May
1972, p6.

391 *Times*, "School kids issue": editorial,
17 May 1972.

392 B Park, R Herd and C Wnebell (1972),
"Pupil power boss...a teacher of 27",
Daily Mail, 17 May.

393 *Times* (1972).

394 G Wansell, "Arrests and scuffles with
police as 2,500 children join school
strike", *Times*, 18 May 1972.

395 B Park, "Pupil power demo fizzles into
farce", *Daily Mail*, 18 May 1972, p9.

396 R Bourne, "Aimless truants back to
square one", *Guardian*, 18 May 1972, p28.

397 C Price, "Little red schoolkids",
Guardian, 26 May 1972, p16.

398 R Bourne (*Guardian*, 1972), p28.

399 G Wansell, (*Times*, 1972).

400 R Bourne (*Guardian*, 1972).

401 R Handyside, Truants or protesters?
Correspondence, *Times*, 20 May 1972.

402 T Smythe, Pupils' protest
Correspondence, *Times*, 27May 1972.

403 P Wilby, "How to deal with pupil
power", *Guardian*, 21 May 1972, p12.

404 R T Armstrong, Correspondence to
Margaret Thatcher, 16 May 1972,
National Archives, ED 207/125.

405 Security Services Schoolchildren's
demonstrations: May 1972, 18 May
1972, National Archives, ED 207/125.

406 Home Office (1972) Militancy among
school children: Reply to Robert
Armstrong, 24 May 1972, National
Archives, ED 207/125.

407 At a NADWR demonstration against
Heath's Industrial Relations Bill in July
1971, Hunt had been arrested and
subsequently found guilty of assaulting
two policemen and of using insulting
behaviour (he was alleged to have
chanted "Kill the pigs"). The SAU had
attended the demonstration, and senior
figures on the SAU executive who had
been present, including Steyne and Lisa
Dresner, the SAU's Treasurer, gave
evidence in Hunt's defence.
Coincidentally, Hunt's appeal against the
conviction took place on 18 May, in the
midst of the fevered atmosphere that
followed the Trafalgar Square
demonstration. The tabloid press seized
on this to reinforce their message that
he was "a subversive left wing political
enemy of society leading people into
left wing political movements of which
they have no knowledge or wish to be
involved". Hunt's solicitor sought to
persuade the judge that his client's

recent vilification in the press prejudiced his chances of a fair trial, but this was arbitrarily dismissed: B Park, "Teacher in demo attack", *Daily Mail*, 19 May 1972, p9. See also R Herd ("Girl of 13 ordered to give evidence", *Daily Mail*, 20 May 1972, p24. The appeal was unsuccessful, and although Hunt's fine was reduced, his convictions were upheld: *Guardian*, "Judge cuts fines", 23 May 1972, p10.

408 P Halsey, Draft response to Armstrong's request for information on pupil militancy, May 1972, National Archives, ED 207/125.

409 W R Elliott, Note to Mr Hudson on draft response, 31 May 1972, National Archives, ED 207/125. Elliott was a former Chief Inspector of Schools and a passionate advocate of selective education.

410 P Halsey, Response to Armstrong's request for information on pupil militancy, 13 June 1972, National Archives, ED 207/125.

411 M Attenborough, Letter to Margaret Thatcher from the NUSS, 10 October 1972.

412 M Thatcher, Letter to Mary Attenborough, NUSS, 14 November 1972. National Archives, ED 269/100.

413 A Osman, "Child governors plan meets snag", *Times*, 23 May 1972; *Times*, "Brighton to enrol pupils as school governors", 24 May 1972; P Hildrew, "Union may be approved", *Guardian*, 20 June 1972; G Wansell, "Headmasters advised to take a liberal view of student 'general strike'," *Times*, 17 May 1972.

414 P Wilby, "How to deal with pupil power", *Guardian*, 21 May 1972, p12.

415 C Price (1972).

416 V Ironside, "Last night's TV", *Daily Mail*, 15 June 1972.

417 *Times*, "'Pupil power' talks on link", 21 June 1972, p3.

418 The school's head teacher, Madeleine McLaughlin, had already written to the *Times*, expressing her alarm at the NUSS's activities arguing that "Sixth formers needed to be on their guard against this kind of political

engineering and this insidious attack on their moral standards": M McLaughlin, Aims of National Union of Students, Correspondence, 6 October 1972, p15.

419 D Smith, Correspondence with Margaret Thatcher, 15 November 1972, National Archives, ED 269/100.

420 D H Griffifths, Note on Dudley Smith's correspondence, 30 November 1972, National Archives, ED 269/100.

421 J A Reeve, Note on the information requested by the Secretary of State, 5 December 1972, National Archives, ED 269/100.

422 It included calls for greater school democracy; the abolition of grammar schools, corporal punishment and uniforms; an end to compulsory religious education and streaming; the introduction of free state nurseries and school milk; the gradual introduction of a universal grant for all school students and the immediate introduction of grants for all students over the age of 16; the introduction of effective employment rights for school students engaged in part-time work (and the availability of trade union membership); and the opening up of school facilities to local communities: S Keys, Correspondence with Reg Prentice, 6 March 1974, National Archives, ED 269/100.

423 NUSS (1974), Policy statement as amended by national conference, 5/6 May, 1973 National Archives, ED 269/100.

424 R H Bird, Note to G F Cockerill, 20 March 1974, National Archives, ED 269/100.

425 G F Cockerill Note to J A Hudson, 21 March 1974, National Archives, ED 269/100.

426 J A Hudson, Note to G F Cockerill, 25 March 1974, National Archives, ED 269/100.

427 G F Cockerill (1974).

428 G H N Evans, Note to A E D Chamier, 4 April 1974, National Archives, ED 269/100.

429 The "Brockwell Park 3" were Robin Sterling (15), Lloyd James (18) and

Horace Parkinson (19). The NUSS/ Black Students Action Collective march was part of the campaign to have their sentences (and particularly, Sterling's) overturned: *Guardian*, "Coloured youth's conviction over affray is quashed", 1 August 1974, p6.

430 P Avis, "Solidarity plea to students", *Morning Star*, 1 April 1974.

431 A Kent, "Pupil power", *Daily Mail*, 4 April 1974, p20.

432 *Morning Star*, "YCL to set up branches in schools", 17 April 1973.

433 A E D Chamier, Note to G H N Evans, 5 April 1974, National Archives, ED 269/100.

434 B Kavanagh, "NF=No Fun, School Kids Against the Nazis", *SKAN*, 1978, issue 3.

435 J Shepherd, *Crisis? What Crisis? The Callaghan Government and the Winter of Discontent* (Manchester, 2013).

436 Ibid.

437 C Hay, "Narrating crisis: The discursive construction of the 'winter of discontent'", *Sociology*, 1996, vol 30, no 2, pp253-277.

438 L Black, "An enlightening decade? New histories of 1970s Britain", *International Labor and Working Class History*, 2012, vol 82, Fall, pp174-186; L Black, H Pemberton and P Thane (eds), *Reassessing 1970s Britain* (Manchester, 2013).

439 G Stevenson (1982).

440 J Fairhall, "Please, sir, not again", *Guardian*, 5 March 1976.

441 *Sunday Telegraph*, "'Soft' on pupils", 9 June 1974.

442 The other bodies asked to give evidence were the National Association of Schoolmasters (NAS) and the National Union of Teachers (NUT), the Association of County Councils, the Association of Metropolitan Authorities, the TUC, the Association of Teachers in Technical Institutions, the Child Poverty Action Group and the Department for Education and Science.

443 *Sunday Telegraph* (1974).

444 *Guardian*, "Boost to school students union", 27 May 1974.

445 House of Commons Expenditure Committee Educational maintenance allowances in the 16-18 years age group (London, 1974), p83. HMSO. H.C. 306.

446 On the question of uniforms, it is worth noting that the joint-memorandum reaffirmed the NUSS's view that "the general principle of school uniform is objectionable": House of Commons Expenditure Committee (1974). The NUSS's demand for a school student allowance was supported by the Trades Union Congress (TUC), which, in its evidence to the Committee, argued that a final year allowance for school students would tackle hardship and reduce the growing tendency for older children to seek employment outside school hours, a practice that it felt was detrimental to their education. See the TUC memorandum, House of Commons Expenditure Committee (1974). In a subsequently submitted, supplementary joint-memorandum, the NUS/NUSS recommended the introduction of a basic "school student allowance" of £479pa (compared to £505 for an FE student living at home and £655 for an FE student not living at home).

447 G Bowd, "Pupils demand £10 per week", *Guardian* 8 July 1974.

448 G Sheridan, "Unwillingly to school", *Guardian*, 16 July 1974.

449 J Fairhall, "Pupils' union charges 'rubbish,'" *Guardian*, 16 July 1974.

450 Ibid.

451 J Fairhall, "School's 50 percent staff turnover", *Guardian*, 18 July 1974.

452 J Fairhall, (1974).

453 J Izbicki, "Parents ring school to stop pupils' walkout", *Daily Telegraph*, 18 July 1974.

454 J Fairhall, (1974), "Pupils' union charges 'rubbish,'" *Guardian*, 16 July.

455 J Fairhall, J (1974).

456 P Gruner, "Obituary: Death of Laurence Norcross, former head of Highbury Grove boys' comp", *Camden New Journal*, 7 May 2010, http://www.camdennewjournal.com/news/2010/may/obituary-death-lawrence-nocross-former-head-highbury-grove-boys-comp.

457 P Simple, "Horrors", *Daily Telegraph*, 9 July 1974.

458 *Daily Mail*, "Please sir, it's our turn to strike", 8 July 1974.

459 Commons, *Hansard*, 10 December 1975, vol 347, c965.

460 Lords, *Hansard*, 10 December 1975, vol 347, c882.

461 STOPP was formed in 1968 by a group of teachers opposed to the principle of corporal punishment in schools and other institutions. It continued to lobby MPs and governments and produce pamphlets and reports on the issue until it dissolved in 1986, following the formal abolition of corporal punishment in schools. By 1976 it had the support of a number of prominent sponsors including Tony Benn, Lord Beaumont, Lord Boyle, Barbara (Baroness) Wooton, David Steel and the Marxist educational historian Brian Simon: STOPP Corporal punishment in schools: Submission to the Secretary of State for Education and Science (London, 1976), National Archives, ED 269/277.

462 NCCL Protection of minors: A case against corporal punishment, A model Bill (London, 1974).

463 Commons, *Hansard*, 22 July 1974, vol 877, c1260.

464 Commons, *Hansard*, 22 July, 1972, vol 877, c1264.

465 M Wilkinson, "Teachers attack pupil governors", *Daily Mail*, 29 November 1975.

466 Ibid.

467 *Times*, "Pupils say teachers' union is trying to stifle them", 2 March 1977.

468 D Hencke, "Race group sacks school union boy", *Guardian*, 8 March 1978.

469 R Brand, "An unhappy union, correspondence", *Guardian*, 21 March 1978.

470 J Ezard, "Tories woo the young", *Guardian*, 8 November 1976.

471 DfES Background note on the NUSS, 22 July 1974.

472 Cited in G Stevenson (1982).

473 *Times*, "Pupils who cannot find jobs demand £25 per week", 14 July 1975.

474 Young Communist League YCL Congress 1977 (London, 1977), p11.

475 Ibid, p33.

476 Cited in G Stevenson (1982).

477 S Taylor "The National Front: Anatomy of a political movement" in R Miles and A Phizacklea (eds), *Racism and Political Action* (London, 1979), pp134-135.

478 John Rose "The Southall Asian Youth Movement", *International Socialism* (first series) number 91, September 1976, available at www.marxists.org/history/etol/newspape/isj/1976/no91/rose.htm; K Puri "The pool of blood that changed my life", BBC News 5 August 2015, http://www.bbc.co.uk/news/magazine-33725217?ns_mchannel=email&ns_campaign_news_&ns_linkname=na&ns_fee=0. On McKinnon, see "A job for life", *Socialist Review*, January 1995, http://pubs.socialreviewindex.org.uk/sr182/briefing.htm.

479 Weyman Bennett, interview with authors 10 January 2016.

480 John Newsinger, interview with authors 19 January 2016.

481 E Smith, "Are the kids united? The Communist Party of Great Britain, Rock Against Racism, and the Politics of Youth Culture", *Journal for the Study of Radicalism*, vol 5, no 2, 2011, pp85-118.

482 M Power, "Aspects of ideological struggle for the British road to socialism and the Young Communist league", *Cogito*, no 4 1977, p7.

483 School Kids Against the Nazis (1978), *SKAN*, issue 1.

484 Ibid, issue 3.

485 Rehad Desai, interview with authors 6 April 2015.

486 The Archive: A History of Over 30 years of UK Festivals: "The northern Rock Against Racism Festival, 1978", 2015. http://www.ukrockfestivals.com/rock-against-racism-1978.html

487 *Guardian*, "The games that teachers play", Editorial, 17 March 1978.

488 C Cross, "School unions may split", *Guardian*, 19 March 1978.

489 A Chalmers and R Turner, "Rebellion: More pupils held on day two of the

lunch war", *Daily Mail*, 16 March; *Daily Mail*, "A caning for riot children", 17 March 1978; R Boyson, "The one lesson pupils have learned too well", *Daily Mail*, 17 March 1978; A Osman, "Pupils face retribution after brief revolt", *Times*, 17 March 1978.

490 A Chalmers and R Turner (1978).

491 *Guardian* (1978).

492 C Cross (1978), "School unions may split", *Guardian*, 19 March.

493 A Osman (1978).

494 *Daily Mail* (1978).

495 A Chalmers and R Turner (1978).

496 A Osman (1978).

497 *Daily Mail* (1978).

498 A Osman (1978).

499 R Boyson, (1978).

500 *Daily Mail* (1978).

501 Ibid.

502 Commons, *Hansard*, 13 April 1978, vol 947, c1160.

503 Lords, *Hansard*, 21 March 1978, vol 389, c1786, Written Answer.

504 D Geddes, "Pupil power report for Labour party", *Guardian*, 10 April 1978; R Underhill, *The LPYS and National Union of School Students*, People's History Museum, NEC Minutes and Papers, April 1978-July 1979.

505 *Times*, "Inquiry ordered into Young Socialist school leaflet", 23 March 1978.

506 R Underhill (1978-9).

507 R Underhill (1978-9).

508 D Geddes (1978).

509 A Bevins, "You cannot stop school Left, says Trotskyist", *Daily Mail*, 11 April 1978.

510 Green, cited in *Common Cause: A Survey of Left Wing Plans for Transforming Education* (Hampshire, 1980), p30.

511 Rehad Desai, interview with authors 6 April 2015.

512 Erica Laredo, interview with authors 8 April 2015.

513 *Times*, "Pupils present a forthright view of school life", 5 October 1978.

514 *Times*, "School transfers boy over union paper", 6 November 1978.

515 *Daily Mirror*, "Sex shock in school magazine", 5 October 1978.

516 NUSS, *Blot*, issue 2 1978, Working Class Movement Library (Manchester), Shelfmark: Periodicals A-Z, Copy number: 31000553.

517 Ibid.

518 M O'Connor, "Getting involved", *Guardian*, 31 March 1979.

519 Erika Laredo, interview with authors 8 April 2015.

520 *Daily Mail*, "Young 'MPs' heckle Maggie", 26 October 1978.

521 Cited in *Observer*, "Militancy pays", 4 November 1979.

522 Barbara, Islington NUSS, *Blot*, November 28 1978.

523 *Times*, "Red rebel pupils learn the arts of revolution", 10 March 1980.

524 I Bradley, "Ban pupils union from schools, MP urges", *Times*, 11 March 1980.

525 Commons, *Hansard*, 1 April, 1980, vol 982, c193.

526 W Berliner, "Students draft claim for 36pc rise in grants", *Guardian*, 10 December 1979.

527 *Guardian*, "NUS cuts off aid to schools union", 8 December 1980.

528 Steve Marsh, interview with authors 8 March 2015.

529 Ibid.

530 Rehad Desai, interview with authors 6 April 2015.

531 Steve Marsh, interview with authors 8 March 2015.

532 Rehad Desai, interview with authors 6 April 2015.

533 Ibid.

534 *Evening Post*, "Stop anarchy in classroom urges Leeds councillor", 30 November 1979.

535 J Ardill, Commission warns on rising jobs figures, *Guardian*, 30 July 1980.

536 NUSS, "Oct 10th Right to work: NUSS demo", *Blot*, cSeptember 1980.

537 Daily Mail "Children incited to riot", 15 October 1981.

538 M Morris, "Pupils face discipline after sit-in at school", *Guardian*, 7 January 1981; C Rowlands, "Police curb pupils' lunchtime riot", *Daily Mail*, 13 March 1982; W Berliner, Pupils protest as teachers ban lunch-time duty,

Guardian, 12 March 1982; *Guardian*, "Pupils at Fume school protest over bussing", 6 July 1982; *Daily Mail*, "Socks protest girls punished", 11 March 1982; *Daily Mail*, "School on the rampage", 9 December 1982.

539 S Cook, "Sixth formers excluded after anti-nuclear protest", *Guardian*, 16 April 1981; *Daily Mail*, "Walkout by pupils in race protest", 14 February 1984.

540 S Tirbutt, "Defence politics", *Guardian*, 7 June 1983. For allegations of left wing influence in encouraging pupils to embrace CND, see C Cox, (Lady) "Cracking down on 'peace studies'", correspondence, *Times*, 9 January 1984; *Daily Mail*, "Schools most sinister lesson", 26 January 1984.

541 Dave Gibson, interview with authors 30 June 2015.

542 Ibid.

543 Ibid 30 June 2015.

544 A Bennett "The playground revolution", *Times*, 2 May 1985.

545 Ibid.

546 Ibid.

547 *Daily Mail*, "Pit protest pupils banned", 18 February 1985.

548 See F Arrowsmith, "Miners strike—30 years on: 'We won't stop until we've got justice,'" *Morning Star*, 1 March 2014, http://www.morningstaronline.co.uk/a-a467-Miners-strike-30-years-on-We-wont-stop-till-weve-got-justice#.VTjsZo1oyUk.

549 Keir McKechnie, interview with authors 16 April 2015.

550 Hannah Sell, interview with authors 21 May 2015.

551 Lois Austin, interview with authors 21 May 2015.

552 Angela McCormick, interview with authors 9 April 2015.

553 Cited in Commons, *Hansard*, 16 May 1885, vol 79, c 555.

554 Cited in B Clement, "Bleak picture of rising unemployment and more time on the dole", *Times*, 1 August 1985.

555 D Raffe and P Mith "Young people's attitudes to YTS: The first two years", *British Educational Research Journal*, 1985, vol 13 (3), pp241-260.

556 D Finn, "The Manpower Services Commission and the Youth Training Scheme: A permanent bridge to work?" *Compare: A Journal of Comparative and International Education*, 1984, vol 14, no 2, pp145-156.

557 Vincent "The Conservatives Diary: Policies Affecting Poor Families: June 1979-July 1991" in S Becker (ed), *Windows of Opportunity: Public Policy and the Poor* (London, 1991).

558 Welfare Rights Bulletin "YTS round up", no 58, pp2-3, February 1984.

559 Section 20(1) (e) of Labour's 1975 Social Security Act allowed for the disqualification of unemployment benefit for a period of six weeks if, without good cause, a person refused the opportunity of training "for the purposes of becoming or keeping fit for entry, or return to, regular employment": Commons, *Hansard* (W), 10 June 1985, vol 80, col 365-6.

560 Commons, *Hansard*, 10 June, 1985, vol 80, c 365W.

561 M Hill, "Government Responses to Unemployment", in M Loney, D Boswell and J Clarke (eds), *Social Policy and Social Welfare* (Milton Keynes, 1983).

562 D Finn (1984).

563 D Lee, "Poor Work and Poor Institutions: Training and the Youth Labour Market" in P Brown and R Scase (eds), *Poor Work: Disadvantage and the Division of Labour* (Milton Keynes, 1992).

564 P J Little, "Social Security Policy Inspectorate Inquiry onto YTS: Initial Impressions" (1984), Social Security Inspectorate: Youth Training Scheme Report, National Archives, AST 37/126.

565 A A Brown, Note to Mr Chatten, 14 March 1985, Social Security Inspectorate: Youth Training Scheme Report, National Archives, AST 37/126.

566 Note to G A Brand, Department of Employment, 23 October 1984, Social Security Inspectorate: Youth Training Scheme Report, National Archives, AST 37/126.

567 Commons, *Hansard*, 2 February 1983,

vol 36, c 319 and 323.

568 K Harper, "Labour and TUC leaders unveil £6b youth employment plan", *Guardian*, 16 August 1985.

569 Commons, *Hansard*, 16 May 1985, vol 79, c 555-6.

570 J Hird, "Wanted: Real jobs", *Militant*, 1 February 1985.

571 J Hird, YTURC/LPYS Lobby of Parliament, Briefing by the LPYS Chairman for the NEC of the Labour Party, 4 March 1985, People's History Museum, Salford.

572 M Wainwright, "Rebel parents guard against race 'strike' retribution", *Guardian*, 11 March 1985.

573 D Rudd, "Schools rocked by school student strike", *Militant*, 22 March 1985.

574 *Daily Mail*, "Pupils storm city hall in school dinners demo", 16 February 1985.

575 Hannah Sell, interview with authors 21 May 2015.

576 Nancy Taaffe, interview with authors 21 May 2015.

577 Socialist Youth, "Schools in revolt" May 1985.

578 I Wilson and D Steele, "Young socialists unrepentant over pupils' protest", *Glasgow Herald*, 22 March 1985, p5.

579 J Galbraith "School strike" *Militant*, 29 March 1985.

580 Ibid.

581 B McDowall, "Demo Chaos", *Evening Times* (Glasgow), 21 March 1985.

582 James Doleman, interview with authors 16 April 2015.

583 Angela McCormick, interview with authors 9 April 2015.

584 I Wilson and D Steele, "Young socialists unrepentant over pupils' protest", *Glasgow Herald*, 22 March 1985.

585 Keir McKechnie, interview with authors 16 April 2015.

586 Socialist Youth (1985).

587 P F Drake Letter to M J Martin MP, 11 April 1985, People's History Museum, Salford.

588 I Wilson and D Steele (1985).

589 M J Martin, Letter to James Mortimer, General Secretary of the Labour Party, 15 April 1985, People's History Museum, Salford.

590 J Allison, Letter to David Hughes, 15 April 1985, People's History Museum, Salford.

591 Keir McKechnie, interview with authors 16 April 2015.

592 Ibid.

593 Angela McCormick, interview with authors 9 April 2015.

594 Ibid.

595 Keir McKechnie, interview with authors 16 April 2015.

596 Socialist Youth, "LPYS conference: Come to the Event of the Year!" March 1985, p3.

597 Nancy Taaffe, interview with authors 21 May 2015.

598 Lois Austin, interview with authors 21 May 2015.

599 Socialist Youth, "Schools in revolt", May 1985.

600 Labour Party Youth Committee, minutes of the sixth meeting held on 16 April 1985, People's History Museum, Salford. It is unclear which members of the Committee voted against the resolution, but given the subsequent support they would express for the strike, it seems likely that among them were Audrey Wise, Frances Curran and Joan Maynard.

601 Commons, *Hansard*, 16 April, vol 77, c135-6.

602 *Daily Mail*, "Militants call for pupil strike", 17 April 1985, p5.

603 C Edwards, "Militant squads call out children on school strike", *Daily Mail*, 19 April 1985.

604 Ibid.

605 Baroness Cox, "Militants who are getting at your children", *Daily Mail*, 22 April 1985.

606 A Moncur, "Labour pledges £200m boost for schools", *Guardian*, 17 April 1985.

607 Cited in *Militant* "Youth want fighting campaign against Tories", 10 May 1985.

608 A Bevins, "Kinnock condemns Militant-backed school strike call", *Times*, 25 April 1985.

609 P Chorlton and A Dunn, "Thousands join children's classroom strike for jobs", *Guardian*, 26 April 1985.

610 J Hird "250,000 join school strike", *Militant*, 26 April 1985.

611 Labour Party National Executive Committee Minutes, 24 April 1985, People's History Museum Archive.

612 A Bevins (1985).

613 C Hughes, "Heads attack school 'strike' organisers", *Times*, 27 April 1985.

614 C Hughes, "Pupils in 'strike' arrested", *Times*, 26 April 1985.

615 Commons, *Hansard*, 24 April 1985, vol 77, c452-3 W.

616 Lois Austin, interview with authors 21 May 2015.

617 Commons, *Hansard*, 16 May 1985, vol 79, c. 555.

618 C Hughes, "Pupils in 'strike' arrested", *Times*, 26 April 1985 ; B Wade, "Schools revolt: Mass walkout slams YTS", *Militant*, 3 May 1985.

619 Commons, *Hansard*, 16 May 1985, vol 79, col 535.

620 Cited in C Mathews, "Liverpool March", *Militant*, 3 May 1985. For the *Times*'s version of events, see C Hughes, "Support is claimed for pupil strike", *Times*, 20 April 1985.

621 These comments were made by Dave Sinclair, who helped organise and photograph the Liverpool protest: BBC Liverpool school strike 1985: Exhibition at Bluecoat, 2011, http://www.bbc.co.uk/news/uk-england-merseyside-15153305. This article includes pictures taken on the day by Sinclair.

622 *Guardian*, "Thousands Join Children's Classroom Strike For Jobs", 26 April 1985.

623 Commons, *Hansard*, 16 May 1985, c534.

624 Commons, *Hansard*, 25 April 1985, vol 77, c991.

625 Commons, *Hansard*, 11 June, vol 80, c821.

626 C Mathews (1985).

627 *Socialist Worker*, "Why we're striking", 5 May 1985.

628 C Mathews (1985).

629 *Socialist Worker* (1985).

630 J Ford and J Ford, "Birmingham", *Socialist Worker*, 5 May 1985.

631 P Bembridge "Nottingham", *Socialist Worker*, 5 May 1985.

632 *Militant* "Students look to unions", 10 May 1985.

633 *Evening Post*, "The daft wing", 26 April 1985.

634 *Manchester Evening News*, "Support for demo pupils", 26 April 1985.

635 *Manchester Evening News*, "The young protesters: Correspondence from pupils at Loreto school", 29 April 1985.

636 Quoted in *Militant*, "Northern Ireland", 26 April 1985, p14.

637 *Militant*, "Hundreds join strike in southern England", 3 May 1985, p11.

638 *Socialist Youth*, "250,000 school students say no to the Tories", June 1985, p5.

639 P Forrester, "The Right to Fight For A Better Future": Correspondence, Lancashire Evening Post, 2 May 1985. For a more detailed account of the Preston YTS pupil strike see S Cunningham, "The 'Gissa Job' School Strike of 1985", in M Lavalette and P Marsden (eds), *Mark Our Words, We Will Rise: Episodes in Preston's Radical History* (Preston Socialist History Group, 2014).

640 *Times Educational Supplement*, "Militants Help to Establish Pupils' Union", 3 May 1985.

641 *Times Educational Supplement*, "Left Wing Groups Helped To Organise Pupil's Strikes", 3 May 1985a.

642 *Times Educational Supplement* (1985, 1985a).

643 Commons, *Hansard*, 16 May 1985, vol 79, c555.

644 *Lancashire Evening Post*, "The 'Gissa Job' Strike", 26 April 1985.

645 *Militant*, "Youth want fighting campaign against Tories", 10 May 1985, p7.

646 *Militant*, "Schools campaign backed", 2 August 1985.

647 S Cunningham (2014).

648 *Lancashire Evening Post*, "Blame Adults For Youngsters' Strike": correspondence, 29 April 1985.

649 *Guardian*, "Some thoughts on strike": correspondence, 7 May 1985.

650 I Gazeley and P Thane, "Patterns of Visibility: Unemployment in Britain

During the Nineteenth and Twentieth Centuries", in G Lewis (ed), *Forming Nation: Framing Welfare* (London, 1998).

651 Commons, *Hansard*, 11 June 1985, vol 80, c821.

652 Hannah Sell, interview with authors 21 May 2015.

653 Lois Austin, interview with authors 21 May 2015.

654 Nancy Taaffe, interview with authors 21 May 2015.

655 D Sirockin "School students launch a union", *Socialist Youth*, July 1985.

656 N Mullholland "Northern Ireland SSU", *Socialist Youth*, September 1985.

657 T Forrester "School students organise", *Militant*, 4 October 1985.

658 Nancy Taaffe, interview with authors 21 May 2015.

659 SWP SSU leaflet, cited in Commons, *Hansard*, 16 May 1985, vol 79, c534.

660 Commons, *Hansard*, 16 May 1985, vol 79, c534.

661 H Sell and D Maguire, "Wolverhampton schools strike", *Militant*, 15 November 1985.

662 Hannah Sell, interview with authors 21 May 2015.

663 D Sirockin, "School students branches grow", *Socialist Youth*, October 1985.

664 Nancy Taaffe, interview with authors 21 May 2015.

665 Tom Sawyer led the attack against the YTURC and the LPYS, on behalf of Labour's NEC. In an influential, carefully prepared speech given to party members during 1986 he set out the case against both. While acknowledging that "schoolchildren and other young people have legitimate grievances to which the Labour and trade union movement are not adequately responding", he expressed "growing concern at the destructive activities of the Youth Trade Union Rights Campaign". The LPYS, he alleged, was "totally dominated by the politics of the Militant Tendency" and had "little appeal to a wider youth audience". His vision for the future was one where "the main emphasis of the LPYS's activities should be in the area of 'youth culture'" rather than "political education". National decision making conferences would be replaced by "rallies with workshops and practical sessions" widening the appeal of the party to young people: T Sawyer Labour's youth section: Time for change, speech, 1986, People's History Museum, Salford.

666 See, for instance, the letter written to Sawyer by his NUPE advisor/assistant Bill Gilby regarding the forthcoming debate on the party's youth organisation at that year's annual conference. Gilby expresses his concerns that Joe Richardson, the chair of the composite meeting on the party's youth organisation, might be "crazy" enough to allow amendments that made reference to the positive work of the YTURC: B Gilby, Letter on Labour Party Youth Organisation, 12 September 1985, People's History Museum, Salford.

667 S Cunningham and M Lavalette, "'Active Citizens' or 'Irresponsible' Truants? School Student Strikes Against the War", in *Critical Social Policy*, 24 (2), May 2004.

668 B Woodward, *Bush at War* (New York, 2002) p44.

669 N Lemann, "The Next World Order: The Bush Administration may have a brand-new doctrine of power," *The New Yorker*, 2002, http://www.newyorker.com/magazine/2002/04/01/the-next-world-order.

670 Thomas L Friedman, "A manifesto for the fast world", *New York Times*, 28 March 1999, http://www.nytimes.com/1999/03/28/magazine/a-manifesto-for-the-fast-world.html?pagewanted=1 p8 (of 9).

671 A Callinicos, *The New Mandarins of American Power* (Cambridge, 2003).

672 See E Bircham and J Charlton (eds), *Anti-capitalism: A Guide to the Movement* (London, 2001).

673 A Murray and L German, *Stop the War: The story of Britain's Biggest Mass Movement* (London, 2003).

674 Ibid.

675 C Phipps, "Children of the Revolution: Who Can Blame the Decision-makers

of the Future for Taking to the Streets?" *Guardian*, 22 March 2003, p20.

676 Kate Connelly interview in Katya Nasim, "Iraq War Day X: The largest school strikes in UK history", available at http://www.stopwar.org.uk/index.php/video3/iraq-war-day-x-the-largest-school-strikes-in-uk-history.

677 A Johnson and N Pyke, "Pupils urged to leave lessons", *Independent on Sunday*, 23 February 2003, http://www.independent.co.uk/news/uk/politics/pupils-urged-to-leave-lessons-5352606.html.

678 Henna Malik, interview with authors 13 April 2015.

679 Kate Connelly interview in Katya Nasim, "Iraq War Day X: The largest school strikes in UK history", available at http://www.stopwar.org.uk/index.php/multimedia/video/178-iraq-war-day-x-the-largest-school-strikes-in-uk-history.

680 Interview with authors 9 April 2003.

681 Aftab Anwar and Louisa Oram, "No time to lose to stop warmongers: School students lead the way", in *Socialist Worker*, 8 March 2003 https://socialistworker.co.uk/art/3315/No+time+to+lose+to+stop+warmongers.

682 A Stone, "School's out against war", *Socialist Review*, April 2003, http://socialistreview.org.uk/273/schools-out-against-war.

683 A Bloom, "Passion of playground politics", *Times Educational Supplement*, 28 March 2003. This story is also based on direct experience. One of us (Michael) was the parent called by the school, who were dumbfounded by his support for the strike and his assertion that the Stop the War Coalition was fully supportive of any student who took strike action against the war!

684 L Brooks, "Kid Power", *Guardian Weekend*, 26 April 2003, p41.

685 Zoe Pilger, "Generation Apathy has woken up", *Independent on Sunday*, 23 March 2003, http://www.independent.co.uk/voices/commentators/zoe-pilger-generation-apathy-has-woken-up-5352510.html.

686 Murray and German (2003), p179.

687 A Gramsci, *Selection from the Prison Notebooks* (London, 1971), p196.

688 C Barker, A Johnson and M Lavalette (eds), *Leadership and Social Movements* (Manchester, 2001).

689 Interview with authors 9 April 2003.

690 *Socialist Worker*, "Delegates at People's Assembly for Peace call for action to stop war: lessons from school", 22 March 2003, https://socialistworker.co.uk/art/3381/Delegates+at+Peoples+Assembly+for+Peace+call+for+action+to+stop+war.

691 A Stone, "School's out against war" *Socialist Review*, April 2003 http://socialistreview.org.uk/273/schools-out-against-war.

692 Angela Harrison, "Pupils walk out over war" BBC News, 5 March 2003 http://news.bbc.co.uk/1/hi/education/2821871.stm.

693 Alys Zaerin, interview in Katya Nasim, op cit.

694 Kate Connelly, interview in Katya Nasim, op cit.

695 Henna Malik, interview with authors 13 April 2015.

696 Angela Harrison (BBC 2003).

697 Ibid.

698 BBC News, "Pupils suspended over protest", 5 March 2005 http://news.bbc.co.uk/1/hi/england/2822533.stm.

699 BBC News, "Arrests at children's anti-war protest", 7 March 2003 http://news.bbc.co.uk/1/hi/england/2831063.stm.

700 Interview with authors 10 May 2003.

701 Angela Harrison (BBC 2003).

702 Ibid.

703 BBC News, 5 March 2005.

704 Alys Zaerin, interview in Katya Nasim, op cit.

705 Henna Malik, interview with authors 13 April 2015.

706 *Socialist Worker*, "Delegates at People's Assembly for Peace call for action to stop war: lessons from school", 22 March 2003 https://socialistworker.co.uk/art/3381/Delegates+at+Peoples+Assembly+for+Peace+call+for+action+to+stop+war.

707 J Cox, "Anti-war fever is sweeping

Britain", *Socialist Worker*, 8 Feb 2003 https://socialistworker.co.uk/art/3179/ Anti-war+fever+is+sweeping+Britain.

708 *Socialist Worker* (2003).

709 K Connelly, E Cope and Y Bauroubi "The opposite of apathetic", in Murray and German (2003), p189.

710 BBC News, "Children march against the war" 19 March 2003, http://news. bbc.co.uk/1/hi/scotland/2864901.stm

711 A Stone (2003).

712 Brooks (2003).

713 Socialist Party (2009), "School students organised strikes", http://www. socialistparty.org.uk/articles/7360.

714 Adam Riaz Khan, "School's Out!" in Murray and German (2003), p180.

715 BBC News, "School children march against war", 20 March 2003, http:// news.bbc.co.uk/1/hi/education/ 2867923.stm.

716 R Waterhouse, "More Arrests as Pupil Protests Gather Pace", *Daily Telegraph*, 22 March 2003, p11.

717 Kate Connelly, interview in Katya Nasim.

718 Henna Malik, interview with authors 13 April 2015

719 Interview with authors 5 April 2003.

720 Ibid.

721 Ibid.

722 A Dargie, "Pupils Play Truant in War Protests", *Newcastle Journal*, 6 March 2003, p6.

723 S Naqvi, "Warning as Pupils Protest", *Birmingham Post*, 6 March 2003, p1.

724 K Hewitt, "Iraq Crisis: Pupils Defy Rules to Hold Pupil Protests", Belfast Newsletter, 6 March 2003, p8.

725 *The Long View*, "The Pupil Strike of

1911", BBC Radio 4, 8 April 2003 http://www.bbc.co.uk/radio4/history/ longview/longview_ 20030408.shtml.

726 BBC News, "Head Teachers Are Being Warned They Should Take Firm Action against Pupils who Stage Anti-war Protests or Leave School to Take Part in Demonstrations", 20 March 2003, http://news.bbc.co.uk/1/hi/ education/2869147.stm.

727 *Essex News Chronicle*, "School Protest Girl Excluded", 28 March 2003.

728 B Campbell, "Walkout Fracas Spirals", *Irish News*, 27 March 2003.

729 BBC News (20 March 2003).

730 R Waterhouse, "More Arrests as Pupil Protests Gather Pace", *Daily Telegraph*, 22 March 2003, p8.

731 A Dargie (2003).

732 Adi Bloom, "Rebellion? No thanks, we've got homework", *Times Educational Supplement*, no 5136, Friday 6 March 2015, p26.

733 H Williams, "Thousands join Bristol Against Austerity march", *Socialist Worker*, 14 May 2015, http://socialist worker.co.uk/art/40533/Thousands+jo in+Bristol+Against+Austerity+march.

734 Ibid.

735 Hilary Wainwright, "Higher aspirations: politics beyond the ballot box", *Red Pepper*, June 2015, http://www. redpepper.org.uk/higher-aspirations- politics-beyond-the-ballot-box/.

736 Katie Forster, "Teenage anti-austerity protesters in Bristol challenge 'lazy' stereotype", *Observer*, 20 June 2015, http://www.theguardian.com/ business/2015/jun/20/teenage-austerity- protesters-challenge-lazy-stereotype.

Index